BEYOND BIAS

BEYOND BIAS

Perspectives on Classrooms

Jean V. Carew and Sara Lawrence Lightfoot

HARVARD UNIVERSITY PRESS

CAMBRIDGE, MASSACHUSETTS, AND LONDON, ENGLAND 1979

Library of Congress Cataloging in Publication Data

Carew, Jean V   1936-
   Beyond Bias

   Bibliography: p.
   Includes index
   1. Classroom management.   2. Teacher-student relationships.
3. Interaction analysis in education.
I. Lightfoot, Sara Lawrence, joint author.   II. Title.
LB3013.C34   372.1'1'02   78-20997
ISBN 0-674-06882-3

Acknowledgments

WE WISH to extend our gratitude first of all to the four teachers and eighty children without whom this research could never have been done. We cannot express sufficient thanks for their cooperation and good-humored tolerance of our presence in their classrooms. We are especially grateful to the teachers, school administrators, and parents who gave us many hours of their time in interviews and tried to answer honestly our sometimes awkward, convoluted, and intrusive questions. (Names and locations have been altered throughout the book to conceal the identities of the participants in the study.)

Many other people assisted us enormously in this project: in particular, Gloria Chao, who helped to develop the observation procedures, carried out and coded most of the classroom observations, interviewed parents and children, and kept week-to-week friendly contact with participants in the research; Josefa Rosenberger, whose assistance in the administration of the study, in the data analysis, and in the typing and editing of the manuscript was invaluable; Hugh Macdonald, who executed the computer analyses; Kathy Hewett, who helped us sketch the descriptions of the city, neighborhoods, and schools surrounding teachers and children found in chapter 4; and Edward Gondolf, whose scholarship and insights were a great contribution to chapter 2.

We wish also to thank, sincerely and gratefully, the Office of Child Development (now the Administration for Children, Youth and Families), which sponsored this research, and in particular Dr. Maso Bryant, who gave us timely encouragement and support.

Husbands, children, and friends also helped in the enterprise by providing advice and criticism or simply by putting up with our monologues and reveries. We thank these dear people for their loving interest and tolerance of many varieties of researcher's withdrawal and writer's cramp.

Contents

Tables

BEYOND BIAS

PART ONE

Introduction

Sara Lawrence Lightfoot

TEACHERS ARE familiar figures in all our lives. No matter what our age, we can recapture the images of the teachers of our childhood and growing-up years. Memories of caring, dedicated, energetic teachers still make us feel grateful and inspired, and images of boring, deceptive, and unfair teachers make us feel angry for wasted time and injured spirits. Mostly, we tend to remember the good and bad extremes of teacher behavior as our retrospective fantasies obscure the subtleties and erase the complexities of their personalities and relationships to students. The details fade but the general impressions remain.

Just as teachers are caricatured in our memories, so much of the research on teaching gives us a narrow, reductionist vision of who teachers are, what they do, and how they do it. A major purpose of this book is to present a portrait of teachers and children in classrooms that illuminates the intricacies of their interactions, that paints in the subtle, shadowy grays that have gotten lost in our memories of teachers and often in the study of teaching.

Teaching is an extremely demanding job that requires a complex mixture of intellectual capacities, pedagogical skills, personality characteristics, and organizational talents. The interactions between teachers and children seldom have a clear, singular purpose; they encompass a range of meanings and messages as teachers try to keep track of the individual agendas, styles, needs, and capabilities of twenty or more very different children. Teachers seldom act alone. They must work within the context of the schools—highly ritualized and bureaucratic social environments that shape their behaviors, restrict their choices, and often provide sources of support, guidance, and reinforcement. And these schools, of course, exist within communities whose culture, history, physical dimensions, and political life have influence on what goes on inside classrooms. Therefore, before teachers even begin the difficult task of working with children, they must respond (whether consciously or not) to a great variety of impinging forces that guide their decision making and shape their relationships with children.

The purpose of this study is to reveal the rich and dynamic life of classrooms, with a primary focus on teachers. We present teachers through the lenses of various observers and participants and tell a story that integrates the variety of perspectives we have gathered. Our aim is to create a multifaceted, multilayered picture of teachers by adopting, one at a time, and then synthesizing diverse ways of perceiving, recording, and interpreting what they said and did. Our methods were purposely eclectic. For instance, one of the unique aspects of our study was the integration of systematic observational data taken from time-sampled behaviors and communications between teachers and children and comprehensive, qualitative data taken from a series of in-depth, thematic interviews with teachers. Both of these methods of documentation and analysis were used over the course of the school year, offering the opportunity to record changes and developments in patterns of interaction within the classroom. The two sources of data created an interesting range of contrasts, validations, and comparisons.

A major theme weaving throughout our work is that of the teacher as a primary source of knowledge for researchers. We strongly believe that teachers have an understanding of children and classrooms that is both more subjective and intimate and more realistic and comprehensive than that of researchers. Teachers are the authorities on their own feelings, motivations, and personal and intellectual histories. Our research seeks to capture their insider's perspective, to understand the origins of their reasoning, and to get them to offer retrospective, reflective analyses of life in their classrooms. In a sense this research orientation creates a very personal document—one that reveals the person and the teacher, the present and the roots of the present, and the internal and external forces that shape the teacher's interactions with children.

A secondary concern of our research focused on understanding how teachers, with limited resources of time, space, energy, and emotion, distribute their attention to some twenty children in the classroom. How do teachers make judgments about who needs special help with reading, a firm reprimand, or a fond word of encouragement? Over time, can we see patterns of positive discrimination (discerning and responding to the individual needs of children) or negative discrimination (reacting prejudicially to children as members of low-status categories)? Is there evidence of the teacher discriminating against groups of children on the basis of sex, race, or social class?

The organization of this book is designed to reveal the sequence and structure of our research in four first-grade classrooms in two public elementary schools in the same city. We trace our movements and the development of our ideas through a self-conscious reflection on the research process. The first chapter, therefore, offers a critique of selected literature written about teaching. In reviewing these works, we summarize the descriptions of teachers that have dominated educational research on classroom life. This review does not include the entire range of studies on teachers in classrooms, but rather sketches the images of teachers and teaching that have prevailed in many of the major works—images often lacking in depth, subtlety, and complexity. It is in response to much of this literature that we felt inspired to pursue this study.

Research on teachers and children in classrooms can be better understood through an examination of the intellectual history that has shaped the nature of the research inquiry. The design, methods, and goals of research on educational process are informed by a set of theoretical assumptions that often remain covert and unarticulated but nevertheless have a powerful influence on investigators' perceptions of classroom environments and the roles and actions of teachers and children. Chapter 2 explores some of the theoretical frameworks that underlie the educational literature and shape the methods of inquiry. We argue that an awareness of the assumptions one brings to the research task leads to greater clarity and objectivity in reporting what takes place.

Researchers bring with them not only theoretical assumptions but also their own persons. As researchers move into schools, they have an impact on the environment they enter and the people they encounter. They are not merely well-placed hidden cameras snapping photographs of an unchanging scene, but observers who intrude upon others' territories and selectively record certain aspects of the environment. Additionally, it is becoming increasingly difficult for researchers to gain entry into schools. Parents, teachers, and administrators have grown wary of researchers who scrutinize their behaviors but who rarely offer anything of practical value. Because we viewed the process of our entry into schools as an integral part of our research, in chapter 3 we describe our long search for schools and teachers to participate in this study. The narrative of our entry into schools offers an important backdrop for understanding the research findings that follow.

Chapter 4 offers a journalistic, sociological account of the city, neighborhoods, and schools in which the children and teachers we studied live each day. These more macroscopic, institutional, and structural surroundings have a profound influence on both teachers and children. As children negotiate the path from home to school each day, they experience the familiarity, vitality, and potential dangers of the streets, and they may see school as a place of solace or of boring isolation from community life. And behind the classroom doors teachers are keenly aware of the external forces that make their way into the school. Chapter 4 gives a sense of the worlds that surround teachers and children, drawing the outlines of the political, cultural, and economic realities that shape their patterns of behavior.

One goal of this study was to capture the vital dialectic between qualitative and quantitative ways of knowing. We wanted to look in on the classroom through many windows, by recording the views of external observers (through systematic behavioral observations), the reasoning and motivations of teachers (through a series of in-depth interviews), the experiences of children (through focused conversations and interviews with selected children), and the opinions of parents about their child's school experience (through parent interviews of the focal children). Each of these groups of people—researchers, teachers, parents, and children—spoke from different perspectives and with different voices. Their combined story offers a kaleidoscopic vision of classroom realities. Chapter 5, therefore, begins with a description of the various observational methods used to record life in these classrooms and ends with a report of the quantitative data gathered through systematic observations of teachers and children. From these data one can begin to get a sense of gross differences in teacher styles, interactional strategies, curriculum emphasis, reward systems, grouping and seating patterns, organizational and procedural characteristics—differences that are given greater depth and meaning when integrated with the qualitative data presented in later chapters.

The second half of the book (chapters 6-9) presents portraits of the four teachers with whom we worked very closely over the course of our study. Our analysis was designed to reveal their unique character, the complex institutional and interpersonal forces affecting their teaching, the varied strategies they use to work with children, their differing ideological and philosophical visions that often pierce through the classroom environment unsaid. The themes that emerge in each teacher portrait reflect the issues and concerns that seemed to dominate their perceptions of teaching and classrooms. Those things the *teachers* seemed to care about most are expressed in these chapters, define the themes, and shape the narratives we tell. The qualitative portrayal of each teacher is followed by the quantitative data taken from behavioral observations, which provide contrast and validation for the more subjective, personal accounts. It is also in these chapters that we trace the interactions and unique relationships that teachers formed with ''special'' children in their classrooms. For four teachers, four tapestries are woven, each with its own unique color scheme, pattern, and texture. The weavings illuminate and celebrate the differences among the teachers and children, the differing perceptions of the scene, and the different windows through which we look to capture the complex reality.

The Teacher as Central Figure

Sara Lawrence Lightfoot

THE TEACHER has been the central and dominating figure of classroom research. She has been described as the all-powerful determining force who is
there to "make education happen" (Farber 1969), and her dominance has
been affirmed by the theoretical concepts and methodological strategies
used by researchers studying classroom procedures. Research on teacher effectiveness and teacher expectations has been a primary concern in the literature on classrooms and it has focused on documenting the attitudes and
behaviors of the teacher almost exclusively. This focus is not in itself surprising, since the explicit purpose of much of this research is to assess the effects of teacher characteristics on student outcomes such as reading or IQ
scores. But behind this purpose is a critical assumption that is very much
open to question. It is that the teacher is the primary initiator and ultimate
determiner of all that happens in the classroom. The teacher is thought to be
the only person who "teaches" and the only one who has a significant impact on the child's learning and development. Teaching is seen as a unidirec-
tional process with power and authority resting securely in the hands of the
teacher. The result is a severely oversimplified picture of life in classrooms,
one in which the teacher stands large and imposing at the front of the room
and all activity emanates from or is directed toward her.

   Closely linked with this view of the teacher as central figure in the classroom is the overriding concern in past research with identifying the teaching
techniques that create the optimal child product. The literature is replete
with metaphors of industrial efficiency, productivity, technology, and standardization, as if children were refrigerators or television sets that are just
meant to work when we plug them in. In this school-as-factory conceptual-
ization, the teacher is seen as a manager or assembly-line worker and the

child as a manufactured item whose quality can be measured by applying standardized tests. The teacher may be held accountable for the child product in much the same way as a garment worker may be held responsible for the cut of a dress. A basic but hidden assumption here is that the teacher follows some standard routine in his interactions with children just as a factory operative follows a set sequence of steps in assembling a machine. At the very least, the teacher is thought to have a characteristic style or pattern of behavior which varies so little from child to child that it can fairly be represented by averaging his responses to the individual students composing his class. This assumption flies in the face of reality. It ignores the wide variation in teacher behavior toward individual children that is often strikingly apparent in classroom observations and the wide variation in the personalities, needs, and behavior of children; it also ignores the fact that the former is often contingent on the latter.

Teachers treat individual children differently. They may do so out of dislike or prejudice or they may do so because they perceive them as having different needs, abilities, and temperaments. Teachers do not necessarily strive to create the same product with all children, nor do they necessarily adopt the same strategies to fashion the product they have in mind. Indeed, teachers probably vary greatly in how much influence they think they have on children, in their desire to create a product that is homogeneous and standardized or varied and diverse, in their sensitivity to individual differences in children, and in their ability to adopt appropriately different modes of treating them. These sources of variance make it entirely unrealistic to assume, as does most research, that teachers have typical styles of behavior which they display equally to all their students, or, the implicit corollary, that teachers exert the same impact and influence on all children.

The concept of the teacher as the central actor in the classroom and as the maker of a child product is also clearly expressed in the methods typically used in classroom research. The teacher is nearly always the main subject on whom data is collected, and observations or ratings of her behavior are often the primary or only method used to document classroom processes. These procedures are themselves often unsatisfactory even as methods of describing teacher behavior. For example, in studies of teacher effectiveness, researchers have employed both high- and low-inference methods. High-inference methods such as rating scales typically require the observer to make large interpretive leaps in judging the teacher's style, personality, or pedagogy. For example, an observer may be asked to rate a teacher as authoritarian or democratic, warm or cold, integrative or dominative merely from observing her teach or interact briefly with children in the classroom. What the observer actually witnesses may be statements such as: "Johnny, give me an 'at' word!" "Susan, stop that silly whispering!" "Tim, you look tired today." But what she is required to rate are stable and general aspects of style or personality such as "warm or cold," "authoritarian or democratic." High-inference rating scales encourage so much subjectivity that the scores are likely to reflect more about the observer's perceptions and biases than about classroom realities. The forced choice that such scales often demand may also compel the rater to think in terms of jargonized, good-bad dichotomies and degrade the observer's perceptions, which may in fact be more precise and subtle than the scale allows.

The obvious subjectivity of such rating scales has led many investigators to turn to low-inference methods. These methods typically require only the counting of discrete, directly observable behaviors, ostensibly keeping interpretation, intuition, and judgment on the part of the observer to a minimum. Using prescribed behavior categories, an observer may record the number of times the teacher praises the child, gives negative reinforcement, provides feedback, and so on, or, if such categories are regarded as still too inferential, he may limit himself to counting the number of times the teacher smiles or frowns, says "correct" or "incorrect," and so on. Unfortunately, behavior counts, although usually more objective and reliable than high-inference ratings, may also grossly misrepresent the behavior and influence of teachers. Only those behaviors that can be counted easily and reliably tend to be recorded in these observation systems. But countable actions are not necessarily significant ones, nor are significant behaviors necessarily countable. Many aspects of teacher communication that are subtle, fluid, and difficult to measure may reliably represent the more interesting and crucial dimensions of teacher-child relationships. Indeed, there is some evidence indicating that ratings of teacher characteristics that are less closely linked to actual, discrete behaviors are more predictive of child outcomes than are counts of specific behaviors (Rosenshine and Furst 1973).

Another major focus of classroom research—the self-fulfilling prophesy —further exaggerates the teacher as the dominant, overpowering, even malicious figure in the classroom. This research has been primarily concerned with documenting the strong relationship between the teacher's expectations of a pupil's academic performance and the actual performance of that pupil. More broadly, researchers have traced the powerful effect that a teacher's conscious and unconscious values, attitudes, and expectations toward students have on his classroom behavior and teaching style and subsequently on the academic and social achievement of his pupils. Although a few investigators have recognized the potentially positive impact of teacher expectations, much of the research on the self-fulfilling prophesy in education has come to have predominantly negative connotations. The teacher is seen to be an all-powerful being who determines the life chances of his defenseless children, sometimes making the critical judgments in the first few hours of the school year.

In his attack on the all-encompassing power of the school in an industrial society, Ivan Illich (1970) discusses the impact of the professionalization of the teacher's role. He claims that teachers now have exclusive power to decide whether a child has shown a sufficient degree of mastery. These judgments by teachers are not limited to evaluations of the academic and conceptual skills of the student but encompass a wide range of characteristics, enabling the teacher to become custodian, master of ceremonies, preacher, and therapist as she controls and manipulates the psychosocial and motivational aspects of the child's life.

Few social scientists are as passionately opposed to the assymetric power of teachers and children within schools as Illich, but many have focused their attention on teachers as the primary judges of deviance and on the forces that shape their judgments. These judgments, in turn, influence the social and cognitive learning that is consciously or unconsciously transmitted to pupils. For example, in his study of classroom interaction patterns, Jules Henry (1957) claimed that the significant aspect of teacher-child communications is the transmission of value orientations from teacher to child. The learning of values does not necessarily proceed through didactic teaching but through systems of reward and punishment. The values that are transmitted depend on the teacher's value orientation, which in turn is determined by her social-class identification.

In a study based on interviews with large numbers of teachers in Chicago, Howard Becker (1952) analyzed the responses of teachers to children from different social class backgrounds. Becker claimed that the teacher's perception of the child's ability to do schoolwork determined her actual teaching techniques: "The teacher expects that the amount of work and effort required of her will vary inversely with the social status of her pupils . . . Such consequences of the teacher's differential reaction to various class groups obviously operate to further perpetuate those class-cultural characteristics to which they object in the first place" (pp. 455-456).

In this very perceptive study Becker was vitally interested in the motivations behind the discriminatory behavior of teachers. He recognized the profound impact of the teacher's self-image on his perceptions of children. Not only did middle-class teachers find it difficult to develop effective pedagogical strategies for conveying information to lower-class children, not only did teachers have a hard time disciplining such children, but they also seemed deeply offended by them. "In terms of physical appearance and condition lower class children disgust and depress the middle class teacher." On the other hand, the responsiveness and similarities of middle-class children to themselves made the teachers feel successful and rewarded in their work and increased their self-esteem as competent professionals. The actions, behaviors, and values of middle-class children were familiar, non-threatening, and anticipatable, while those of lower-class children were viewed as disruptive and threatening. Becker appreciated that teachers have human needs for support and reinforcement and that if deprived of these they are likely to project their negative feelings onto their less powerful students. The teacher's feelings and perceptions about the abilities of children in his class are largely a reflection of how successful he feels at making them learn. In focusing on the teacher as a whole person with his own needs, Becker began to uncover some of the intrapersonal and interpersonal roots of teacher attitudes and behavior and the complexities of classroom processes.

Pygmalion in the Classroom, by Rosenthal and Jacobson, is probably the best known experiment on teachers and children in classrooms. When the data were published in 1968, teachers were suddenly struck with their own sense of power and irreversible influence, parents feared that their children would be labeled losers and doomed for life by careless or hostile teachers, and researchers marveled at the dramatic documentation of the expectation effect. Although the authors' claims have been challenged by more recent research on teacher expectations, the historical and symbolic importance of this study still remains with us today.

The experiment took place in a public elementary school in a lower-class, medium-sized community. Rosenthal and Jacobson wanted to test the proposition that favorable expectations by teachers could lead to an increase in the intellectual competence of children. About one-fifth of the children in the school were alleged to be potential academic bloomers on the basis of a fictitious test. In actuality, the names of these special children were randomly chosen and bore no relation to their actual abilities. "The difference between the special children and the ordinary children, then, was only in the minds of the teachers" (p. 175). Results of IQ tests given to children at the end of the school year revealed that students whom the teachers were led to believe would bloom in their academic performance actually did score higher than other students. In addition, these children were rated by teachers as being more intellectually curious, happier, and less dependent on social approval and reinforcement from teachers. The only plausible explanation the authors could advance for these findings was the differential treatment by teachers of students for whom they had different but false expectations. Rosenthal and Jacobson did not observe the teachers' behavior, so they could only speculate on how teachers brought about these differences in children's intellectual competence.

> To summarize our speculations, we may say that by what she said, and by how and when she said it, by her facial expressions, postures, and perhaps by her touch, the teacher may have communicated to the children of the experimental group that she expected improved intellectual performance. Some communications together with possible changes in

teaching techniques may have helped the child learn by changing his self-concept, his expectations of his own behavior, and his motivation, as well as his cognitive style and skills. (p. 180)

Reaction to this research was immediate and vociferous. Some researchers feared uncritical acceptance of the study's results by the public and worried that people would believe in the automatic, universal impact of the self-fulfilling prophesy in all classrooms at all grade levels. Robert Thorndike (1968) complained, "In spite of everything I say, I am sure it [*Pygmalion in the Classroom*] will be a classic widely referred to and rarely examined critically." Similarly, after an extensive review of the study, Richard Snow (1969) concluded, "*Pygmalion* inadequately and prematurely . . . has performed a disservice to teachers and schools, to users and developers of mental tests and perhaps worst of all, to parents and children whose newly-gained expectation may not prove quite so fulfilling." Many other educators responded to the experimental results with mixed amazement and skepticism. Most were willing to accept the basic premise of the self-fulfilling prophesy (that when we have high expectations of children, they are more likely to thrive than when we have low expectations), but it was difficult to imagine that the achievement of children, regardless of their abilities, could be so greatly shaped and transformed through teacher expectations. Despite the sophisticated research techniques and statistical analysis used by Rosenthal and Jacobson, the process of changing a child's competence and self-image was obviously more subtle and complex than that portrayed by the authors. Researchers, teachers, parents, and laymen voiced many concerns and questions about the process and dynamics of teacher-child interactions that produced these dramatic results. *Pygmalion in the Classroom* had given an incomplete vision of the self-fulfilling prophesy at work—one that emphasized the final child product but did not reveal the process of accommodation and change experienced by the teachers and children in the classrooms during the school year.

In 1970, Brophy and Good explored the processes of interaction and transformation within classrooms that might create the self-fulfilling prophesy (1970b). They were interested in documenting the ways in which different expectations are communicated between teachers and students. The teachers of first-grade children were asked at the beginning of the school year to rank their students in order of their academic achievement, and this ranking constituted teacher expectancy. The six students ranked highest formed the high-achievement group, and the six ranked lowest formed the low-achievement group. Brophy and Good found that high achievers sought out their teachers and initiated interactions more frequently than low achievers; teachers criticized the low achievers more, gave feedback more frequently to high achievers, and were more persistent in eliciting responses from them; and high achievers scored better on standardized tests at the end of the year. The authors concluded that teacher expectation predicted objective measures of classroom performance, objective achievement-test scores, and rate of teacher praise and criticism.

It is important to note that Brophy and Good's operational definition of teacher expectations is quite different from Rosenthal and Jacobson's. In the latter research, teachers are asked to accept an *expert*'s judgments of the children's intellectual abilities (to accept fictitious test scores as valid predictors of their competence), whereas in the Brophy and Good study they are asked to give their *own* expectations of children's abilities, which may have been based on perceptions of real differences among children that were apparent even in the first few weeks of school. Thus, Brophy and Good's observations of differential treatment of children whom teachers initially judged to be high and low achievers do not necessarily explain the Pygmalion effect. Expectations induced by relying on the word of experts may have different consequences in the classroom than expectations that teachers arrive at for themselves.

Brophy and Good's observational instrument marks a critical breakthrough in the documentation of classroom processes. In much of the previous observational research, observers had described the teacher's behaviors in relation to the class as a whole. For instance, teacher effectiveness studies had rated the teacher as "warm" or "cold" in her interactions with the class as an undifferentiated group. Teacher characteristics were then correlated with class mean scores on standardized achievement tests. Treating the class as an undifferentiated group conveyed the misleading impression that the teacher responded in the same way to all children. The data did not reveal discriminations in the teacher's relationships with children nor reflect the unique experiences of each child in the class. Using a dyadic approach, Brophy and Good (1970a) were able to record individual interactions between teachers and children and offer a far more differentiated and authentic picture of classroom processes.

That teachers behave differently toward students whom they perceive as differing in academic potential is a highly plausible hypothesis about real-life classroom experiences, although most subsequent studies have failed to confirm the experimentally induced Pygmalion effect. A related question is how these expectations are formed and internalized by teachers in the first place. It is not surprising that two of the factors so far alleged to be determinants of teacher expectancy of student ability are social class and race. Rist (1970) clearly demonstrated this relationship in his report of observations made in an all-black ghetto school (the teachers were black as well). On the eighth day of kindergarten he observed the teacher segregating her students by tables, apparently defining the groups by social dimensions such as the children's physical appearance, interactional behavior, use of language, and family socioeconomic variables. She labeled one group "fast learners" and the other "slow learners" and then proceeded to discriminate systematically in favor of the first group and against the others. The fast learners received much more encouragement, instruction, and privileges from her, while the slow learners were far more often controlled and ridiculed. Moreover, the children themselves internalized the teacher's invidious comparison, the fast learners adopting her tactics of belittlement and contempt toward the slow learners, the latter deflecting their resentment and shame from the aggressors onto each other. Rist demonstrated that the teacher's initial expectations and consequent discriminatory patterns of behavior not only profoundly affected the students' academic performance throughout the kindergarten year, but worse, provided teachers in the later grades with "objective" evidence which became the basis for further discrimination. It is not far-fetched to conclude that these children's chances for academic and occupational success were substantially set in the first eight days of school.

Rist's study made a significant contribution to the literature on classroom processes because it provided an analysis of critical factors in the teacher's development of expectations and documented the process by which expectations influence the classroom experience of teachers and children. Rist's observations also underscored the need to consider expectations that children have of one another. In this study the teacher's expectations were mirrored in and magnified by the behavior and attitudes of children in the classroom, but it is also conceivable that children might reject their teacher's judgments and engage in behaviors that conflict with hers. If one is to understand the impact of teacher expectations, one must also explore the complicated network of relationships among children.

In *Teaching and Learning in City Schools* (1969), Leacock was interested in examining the teacher's assumptions about desirable patterns of socialization for children from different backgrounds. She observed fifth-grade classrooms in middle- and low-income black and white schools and contrasted the teacher attitudes and behavior within these schools. In comparing black and white schools, Leacock found a marked difference between teacher attitudes and behavior with regard to organizing the classroom for leadership and responsibility. The teacher in the middle-income white school had high expectations and placed a strong emphasis on student independence and self-reliance (although the responsibility given was clearly nominal and often superficial). In the low-income black school Leacock found a more relaxed and cooperative atmosphere but an emphasis on discipline and obedience and a lack of academic expectations or explicit learning goals. In explaining the differences in the teachers' attitudes and aspirations, Leacock raised the important issue of the effects of the school and community environments on interactional patterns within classrooms. In the anthropological tradition, Leacock asserted that we must not view teacher expectations as isolated phenomena that relate only to interactions between the teacher and the child. "The way the teacher structures both her relations with the children and their relations with each other sets up a behavioral model for them, the implications of which extend far beyond the classroom" (p. 117). Expectations pervade the entire school population, and researchers must seek to identify how the social and behavioral norms found in schools influence the individual teacher's conception of the ideal and successful student and shape the interactional patterns within classrooms.

This review of research is not meant to be an exhaustive account of the literature on classroom processes but serves to identify studies that have offered different conceptual perspectives on teacher-child interactions. For instance, Becker's work is important in its recognition of the teacher's needs for positive self-esteem and feelings of competence and of the negative and pejorative projections she often makes onto children when she is feeling threatened or unsuccessful with them. Brophy and Good offer an observational approach that records classroom processes, focuses on individual interactions of teachers and children, and documents the different experiences of children in the classroom. And Leacock gives a much broader perspective to the study of classroom processes by referring to the powerful impact of social context. Teachers do not act in isolation (even behind classroom doors), but are greatly influenced by the norms, values, and culture of the school and community that surround them.

After reviewing the dozens of studies on teacher expectations that have accumulated since *Pygmalion in the Classroom,* one must agree with Brophy and Good (1974) that this research has raised many more questions than it has answered. Rosenthal and Jacobson's original findings on the effects of teacher expectations on student outcomes have never in fact been fully replicated. Results seem to depend on a large number of variables, including when and how the teachers' expectations are formed (whether experimentally induced or naturally arrived at); the kind of evidence that is supplied or used in forming these expectations and how consistent these are with later observations of students in the classroom; various teacher characteristics including aspects of personality and coping abilities; various student characteristics including race, sex, and age and also classroom behaviors that confirm or contradict teacher expectations and those that reward the teacher in his interactions with students; and various combinations of teacher, student, and classroom characteristics that encourage the teacher to be relatively proactive, reactive, or overreactive vis-à-vis individual pupils. As Brophy and Good wisely point out, teacher expectations—judgments of students' abilities and personalities—are normal, ubiquitous, many-sided, and necessary. Teachers typically form impressions of individual students within a few days or weeks of school and these impressions vary in elaborateness, in the particular dimensions considered salient, in their openness to change in the face of later, contrary evidence, and most important in how teachers act upon them. Teachers vary in whether or not they are likely to act so as to fulfill the prophesies implicit in negative judgments. Some are challenged to reverse these judgments through special intervention; others react simply in accordance with student behavior that is consistent with the judgment; others overreact, as if exaggerating the initial judgment and treating the child in question more negatively than his behavior warrants. Only in the latter case can the teacher be truly said to be bringing about a self-fulfilling prophesy. Which teachers are prone to do this, why, and with respect to what types of students is a research question that needs to be seriously investigated.

The Child as Initiator and Creator

The lives of children have been significantly absent from the studies on classroom processes. Since schools and classrooms are settings that are created as special places for child learning and growth, it is very strange not to hear the voices of children in the research literature. Throughout the research we hear about children through class mean scores on achievement tests. Not only is our vision of children limited to results of narrowly constructed standardized tests, but we are rarely given any information on the individual child.

Class mean scores mask individual differences. Research findings on ability grouping, for instance, show that it is virtually impossible to create homogeneous groups of children. If children are selected to be homogeneous on a single variable such as achievement, reading scores, or IQ, they are found to vary widely in other social, psychological, and intellectual dimensions. Even if one focuses solely on the variable on which the children were homogeneously selected, their different rates of growth and development create variation in this dimension after a few months of school (Olson 1966). It is a distortion of reality, therefore, to represent children's learning in terms of class mean scores on standardized tests. Children possess different constellations of abilities that cannot be captured by an aggregate score; neither can patterns of learning be captured by summary, end-of-the-year scores on standardized tests.

Not only does research on classrooms neglect individual differences among children in ability and learning styles, but it also fails to record the children's responses to the classroom environment. Student-gain scores tell us nothing about the children's perceptions of the learning experience, their views of the teacher, or their accommodation to the social context. We do not know how the children perceive the environment, nor do we get any sense of what they perceive as salient and important. Intuitively, we all recognize that our retrospective view of our early school experience evokes particular events. Those special moments capture our memories—not necessarily the repetitive patterns of interaction that we experienced daily. The frequencies of certain kinds of interactions may not determine their relative importance to the experience of a child.

In probing the complexities of teacher-child interactions, it is also crucial to recognize that all children in a classroom do not share a common experience. In an interesting observational study, Philip Jackson and Henriette Lahaderne (1970) warn observers about the dangers of perceiving the classroom experience as one that is shared by all children equally. The authors recorded the different interactions of teachers in four sixth-grade classrooms:

> The findings reveal a range of differences in each classroom broad enough to weaken any hopes of making facile generalizations about what goes on there. In each classroom there are a few students who are almost always out of the teacher's range of vision, so to speak, and a few others who are almost always underfoot. What this difference means and how it comes about is anybody's guess, but it is fair to conclude that by the end of the year some students likely will be more familiar to the teacher than will others, even though they have all lived together in the same room for about the same number of days. This observation calls into question the conventional view of looking upon each classroom as a unit whose participants have shared in a common educational experience. In a sense, each classroom contains as many environments as it does pairs of eyes through which to view them. (p. 103)

Teacher expectations are not formed in a vacuum. Ray Rist (1975) emphasizes the need to consider even the labeling of children as an interactive process that implies behavior and choices by both teachers and children. Labeling is a social process in which individuals are involved in negotiating, rejecting, accepting, and modifying each other's perceptions. "For expectations to become realized, both teacher and student must move towards a pattern of interactions where expectations are clearly communicated and the behavioral response is consonant with the expected pattern."

This point is well illustrated by Brophy and Good's (1974) description of the characteristics of four groups of students whom teachers tend to perceive very differently. "Attachment," "concern," "indifference," and "rejection" are the labels they used to refer to the feelings teachers report about the four groups. "Attachment" students are model students academically and behaviorially; they reward the teacher by conforming to his ideal of a good student. "Concern" students are typically weak academically and very dependent on teachers; but they too reward the teacher by frequently asking for his help and providing him with evidence that this help is beneficial. "Indifference" students are typically no weaker than "concern" students but their passivity and apparent lack of interest in the teacher's overtures "turn him off." "Rejection" students are often students who are academically able but present behavior problems. They may seek the teacher's attention no more often than "concern" students but do so in ways that teachers dislike. This group is the one most likely to be victimized by teacher action leading to self-fulfilling prophesies. Teachers tend to underrate these students' academic abilities and exaggerate their misbehaviors and consequently to overreact to their objective characteristics.

It is true that teachers and children are not equally powerful. Children do not have an equal chance to determine the nature of their school environment or shape the substance of their curriculum. But children do have very subtle and sophisticated ways of denying categorization and defying labels. Expectations, even prophesies, develop out of interactional experience, and research must document the behavior of both actors in the process: teacher and child. In undertaking such an analysis, one must recognize that children are individuals with different talents, skills, needs, and desires, and that when teachers treat children dissimilarly, they may be responding rationally and sensitively to manifest differences. In fact, one of the hallmarks of good teaching is learning to diagnose individual needs of children and to tailor one's behavior appropriately to their needs. Teachers must discern differences among children in order to do their job effectively.

In tailoring her responses to the individual needs of children, the teacher is likely to develop special relationships with individual children in the class —relationships of greater intensity, commitment, and depth. The special quality of this relationship may be reflected in the teacher's giving the child more attention, more positive reinforcement, more privileges and affection, but the relationship itself may depend on complex and subtle matches between the personalities, styles, values, and histories of teacher and child. It would be unrealistic to expect that even the most reflective and sensitive teacher would develop relationships of equal intensity with all the children in the classroom. Building and sustaining human relationships is a complex, dynamic process that requires a great deal of commitment and energy on the part of both participants. Rather than developing equal and similar relationships with all children, it is more likely that the teacher will feel closer and more committed to a few children—often children who have pursued and initiated contacts with her or worked hard at becoming the focus of her special attention and favors. The teacher's relationships with special children should be viewed as one of the inevitable consequences of a single person relating to a large group of persons, and not necessarily perceived as dysfunctional to the creation of a just and comfortable classroom environment.

The Teacher in Context

Although several studies of classrooms point to the fact that teacher behavior is shaped by the culture and organization of the school, very few have sought to describe the social contexts which surround the interactions of teachers and children in classrooms. For the most part, classroom research has given a very limited definition to social context—one which defines the focus of the activity being engaged in (work-related context, procedural context, behavioral context) or the number of people engaged in the work (individual seatwork, small group, lecture). Researchers have also referred to serial context, an observational strategy that records more than isolated and discrete teacher emissions by encompassing the sequence of extended interactions or episodes (for example, teacher question, student response, sustaining or terminal feedback from the teacher). However, these definitions of social context barely take into account the institutional and structural forces surrounding teachers and children that limit and shape their behaviors.

As one's vision expands beyond the interactions of teachers and children within classrooms, the image of the teacher as an autonomous, powerful, and central figure changes. Within the broader contexts of school systems, communities, and occupational structures, teachers tend to be described as powerless, isolated, and subordinate. Their image suddenly shifts from victimizer of helpless children to victim of an impersonal and unresponsive bureaucracy. Primarily, this wider lens has been used by sociologists interested in documenting the social and institutional contexts within which teachers function and the influence of these environmental factors on teacher behaviors and attitudes, professionalism, and identity. This perspective stresses the teacher as reactor within a larger universe, as one who is not completely in control of his environment nor responsible for his charges. If one can identify the constraining norms and structures that surround the daily lives of teachers and children, then the teacher's influence, power, and centrality can be more realistically assessed. A broader perspective on teachers in context can illuminate the forces that shape their professional lives and may uncover some of the origins of their behaviors *within* classrooms.

In *The Sociology of Teaching* Willard Waller offers an insightful analysis of the historical, cultural, social, and economic forces that impinge upon the teacher's work. Although the book was written in 1932, the cultural dogma, professional rhetoric, and institutional norms that Waller describes seem strangely contemporary and vivid. Through a sociological analysis of the concentric circles of structure and power surrounding the teacher, Waller reveals the enduring environments and prominent actors who influence teachers' lives. This description offers a balanced view of the influential dimensions of personality and structure. Although a sophisticated and comprehensive analysis, his work is pragmatic and clear. He seems to be talking to teachers as he talks about them; he identifies with teachers and his illustrations are poignantly descriptive, almost visceral—as if the experience had been his own.

Few researchers have continued the tradition of Waller's work. An exception is Gertrude McPherson, whose *Small Town Teacher* (1972) documents the daily lives of elementary school teachers in a school in which she herself was a teacher. Using participant observation, McPherson offers the intimacy and insights of an insider, the external perspective and distance of an investigator. Borrowing the conceptual framework of role theory, she describes the multiple, often conflicting roles that teachers are asked to perform in relation to children, parents, colleagues, and administrators. Teachers are also faced with the conflicts implicit in the idealized visions of teachers and their real-life status.

> It is . . . necessary to distinguish two types of role-expectations that teachers have, both of which are normative, one of which is "idealistic," the other "realistic." What a teacher expects depends on her past experiences and her assessment of present reality. So the "idealistic expectations," what one would hope to find if one could have anything one wanted, and the "realistic expectations" that one will settle for in the world as it is, do not always coincide. The realistic role-expectations emerge over time, through continual change and redefinition, as a compromise between idealistic expectations that have grown up on the basis of reading, moral training, utopianism, or nostalgia, and the actual behavior encountered so frequently as to be regularly anticipated. (p. 9)

McPherson's description is not an apology for the overworked, overwhelmed, and ambivalent teacher. It is an extremely sensitive account of teachers in action and in context.

Dan Lortie's book *Schoolteacher* (1975), using a much broader and more extensive data base, examines many of the same phenomena as Waller and McPherson. On the basis of hundreds of teacher interviews and questionnaires, Lortie paints a more detached and analytic view of the teaching culture. He identifies dimensions of the school environment, qualities of the teaching experience, issues of occupational status, aspects of teacher training and professional development, and long-term sociohistorical continuities that combine to shape teachers' conceptions of their role, their social and cultural purpose, and their sense of self. Feelings of isolation, for instance, fill the daily experiences of teachers. Behind closed doors, they are asked to perform a complex and demanding job alone, without companionship and supportive criticism, often without reinforcement and reward; and their lack of adult contact and interaction gives them a distorted view of their own power and maturity.

Robert Dreeben (1968) echoes Lortie in his perceptions of the feelings of isolation that teachers experience in their work. Dreeben argues that although school systems are bureaucratically organized, the work of teachers in classrooms is largely independent of administrative direction or supervision. The main work of teachers is to elicit from students compliance with, participation in, and commitment to rules and goals of a school which they attend involuntarily. Specifically, the teacher has to develop strategies for implementing her instructional plan, maintaining order, and responding to individual needs of many children of varying ability, in a small space and often with inadequate inducements at her disposal. Teaching is for the most part a solitary, play-it-by-ear occupation. Unlike many other professionals, teachers do not have a strong craft tradition, a highly developed technology, or a set of occupational guidelines based on collective experience to enable them to cope with or evaluate their work. The rapid pace of classroom events, the simultaneous nature of many ongoing activities, and the sheer numbers of children may allow the teacher little time for diagnosis, evaluation, or reflection. One way of adapting to the situational demands of the classroom is to keep talking, lecturing, demonstrating, questioning. Another is to simply react to events as they unfold, abandoning the role of initiator and shaper of student behavior (Dreeben 1972).

Philip Jackson documents many of the same dimensions of the teacher culture as Dreeben, but his descriptions focus less on structural variables and more on the psychosocial issues of schooling for teachers and children. In *Life in Classrooms* (1968) Jackson describes the dynamic culture and ecology of classrooms that present teachers and children with a unique set of influences that require accommodation and change. Children must learn to adapt to crowds, praise, and power. And teachers experience the ambiguities and tensions of their "individualistic" orientation. On the one hand, they perceive the class as a group of individuals with different needs, competencies, and personalities while on the other hand they recognize that their social and cultural role requires that they harness and constrain individual differences and create a smoothly functioning and relatively stable and homogeneous social group. Despite the conflicts created by the institutional and societal demands, teachers perceive the individuality of their work as the source of greatest pleasure. Responding to individual needs and watching the progress of particular children is especially exciting within the context of group experiences in classrooms.

> Thus, paralleling the teacher's delight in observing the progress of individuals is his insistence on having a group with which to work. At first glance these conditions may appear contradictory, but on further reflection the apparent contradiction disappears . . . They do not talk about their class as if it comprised a social unit with integrated parts and differentiated functions. Rather, they seem to be calling for a collection of individuals, a collection large enough to preserve the visibility of individual members. Stable social relations commonly develop within these collections of students and some classes surely evolve into groups in the functional sense of the term. But the primary unit of the elementary school teacher's concern and the major source of his satisfaction remains the individual and his development. (p. 143)

In *The Complexities of an Urban Classroom* (1968) Smith and Geoffrey offer a creative methodological strategy for analyzing and comprehending the evolving classroom social structure. Their study not only documents the teacher's place in the surrounding social contexts but also pursues the dynamic interactional patterns within classrooms—gaining a view of the double lives of teachers as powerful and powerless, victim and victimized, independent and isolated. Smith, a university professor and researcher, and Geoffrey, a classroom teacher, collaborate in an analysis of the developing structures, roles, and relationships that emerged in Geoffrey's classroom over the course of the school year. Their documentation is highly descriptive and behavioral, revealing the harsh realities and everyday experiences of a teacher who is working hard to establish structure and control in the classroom, to respond personally and meaningfully to his charges, to teach substantive curricular material, and to relate comfortably with his colleagues. The realism and subjectivity of Geoffrey is counterbalanced by the pursuit by Smith of a theoretical model of teaching based on systematic observations and analysis.

The Teacher as Knower

For a long time clinicians have been interested in understanding the motivational roots of human behavior, and in the psychoanalytic tradition they have probed personal histories in an attempt to better interpret present behaviors. Therefore, it is surprising that most researchers focusing on the classroom have neglected to recognize and document the psychodynamic origins of behavior but have followed the behaviorist model of looking only at visible and countable behaviors. They have been content to represent life in classrooms by describing actions and interactions, and in the process they have often ignored the character, motivations, attitudes, and values of the actors. (For an exception, see White, *Psychosocial Principles Applied to Classroom Teaching,* 1969.) Teachers are thought of as one-dimensional human beings whose behavior is determined by patterns of reward and punishment. They are viewed as technicians who perform specific actions on children, who in turn are seen as essentially passive human beings to be shaped and controlled by powerful adults.

For the most part, the literature on classroom products and processes adheres to this behaviorist orientation. Even those observers who have been interested in documenting the details of teacher-child interactions have not sought to describe and analyze the forces within the teacher and surrounding the teacher that shape his different responses to children. It is therefore not surprising that although the teacher is regarded as an all-powerful judge, virtually the maker and breaker of children's lives, very little attention is paid to what he thinks about his students, about his behavior toward them, or about the reasons, motives, or purposes governing his actions. Even in the literature on teacher expectations where artificially induced changes merely in the teacher's perceptions of children allegedly have momentous consequences, teachers are seldom asked what they thought of the children for whom they had different expectations or how these expectations affected their own behavior. Yet we suspect that for one teacher, information from an expert that a child is a low achiever may be a challenge to work harder at teaching, motivating, or disciplining her; for another it may be an excuse to give up; and for still a third it may be irrelevant. We cannot know how such information is regarded unless we ask teachers. Scrutinizing only their behavior is insufficient because the same behavior can be governed by quite different motives, and conversely, radically different behaviors can be governed by the same motives. Thus, it seems to us only fair and sensible to find out what these are before we judge a teacher as more or less sensitive, more or less skillful, or more or less effective.

Researchers deprive themselves of a most important resource for understanding classroom processes when they ignore the motivations behind teacher behavior. Teachers are the most profound and experienced knowers of the classroom scene, and their perceptions and reasoning should be an integral part of research. Teachers have a unique insider's view into what is going on in the classroom, a view that is at least as valid to understanding the educational process as an outside observer's.

Many aspects of what teachers know need to be considered. First of all, we need to find out what teachers know and think about the children in their class. How do teachers perceive their pupils? On what are these perceptions based? How do teachers acquire the relevant information? What sources are used? How quickly are initial judgments formed? How open are they to later elaboration or change? What effort does the teacher make to verify her judgments, perhaps by observing the child in a variety of contexts or checking her opinions with others? How differentiated are the teacher's perceptions of children? Does she apply only a few gross categories or does she make subtle, complex discriminations? Does she pay attention to social and emotional functioning or mostly to intellectual and academic performance? How do social class, race, and sex influence her judgments? Are her opinions reasonable and justifiable or are they secret, vague, stereotypic, or irrational?

We also need to find out what teachers know and think about themselves. What do they see as their strengths and weaknesses? What are their values, beliefs, and pedagogical priorities and objectives? How are these related to their life histories, experiences, and training? How self-critical are teachers? How inclined are they to scrutinize their own behavior, to assess themselves, to question their beliefs, to probe their own motives?

Finally, we need to examine the relationship between what the teacher thinks and how he acts. What range of characteristics or behavior on the part of children is considered valuable, acceptable, and not in need of change? Having perceived a child as possessing certain characteristics the teacher wishes to develop or change, what does he then do? What actions on his part are considered warranted and appropriate? How does the teacher check to see whether or not the strategies he uses to bring about change are successful? If there are conspicuous differences in his treatment of individual children, is he aware of them? If so, how does he justify these differences? These are some of the questions that we shall explore in this research when we consider the teacher as a thinking, reflective human being whose perceptions, ideas, and reasoning are indispensable to understanding and interpreting what we observe in classrooms.

Finally, the development and pattern of interactional processes between teachers and children cannot be revealed in a single observation. Actions and reactions must not be seen as isolated events in the classroom but must be viewed as part of a pattern and constellation of behaviors that evolve over time. One cannot, for instance, judge a teacher to be cold and heartless just because she is observed harshly scolding a child for leaving his seat. Neither can we view her goals as positive and nurturant just because her behavior seems immediately rewarding to the child. Education is a cumulative, changing, and transforming process that cannot be captured by a single behavior snapshot. In order to interpret a specific teacher's behavior responsibly, the observer needs to know more about the history of interactions that preceded the behavior, the cognitive and social needs of the child with whom the teacher is communicating, and the teacher's perceptions of the social structure of the classroom.

Objectivity in Classroom Research

Researchers are not merely the lens of a camera; they are selective interpreters of the classroom scene. No matter how quantitative and objective the research strategy appears, there is a point when researchers offer their interpretations, use their intuitions, and apply their values. Research, therefore, is a selective process that combines empirical data, rational thinking, judgment, and intuition. Each of these modes of understanding and analyzing phenomena are valid and valuable and can be made conscious parts of the research process.

Research is also a temperamental process that reflects an individual's style, personality, and predispositions. Research decisions are not made solely on the basis of intellectual or academic arguments. Certainly the path of questioning and focus of inquiry is guided by the need to know and the skills one possesses. But researchers are also directed by what they like to do, and their decisions are often shaped by the ways they feel most comfortable functioning. Consciousness of the motivating forces that shape the questions researchers choose to ask and the strategies they use can help them become more aware of their role and increase the objectivity of their work.

Our view of objectivity, therefore, is somewhat different from the one proposed by most research in the social sciences. We do not believe that one is able to gain an objective picture of classroom processes by using a single instrument of high validity and reliability. Certainly we would want to be sure that any research tool was gathering accurate and authentic data. But our main concern here is that the single vision gained by using one methodological approach cannot encompass all the important aspects of the phenomena we wish to analyze. Traditionally, objectivity has been synonymous with the researcher's perceptions and descriptions of the behaviors of subjects. We consider this approach to present a narrow and often distorted picture of classrooms. At best it provides us with the perspective of a nonparticipating, dispassionate outsider, but the price we pay is that only visible actions are recorded and the rationale and meaning of these actions to those who initiate or respond to them are ignored. The perspective of the uninvolved outsider is important, but it is not the only valid view. The views of participants—teachers, children, parents—are equally valuable, and truth is more likely to emerge when all of these perspectives are balanced and synthesized.

We are also skeptical of research that presents lyrical accounts of classroom life without serious attention to systematic and sustained inquiry. These descriptions attempt to capture "realism," but the passion and subjectivity of the narrator often obscure our understanding of the actual events, behaviors, and activities of teachers and children. Many of these pieces of experiential research are inspired by the political and ideological concerns of the author/observer, expressing themes of oppression and degradation experienced by children who are at the mercy of malicious teachers or unjust school systems (see Kozol 1967; Farber 1969; Hentoff 1966). Although one is often inspired by the dramatic force of the narrative and moved by descriptions that bring teachers and children to life in a way that can never be gained through quantitative tabulations of behavior, these accounts express biased and singular visions.

In the research to be described in this report we reject both the traditional, behavioristic approach to the study of classrooms and the loose narrative model. Our purpose is to gain both objectivity and comprehensiveness by capturing the perceptions of many different participants in the classroom drama and by integrating several methodological approaches and data sources: longitudinal observations of teachers and children, conversations and interviews with teachers, administrators, parents and children, quantitative and qualitative analyses, factual description, and subjective interpretation. We do not claim that our rendition is complete or definitive. Our aim is simply to increase the number of windows through which one can glimpse teachers and students in a space where daily they must meet. Brought together willy-nilly by law and custom, teachers and children have no option but to set about the task of living, working, influencing, and caring about each other. The resulting drama, often mundane, ritualistic, and routinized, occasionally comical, tender, and violent, sets the form and substance of this book.

2

Difference and Deviance

Sara Lawrence Lightfoot

THE NARROW constructions of the teacher's role that dominate the research literature are related to pragmatic, methodological considerations. It is easier to focus primarily on the teacher and avoid recording the less predictable, fast-moving actions of children. It is also more efficient to count visible and discrete behaviors than to probe the reasoning and history that produces those behaviors. The quantifiable data can yield clearer, more reliable and objective analyses. And it is less costly and time-consuming to do short-term, behavioral observations than to engage in the more expansive studies using a range of methodological approaches.

But decisions about how a researcher undertakes a study of classroom environments are not exclusively shaped by pragmatic and methodological considerations. Empirical investigations of teacher-child interactions also have an intellectual history that has had a powerful influence on researchers. The theoretical frameworks of social science have shaped (whether consciously or not) researchers' perceptions of what is important to study, who are the central actors, what are the critical questions to ask, and what is the scope of the universe under study. Forceful intellectual traditions, often covert and unarticulated, guide our lens and determine the focus and frame of the pictures we take of teachers, teaching, and classrooms. In this chapter we will explore some of the central conceptual themes that have provided frameworks for much of the research on classroom life.

One of the major preoccupations of social science has been describing the balance between individual expression and social organization. Theorists have sought to conceptualize the optimal state of equilibrium between the constraints of the social context and the needs of individuals for autonomy and expression. Psychoanalysts, for example, following the rather pessimistic tradition of Freud, have emphasized the oppressive and inhibiting forces of society that rob the individual of his instinctive wish to act spontaneously, creatively, emotionally, and sexually. Structural-functional sociologists, in the spirit of Talcott Parsons, have stressed the importance of a stable social system (almost static in its weightiness) that dynamically responds to individual initiative and social change but has its own momentum that must be maintained in order to avoid social disorganization. Spontaneous, individual expression is permitted within certain boundaries but is feared when it threatens the equilibrium of a smoothly functioning system.

Although various theorists may have given greater or lesser weight to the needs of the individual and of the society, these needs are most often seen in opposition to one another. Focusing on the contrasts and conflicts between the opposing forces of the individual and society seems to be related to another major preoccupation of the literature: deviance, pathology, and disintegration. It is easier to define and document disease than health, to record patterns of deviance than to describe patterns of normality. For the most part, theorists and researchers in the social sciences have defined and described social deviance rather than difference and variety and have focused on documenting the behaviors, values, and attitudes of those who do not accommodate to the norms of society and its various institutions. School structures are perceived as normal (and therefore correct) and individuals (whether teachers or children) as the negative forces who are likely to threaten the equilibrium.

Several major theories have shaped researchers' conceptions of normality and deviance in classrooms: theories of negative differentiation or prejudicial discrimination and theories that relate to the expression of individuality and positive forms of discrimination. These theoretical frameworks are directly related to the questions of how the teacher makes decisions about the distribution of scarce resources (time, space, energy, affection) among the children in her classroom, how she discerns differences among her pupils, how she decides who needs nurturance and reward or punishment and scolding, how she describes and rationalizes the different patterns of positive and negative reinforcement that emerge, and whether her behavior reflects discriminatory patterns toward categories of children or whether her interactions reveal changes and adaptations based on the developmental shifts, competence, and needs of individual children.

Social-Systems Theory

Fundamental to classical sociological theory is the concept of a normative order. The founders of this tradition—Durkheim, Merton, Parsons, in particular—see society differentiating itself for survival. Differentiation in the form of "specialization" allows individuals to fulfill themselves while serving the collective good. A precarious balance exists between individual autonomy and expression and the need for social cohesion and productivity. This tension between "aggregate" (collective) and "distributive" (individualistic) values must be resolved in the direction of maintaining a stable social order if society is to function without major upheaval.

Without social norms to regulate a cohesive social system, society would regress and disintegrate into chaos. Social discipline sustained by regulatory norms, therefore, is considered necessary, beneficent, and good for individual survival, safety, and development. Although the major protagonists of this view see the regulatory mechanisms as benign, many critics see a preoccupation with order, equilibrium, and control that reflects a middle-class bias favoring the status quo.

If social norms are suspended, obscure, or unattainable, individuals deviate. Norms are strained and break down during major crisis periods or rapid social transition, and the social disorganization that results brings about "normlessness," a condition referred to as "anomie." Deviation occurs as individuals attempt to adapt to this anomie. Social-systems theory, therefore, views deviance as a response to social conditions that are not deliberately imposed by individuals, but rather reflect a dysfunction of the system induced by the inadequacy or inappropriateness of its norms. In order to diminish deviance, norms need to be refurbished.

The focus of this orientation is vividly expressed by Robert Nisbet (Merton and Nisbet 1966, p. 4): "Modern sociology . . . maintains simply that social behavior, whether moral or immoral, legal or illegal, can be understood only in light of the values that give it meaning and the institutions that provide the channels of these values."

Emile Durkheim, noted French sociologist, fathered this traditional theoretical framework. Differences are described as responses to a prevailing set of values, beliefs, and ideals, and this "morality" is categorically above state and people. In *The Division of Labor in Society* (1893) Durkheim outlines the conditions of his "ideal" society. In the presence of generalized, consensual norms, a society of "organic solidarity" is possible where a wide range of differences can be tolerated as these norms integrate self-interests into a cohesive whole. In contrast, an undifferentiated society is one in which repressive conformity is imposed by rigid, unbending social norms. At the extremes of rigidity, societies function under a "forced division of labor" that leads to totalitarianism.

In social-systems theory, individual needs are never clearly defined, but they evidently approach the biological cravings and instinctual drives that are at the basis of Freudian theory. In the absence of regulation, needs are perceived as "a source of torment" (Durkheim 1897, pp. 247-248). Social control, therefore, is necessary to restrain this festering passion as well as integrate behavior. Although Durkheim claims that the individual becomes "autonomous" in the society of "organic solidarity," the person is always perceived as subservient to the social will.

In his article "Social Structure and Anomie" of 1939 Robert Merton modifies and expands Durkheim's theory by giving some initiative to the individual. In Merton's view it is the individual's adaptation to anomie that makes for different kinds of deviance. A person is responsive to, rather than locked into, social conditions, and his needs are prodded by social circumstances; they are not just consuming desires that must be contained. "Whatever the role of biological impulses, there still remains the further questions of why it is that the frequency of deviant behavior varies within social structures and how it happens that the deviants have different shapes and patterns in different social structures" (Merton 1957, p. 131). Therefore, social norms, though still paramount, serve not so much to regulate and restrain the individual as to prescribe appropriate and worthwhile objectives ("cultural goals").

Talcott Parsons (1951) gives these fixed norms a more flexible and adaptive character in his theory of social action. He claims that the individual takes an active role in the social system and contributes to the formation and alteration of social norms rather than merely submitting to a normative straightjacket (Durkheim) or adapting to cultural goals (Merton). As an "actor," the individual is also charged with transmitting social norms through the process of socialization. Although Parsons introduces themes of individual motivation and action, the individual is still seen mostly as responding rather than initiating action and creating social change. Social disorganization is still viewed by Parsons as malignant and threatening; and deviance is still considered a mere dysfunction of social norms, while opposing theorists think it may be a warranted challenge to oppressive social conditions (Bonger 1969).

Those who apply this theoretical framework to schools see the classroom as a microcosm of the wider society—a reflection of the norms and values of the corporate world beyond school. In *On What Is Learned in School* (1968) Dreeben suggests that schooling experiences impart to children the norms necessary to sustain "organic solidarity" in society. He summarizes the socialization process in schools and gives it prominence in perpetuating the existing social order: "The argument of this volume rests on the assumption that schools, through their structural arrangements and the behavior patterns of teachers, provide pupils with certain experiences largely unavailable in other social settings, and that these experiences, by virtue of their peculiar characteristics, represent conditions conducive to the acquisition of norms" (p. 84). Individuals will supposedly achieve a "meaningful" position in the differentiated society that these "democratic" norms ensure. But Dreeben does not give us a picture of how these societal norms are interpreted and integrated by the child. He offers no theories of identification or internalization, no way to understand the dynamic process of the development and acculturation of children. Rather he presents a vision of an all-powerful, determining social system that imposes values and norms on the passive, totally malleable child. Socialization of children is perceived as complete and irreversible.

In Dreeben's characterization the individual nature of the teacher is also given minimal attention. Teachers as well as children are regarded as passive agents of a static and controlling system rather than as persons with motivation and reason. They serve as an auxiliary or agent in the transmission of established norms. A teacher not fulfilling her part in the process might inhibit vital socialization of society's young, and without sufficient acculturation of norms, children are likely to deviate.

There are grave implications for those children who do not adopt the prescribed norms. William Ryan (1968) reveals the value orientation implicit in social-systems theory: "Within such a framework, then, deviation from norms and standards comes to be defined as failed or incomplete socialization—failure to learn the rules or the inability to learn how to keep them. Those with social problems are then viewed as unable or unwilling to adjust to society's standards, which are narrowly conceived by what Mills calls 'independent middle class persons verbally living out Protestant ideas in small town America' " (p. 84).

Much classroom research originates from the perspective of social-systems theory, which considers the social order of the school and classroom of prime importance and never describes individuals (whether teachers or children) as self-assertive, conscious beings with needs and strengths of their own.

Social-Learning Theory

Social-learning theory explores the role of socialization in the formation of deviance. It examines the process by which individuals prescribe roles for one another in an effort to clarify their identity and establish boundaries. Lemert, Becker, and Goffman in particular have exposed the tendency in this process to categorize others on the basis of superficial observations, and thereby impose deviance.

Conformity to a collective image helps individuals know what to expect from one another, and labeling some as deviants helps maintain the community boundaries. Deviants become scapegoats who mark out what is not acceptable behavior. "Deviant forms of behavior, by marking the outer edges of group life, give the inner structure its special character and thus supply the framework within which the people or the group develop an orderly sense of their own cultural identity" (Erikson 1966, p. 13). Prejudicial discrimination is illustrated particularly well in this analysis. Our misguided judgments, often the outcome of our haste to define our own positions, are transmitted through social interactions. The recipients of these judgments are often transformed and molded into something they may not be or want to be. Their individuality, their need for self-expression and autonomy, may not only be denied but destroyed.

Lemert (1951), responsible for the currency of labeling theory, argues that the collective response to a deviant act is the most important factor in the formation of a deviant personality. Society reacts to the deviant act, making the person into a confirmed deviant. And the rules that a deviant happens to violate initially do not just appear (as Durkheim's norms and Merton's cultural goals do), but "rules are the product of someone's initiative." They are made by presumptive rule makers that Howard Becker (1963) refers to as "moral entrepreneurs."

> The central fact of deviance is that it is created by society. I do not mean this in the way it is ordinarily understood: in which the causes of deviance are located in the social situation of the deviant, or the social factors, which prompted his action. I mean, rather, that social groups create deviants by making rules whose infractions constitute deviance, and by applying those rules to particular people and labelling them as outsiders. From this point of view, deviance is not the quality of the act the person commits, but rather a consequence of the application by others of rules and sanctions to an "offender". The deviant is one to whom the label has been successfully applied. Deviant behavior is behavior that people so label. (p. 9)

The "deviant" act of a relatively innocent person is reinforced with social control measures that mold a "different" person into a deviant role with a corresponding self-concept. The one who has transgressed a rule becomes a habitual outsider, and the manner in which people relate to him reinforces and finally crystallizes that role.

In this view deviance is essentially created through social interaction. One or two acts or superficial attributes are assumed by the labeler to represent the deviant's true character. Goffman (1963, p. 3) describes how evidence is misused in an effort to differentiate deviants from the dominant, insiders group. "While the stranger is present before us, evidence can arise of his possessing an attribute that makes him different from others in the category of persons available for him to be, and of a less desirable kind—in the extreme, a person who is quite thoroughly bad, or dangerous, or weak. He is thus reduced in our minds from a whole person and an unusual person to a tainted, discounted one. Such an attribute is a stigma, especially when its discrediting effect is very extensive; sometimes it is also called a failing, a shortcoming, a handicap.''

Although social-learning theory moves beyond the rigid moralizing of social-systems theory, we are still left with the ambivalence of cultural relativism. There is no overriding notion of ''good'' to guide individual differentiation, and the evaluation and labeling of deviants appears arbitrary, confusing, and pejorative. Most important, social-learning theory overlooks the personal motivations, consciousness, and will of the deviant, who appears as an innocent and passive victim of the discriminatory labeling process. The rule makers (teachers, welfare workers, judges, psychiatrists, prison guards), categorizing individuals for their own convenience, seem entirely responsible and irreversibly influential.

The literature on teacher expectation reviewed in the previous chapter reflects the conceptual orientation of social-learning theory, exposing how teachers impose unsubstantiated labels on their powerless pupils. The teacher is described as selecting those children sure to succeed in the dominant, middle-class society (Becker 1952; Rist 1973; Leacock 1969; Rosenthal and Jacobson 1968). An ''ideal type,'' clothed in middle-class behavior and values, serves as the model for success in most teachers' eyes; and the degree to which the student conforms to this ideal in appearance, background, and interactional style is the degree to which he is expected and allowed to advance academically and socially in the classroom.

Personality Theory

Personality theorists consider prejudicial discrimination to be a manifestation of one's psychological disposition. Prejudiced individuals displace social anxiety, project frustration, and resolve ambiguity through their prejudicial attitudes and discriminatory actions. Prejudice is often characterized by its irrational and vicious nature. It is deeply rooted, unconscious, and complex, a condition that makes it difficult to understand. Prejudiced individuals themselves often are not completely aware of the origins of their discriminatory attitudes and behaviors.

Victimized people (usually from powerless minority groups) become the scapegoats for these internal tensions. They are simply considered innately inferior in the eyes of the prejudiced person—supposedly they were born that way. Frequently, there is no social contact at all between the prejudiced individual and his scapegoat; rather there is deliberate isolation. Prejudiced attitudes, therefore, are expressed and reinforced most often in social avoidance rather than through social interaction, as is the case in social-learning theory. The distance is enforced through institutional discrimination that denies minorities access to educational, employment, and housing opportunities for integration. In essence, minorities are blamed, punished, and suffer for the anxieties and fears of the prejudiced person.

The most important single study into the nature of prejudice has been the examination of "the authoritarian personality." Frenkel-Brunswick and Sanford (Adorno et al. 1950) presented this personality type in an effort to diagnose the antisemitism of Nazi Germany. Their "F" scale, measuring the degree of authoritarianism, found that prejudice tends to accompany ethnocentrism, political conservatism, chauvinism, and pseudopatriotism. Prejudiced people show a great deal of "social anxiety." They are uneasy and fearful about other people and try to diminish their social anxiety through discrimination, which reduces those they fear to an inferior status. The authoritarian personality also tends to worship his parents at the same time as he has strong repressed hostility toward them. The intrapsychic tensions manifested in prejudice often reflect an unresolved history of parent-child conflict.

Social, legal, political, and economic factors often stimulate the internal dissonance that leads to prejudice. In his classic work *The Nature of Prejudice* (1953) Gordon Allport cites various historical, religious, and cultural circumstances that cause festering ambiguity and feelings of threat and frustration. Interestingly, he blames the state of democracy for some of the strain.

> Democracy, we now realize, places a heavy burden upon the personality, sometimes too great to bear. The maturely democratic person must possess subtle virtues and capabilities: an ability to form properly differentiated categories in respect to ethnic groups and their traits, a willingness to award freedom to others, and a capacity to employ it constructively for oneself. All these qualities are difficult to achieve and maintain . . . it is easier to succumb to oversimplification and dogmatism . . . to repudiate the ambiguities inherent in democratic society, to demand definiteness, to "escape from freedom." (p. 515)

Social psychologists, in their extension and elaboration of the psychodynamic view, document and analyze the supporting social interactions. Most prejudiced individuals are sustained by an elaborate social network that comprises people who share similar lifestyles, and these personal relationships are sustained by institutional structures that reinforce the interpersonal and intrapersonal patterns (Erlich 1973).

Personality theories do a great deal to uncover the individual motivational dimensions of discriminatory behavior. Other theories focus on the condition of the relatively powerless deviant or victim rather than on the more powerful aggressor. Personality theory also helps to explain the varying intensities and forms of prejudice in different individuals. It honors the complexity of the human psyche and searches for the origins of prejudice in frustration and fear. The psychodynamic orientation of personality theory, however, does not adequately explain the interactional behaviors and dynamics of the discriminatory process. It does not explain how prejudicial attitudes are conveyed and transmitted. Social-learning theory may be better equipped to interpret this interactional process.

The psychological strains of frustration, uncertainty, and overwork influence the way teachers relate to children in the classroom (Waller 1932; Becker 1952; McPherson 1972; Lortie 1973; 1975). Teachers, pressed by the overwhelming circumstances of their job, can unintentionally misjudge and mistreat students. Personality theory gives a more generous perspective, lifting some of the blame that victimizes teachers in social-learning theory. As he often unconsciously oppresses children, the teacher emerges a victim himself rather than a perfunctory perpetrator of the self-fulfilling prophecy. In *What's Happened to Teacher?* (1970) Brenton interviewed hundreds of teachers and revealed some of the psychodynamic origins of teacher prejudice and discrimination. "Teachers have yearnings and frustrations that go back to childhood days," and the harsh realities of school life merely reinforce these.

In sum, personality theory offers an analysis of the intrapsychic and psychodynamic origins of negative discrimination on the part of teachers. Social-systems theory refers to the power of the social context in determining the normative behavior of teachers and children and considers deviant patterns a reflection of social disorganization and normlessness. And social-learning theories document the interactional processes in classrooms that lead to the discriminatory labeling of children who do not match the teacher's ideal image.

But differentiation can be positive as well as negative. Rather than leading to distinctions that serve social demands at the expense of individual strengths, differentiation often occurs in response to individual needs and furthers the development of each person. In this more tolerant view, differences can be seen not as deficiency but as distinctiveness. Appraisals and evaluations are generally flexible, more objective, less egocentric, and less imposing than the prejudicial judgments that lead to negative discrimination. This second type of differentiation we refer to as "individuation." There are three theoretical perspectives that hold the individual central in their approach.

Differential Psychology

"Wide individual variation has been found in every phase of behavior investigation" (Anastasi 1958, p. 49). Differential psychology has probably best portrayed the variety and complexity of the human species not only by claiming individuality for man but also by illustrating its type, degree, and form through quantitative measurement.

As the theory of natural selection suggests, all living organisms are differentiated by nature, and differences are essential for the survival of the species. The greater the variation among humans, for instance, the more likelihood there is of a successful adaptation to the changing and diverse circumstances that surround us. The fittest will dominate, passing along their appropriate adaptations to future generations. In his *Origin of Species* (1859) Darwin shattered the view of a static, God-created world by presenting an ever-evolving and transforming view of nature. Individual differences were thought to be inherited from previous generations and to move toward positive differentiation in accordance with laws of natural selection. Detrimental traits were trimmed away in the adaptation to environment. "This preservation of favorable individual differences and variations, and the destruction of those which are injurious, I have called Natural Selection, or the Survival of the Fittest. Variations neither useful nor injurious would not be affected by natural selection, and would be left either a fluctuating element, as perhaps we see in certain polymorphic species, or would ultimately become fixed, owing to the nature of the organism and the nature of the conditions" (p. 88).

This life-adjustment process has been elucidated by numerous scientists studying the behavior of living organisms. E. L. Thorndike, the father of modern educational psychology, formulated scale units to measure the difference that nature cultivates in each person. With Thorndike's studies, individual differences were no longer a matter of speculation but became quantifiable characteristics and traits—an undeniable aspect of the human condition. "Sharp, qualitative distinctions among people are encountered every day. Closer observation reveals, however, that all individuals are distributed along a continuous scale in every characteristic. In other words, people do not fall into clearly differentiated types. Differences among people are said to be quantitative rather than qualitative" (Anastasi 1958, p. 23).

What was to follow was an array of IQ tests, standardized achievement exams, attitude inventories, and aptitude measures that helped to describe, diagnose, and predict differences in individual nature and performance. With quantitative testing, individuals could be classified in relation to statistical norms. The mean of the distribution suggested the most prevalent tendency of the population, which was then considered to be the ideal dictated by nature.

The apparent efficiency of this quantitative approach is appealing because it introduces objective criteria for measuring individual performance on specific tasks and in accomplishing concrete goals. This approach may be beneficial in that the needs of the individual can be assessed by comparing him to the functional standards of the group, and appropriate remedies undertaken. But the attempt to fit the individual to society (rather than the other way around) runs the risk of merely perpetuating the status quo rather than assuring social progress or encouraging personal development. Moreover, the survival-of-the-fittest notion presupposes a somewhat ruthless competition of winners and losers, and those varying excessively from the norm may be considered deficient and dispensable rather than different and precious. Finally, the variations that differential psychology defines include only those that can be readily observed and measured. Many of the enlivening inclinations of human variation escape these scientific tests. Creativity, empathy, spontaneity are all capacities that slip by the instruments and often out of consideration.

In the view of differential psychology, education is a training process for human faculties bestowed by nature. The teacher acts as a diagnostician, assessing the strengths and weaknesses through various testing strategies and offering appropriate remedies for the child's deficiencies. Most of the responsibility and direction for the learning process rests with the teacher, as the child remains a passive recipient of the instructor's systematic direction. Robert Glaser, one of the masterminds of this type of instruction, characterizes it this way: "An effective technology of instruction relies heavily upon the effective measurement of subject matter competence at the beginning, during, and at the end of the educational process. Well-defined sequences or progressive, behaviorally defined objectives in various subject areas must be established as guidelines for setting up the student's program of study. The student's achievement is defined by his position along this progression of advancement" (Silberman 1970, p. 199). This mode of individuation might be represented in the teacher who characterizes her students by describing their functional ability and developing pedagogical strategies based on the assessed needs of the individual child. Such a teacher, too, is likely to be very conscious of the societal demands that her students must be prepared to face in the future and will see her role as a preparatory, acculturating function.

The Humanistic Approach

The humanistic approach holds that the individual's perception, awareness, and understanding of himself is the only valid measure of personal worth. Contemporary humanism gained impetus from existential philosophers like Kierkegaard, Sartre, and Buber and was translated into interpersonal dynamics by psychologists like Rogers and Maslow. From their writings grew a concern with a reflective, inward search for oneself. Rather than observable behaviors and skills, one's feelings and emotions became the vital indicators of personal growth.

Each individual in and of himself is thought to be unique. He is optimistically depicted as naturally inclined toward fulfilling a need for personal meaning and is impelled by a growth principle that moves him toward self-expression. This drive, however, is not for mere survival, as the Darwinists would suggest, but for the fulfillment of the individual's nature. To be fulfilled, man's higher needs—his cravings for love, "belongingness," and dignity—must be met. Each must discover his whole self through a process of "self-actualization" rather than merely function efficiently in the process of adjustment.

Self-actualization (or positive differentiation) is possible only as persons suspend their expectations, directions, and evaluations of one another so as not to impinge on self-discovery. Others can offer little guidance, only support, for there is no way of ever really grasping the meaning of another's experience. The humanistic approach, therefore, calls for freedom and autonomy that allow for the individual to make his own choices. Rather than supply external stimulation, direction, or input, one should accept and confirm the output of others.

From the perspective of interpersonal psychology, Rogers (1961, p. 34) describes what could be called a process of individuation: "There is implied here a freedom to explore oneself at both conscious and unconscious levels, as rapidly as one can dare to embark on this dangerous quest. There is also complete freedom from any type of moral and diagnostic evaluation, since all such evaluations are, I believe, always threatening. Thus the relationship which I have found helpful is characterized by a sort of transparency on my part, in which my real feelings are evident; by an acceptance of this other person as a separate person with value in his own right; and by a deep empathic understanding which enables me to see his world through his eyes."

The humanistic approach offers a shift in the emphasis of education because it considers knowledge to be a human fabrication that is subjective and incomplete. Discipline and structured curricula are unjustified, and the educational process becomes an exploration of personal feelings, individual consciousness, and our shared humanity. The humanistic educator becomes a "facilitator," in Carl Rogers' terms, and sets in motion the relationships that promote trust, cooperation, and acceptance. Such a teacher should be nonjudgmental and nondirective, allowing each child to make his own decisions, evaluations, and discoveries. The all-important element in this mode of education is not teaching but the creation of a "learning environment" where children are free to explore, discover, and express themselves (Dennison 1969). As Arthur Sheldon describes it,

A classroom climate of permissiveness and understanding provides a situation free of threat, in which the student can work without defensiveness. The decks are kept clear for him to consider the material being discussed from his own internal frame of reference. His desire for acceptance is realized, and because of this he feels the demand upon himself to be responsible for his own interpretations and insights. He feels the full strength of another person's belief in his own integrity. An interesting and important outgrowth of this self-acceptance is the observable improvement in his inter-personal relations with others. He will tend to show greater understanding of them and develop freer, more real relationships with them. This has great importance from the standpoint of the communication and extension of the basic classroom mood. (Rogers 1951, p. 393)

The humanistic approach is vulnerable to criticism on a number of counts. Humanism often appears diffuse and even contradictory—more like an attitude that pervades a number of different fields of thought rather than a systematic theory. The view that the individual is the seat of authority and direction makes for what is often considered an "anything goes" attitude. Preoccupation with personal freedom can lead to a neglect of social responsibility, as individuality lapses into egocentricism. Some concession to social consensus seems necessary to avoid chaos; yet humanism, in its staunch rejection of tradition and social precedent, proposes no guidelines. The lack of structure and objectivity makes it difficult for many teachers to fully accept this perspective. In their estimation, humanism appears naive to the demands of social reality. Children frequently need to be disciplined rather than indulged, and structures and norms often help restrain childhood egocentrism.

Developmental Theory

The educational philosophy of John Dewey and the child psychology of Jean Piaget have had a profound impact on social-science theory and educational practice. Developmental theory, like the other perspectives, values individuality and freedom. It sees man confronted by his environment but not at its mercy, as those who honor the laws of natural selection do. The individual acts on his surroundings, modifying them continually. Education, therefore, has the capacity to reform society, as the individual—empowered and activated—not only survives but transforms.

Developmental theorists believe, like the humanists, that man is inclined toward growth. For Dewey, education *is* growth. But growth is a disciplined process that has direction, not a culminating aim of normality nor an illusive ideal of self-discovery. "We have been occupied with the conditions and implications of growth . . . When it is said that education is development, everything depends on *how* development is conceived. Our net conclusion is that life is development, and that development, growing, is life. Translated into its educational equivalents, this means that (i) the educational process has no end beyond itself; it is its own end; and that (ii) the educational process is one of continual reorganizing, reconstructing, transforming" (Dewey 1916, pp. 49-50).

Curiosity leads one into activity that he can appreciate and absorb. The greatest need of the individual is to have his curiosity nurtured at developmentally appropriate intervals, rather than to acquire skills or have his feelings catered to. Individuation occurs as a teacher actively diagnoses, stimulates, and sustains the child's interest. This requires an active and disciplined guidance on the part of the teacher, but not the imposing of an "objective" structure.

Piaget (1932) bore out many of Dewey's theories in his years of observing children. He offered an alternative to the stimulus-response model of learning and reinforced the notion that the child is the principal agent in her own education. Piaget's theories expose the structure of children's thought. The child continually recasts the mental structures that order the images she beholds. She progressively accommodates and assimilates new experiences into her expanding framework or world view. Piaget grouped these evolving structural changes into developmental stages.

It is critical that individuals have the structures to accommodate new knowledge, rather than merely the skills to perform new tasks. Teaching means creating situations where structures can be discovered: it does not mean transmitting structures which may be assimilated at nothing other than a verbal level. The teacher is challenging the student and responding to the mental structure that is the child's stage of reasoning.

In the open classroom, children learn while dealing with real-life problems. The teacher leads the child to activities that follow his interest and demand his involvement. The student, therefore, collaborates with the teacher in selecting the what and how of his education. The child's curiosity demands careful nurturing, however. The British Infant Schools, referred to by Silberman (1970) and Featherstone (1971), illustrate how the classroom becomes a laboratory for learning without turning into a playground of frivolity. The classroom must be monitored, and the teacher's role is one of mediation. She becomes a mediator between the child and the demands of society, between the child's curiosity and the classroom material, between the child and other children in the classroom, and between conflicting and competing interests within the child himself. Silberman (1970, p. 267) describes the demands of this type of teaching and suggests that the teacher individuates by sustaining development.

Informal teaching makes a number of demands on teachers that the conventional classroom does not. For example, it requires much more alertness. To be able to "maximize the occasion", a teacher must always be "at the ready"—aware not only of what each child is doing at any moment, but of what state of development the child is in. Since anything and everything a child may do can provide the occasion to be maximized, teachers are *always* teaching; the intellectual and emotional demands seem relentless and unending. And teachers need to be informed about many more things, the curriculum is not limited to the teacher's lesson plan, but is as broad and unpredictable as the children's interests.

In sum, theories of individuation offer different views of human nature and imply different clinical prescriptions for treating, relating to, or teaching the growing child. Differential psychology sees human variation as an outgrowth of nature, with each individual needing to adjust to the demands of society in order to assure his own survival. We can assess the needs of an individual by comparing him to the functional standards and statistical norms of a group, and in this way help him compensate for his deficiencies and ensure the use of his strengths. Humanism rejects the imperatives of natural science and focuses on the individual's felt needs. Each person must explore, discover, and express his own individuality through the dynamic process of "self-actualization." And finally, in developmental theory, individuality emerges in one's encounters with the environment. As the child explores the dimensions of objects and persons around him, he progressively recognizes their distinctiveness and his relationship to them and develops his own competence and individuality.

These major theories of differentiation found in the social sciences are closely related to methodological strategies and clinical practice. Sometimes researchers are conscious of the theoretical views that shape their inquiry and analysis, but more often they proceed without recognizing the powerful impact of their conceptual biases. Part of the objectifying process of classroom research lies in understanding the interaction between basic social-science theories and the development of research methods. The more conscious we are of the origins of our conceptual formulations, the more deliberate and critical will be our view of the research process.

The Long Search
for a Research Sample

Sara Lawrence Lightfoot

IT IS IMPORTANT to talk about some of the origins of our collaboration on this research project because our own histories have very much shaped the present inquiry. Carew and Lightfoot have both been interested in describing and analyzing the behaviors of human encounter but from different perspectives. In her previous work as a developmental psychologist, Carew has observed and analyzed the experiences of young children in two settings: the home and the day-care center (White, Carew, et al. 1973; Carew, Chan, and Halfar 1976a; 1976b; 1977). The aim of that research was to describe the experiences encountered by the young child in his everyday "natural" environment, to assess their impact on the child's intellectual and social development over a formative period of his life (from age one to three), and to trace the role played by the human and physical environment in the child's experiences. A major question Carew has sought to answer is to what extent is the child's development of intellectual competence related to his own active construction of "intellectually valuable" experiences for himself, to what extent is it related to his passive assimilation of such experiences provided to him by the environment (from mothers, teachers, television), and to what extent is it promoted by true reciprocal interchanges in which the child and the interactor jointly shape the child's intellectual experience. One distinctive aspect of Carew's work is her interest in the environment as it is absorbed by the child in his moment-to-moment experiences. Environment, for her, is a dynamic force that is defined as much by the child's own behavior in assimilating and accommodating to it as by its own independent qualities considered apart from the child. This perspective has led her to pay relatively little attention, until now, to aspects of the environment that a sociologist, for example, might describe when analyzing the home or school as a social setting.

In contrast, it is a focus on precisely these independent qualities of the environment that characterizes Lightfoot's previous work (Lightfoot 1973; 1975; 1976; 1978; Lightfoot and Carew 1976). As a sociologist, her interest has been in describing how the teacher's world—her personal, cultural, and educational history, her values, attitudes, beliefs, and goals, her professional skills and experience—influences the pedagogical and procedural decisions, the dynamic patterns of interaction, and the social structure that develop in the classroom. A central theme of her work has been the analysis of discriminatory patterns of teacher behavior in the use of authority, power, evaluation, and cognitive stimulation. When the teacher responds to a child's behavior, she necessarily perceives this behavior through a filter of preestablished categories. The same child behavior may be given a different interpretation depending on who the child is and what he represents to the teacher. A black boy racing across the classroom may be seen as aggressive and hyperactive, while a blond, willowy girl doing the same thing may be seen as gliding across the classroom space in a creative and expressive dance. Similarly, a rough, unkempt, working-class child who says of the emperor "He don't have no clothes" may be seen as crude and sexually precocious, while a neat middle-class child making the comment "He's nude" may be seen as clever and sophisticated. Lightfoot believes that children receive many messages from teachers that go beyond or conflict with the interactions an observer might witness. A challenge she has faced in previous work has been to develop interview methods for documenting underlying teacher values and feelings that penetrate the unspoken environment (for example, why does a child say "My teacher is an angry person" when an observer sees no evidence of this in her overt classroom behavior?).

How are our two perspectives related? Why have we thought it truitful to collaborate in the present research? Some of the reasons stem from our cultural and professional histories. Professionally we both have been interested in the study of human interaction, especially the interaction of unequals—the child and her mother, the child and her teacher. Carew has approached this question from the point of view of the child, Lightfoot from the point of view of the adult, but for both of us the central issue is what happens to the mind and personality of the child as a result of cumulative micro-encounters with an environment that has powerful built-in biases, both positive and negative. As black researchers, our interest in this question is more than academic. It is of urgent concern for us to understand and explain how children come to be labeled as different, inferior, deviant, how these perceptions by powerful others shape the child's experiences, and how, in turn, experiences influence the child's intellectual, social, and emotional development. We see this process of stigmatizing through labels as a negative distortion of a more general and positive process of differentiation among children that teachers must undertake if they are to respond to the individual needs of children. A teacher's job, after all, is to judge what children need and try to provide it for them (this does not mean he must do the providing; often children's needs are best served by encouraging them to solve their problems and answer their questions themselves). The theoretical, practical, and ethical challenge, then, is to distinguish teachers whose perceptions and actions are deliberately discriminatory and destructive from those whose perceptions and actions spring from a desire to respond positively to the individual needs of children even though these may sometimes be misguided and unwittingly prejudicial and harmful. Teaching is not merely a behavioral, observable process; it is a reflective, thinking process. Teachers need to be recognized and respected as thoughtful and cognizant people who make deliberate and careful decisions as well as impulsive, and sometimes dangerous, choices.

We think it is important to recognize not only the humanity of teachers but also the complex nature of the researcher's role. One of the great limitations of much ethnographic and ecological work done in schools is its downplaying of the researcher's impact on the classroom environment. Researchers claim an objective, dispassionate relationship, if any, to the subjects of their research, and act as if they functioned like well-placed cameras, mechanically photographing events and behaviors with precision and accuracy. This downplaying of the researcher's role implies lack of impact as a "person," thereby guaranteeing somehow his objectivity as a "researcher." We maintain, however, that it is critical that researchers involved in interactional and ecological research in social settings must be systematically reflective about their presence in the field, and that a process of self-conscious reflection and recording of behavior must begin with their first movements into the field. The search for a research sample thus becomes a significant part of the inquiry, especially when the topic of inquiry is somewhat threatening and controversial and raises basic socioethical issues for both researchers and subjects. Sometimes the odyssey itself is enlightening and may influence the content and design of the research. We strongly argue, therefore, that researchers must look critically at both sides of the intervention process—their own movements into the field and the subject's responses to their presence.

In these times of increasing discretion, professional solidarity, and guardedness, research has become difficult to initiate. For the most part school doors are no longer open to academic inquiry; teachers want to know the immediate benefits to them, and parents are protective of their children's privacy. When the research design not only demands a long-term commitment from participants but also probes some very sensitive and threatening aspects of human relationships, seeking permission to get into schools can become a complex and arduous task. Our situation was further complicated by the fact that for years teachers and administrators had felt abused by researchers who did not seem to recognize their humanity nor offer any practical benefits to the schools in return for their cooperation. Teachers felt overresearched and principals felt responsible for protecting their teachers and children from such encroachments. Our initial inquiries, therefore, were very discouraging.

In the early seventies we began talking with knowledgeable friends and acquaintances in different parts of the country, asking them to suggest school systems and sympathetic contacts, as well as effective strategies for approaching the schools with our proposal. One of our primary dilemmas, for instance, was whether we should try to make our initial contacts with high administrative officials (from the top down) or with enthusiastic teachers who would become our advocates (from the bottom up). Because of the sensitive nature of our research and our concern for not causing trouble or risk to individual teachers, we decided to follow the prescribed bureaucratic procedures, seeking first the blessings of the superintendent's office, then of principals and teachers. We anticipated several possible responses from the superintendent's office: advocacy, support, mild acceptance, indifference, outright refusal. As it turned out, our search required a great tolerance for ambivalence and uncertainty. For the most part, answers were vague, waiting periods long, the process circuitous.

A critical aspect of our research design demanded that the target classroom population be at least twenty percent minority, preferably black. Because most public schools in the United States tend to be relatively homogeneous in terms of class and race, the requirement of heterogeneity substantially reduced our choices. Only two school systems we investigated looked encouraging—Conroy and Richmond. In Richmond our initial contact was with the associate superintendent, Dr. Lane, who welcomed us warmly and seemed eager for us to work in his schools. He appeared less concerned about the substance of our research than about the "growth value" of research to the practice of teaching. He spoke often of Richmond's open and self-critical approach to the development of curriculum, the in-service training of teachers, and the strategies for supporting the intellectual and social growth of children. According to Dr. Lane, Richmond schools were a model of the productive dialectic between knowledge and practice, theory and action. The only drawback he could foresee in our working in his schools was that the student population might not be diverse enough for our research design.

After the positive and enthusiastic encouragement from the superintendent's office, we were surprised to meet a great deal of skepticism and resistance from the principals and teachers in the schools Dr. Lane had contacted on our behalf. Even with his strong endorsement, principals were protective of the privacy of teachers and teachers were almost militant in their demands for the power to make decisions about research that would intrude into their classrooms and influence the lives of their children. In September we began visiting the recommended schools and presenting our proposal to the principals. After receiving a few promising responses, we were told that the final decision would have to be made by a recently-formed research committee composed of teachers elected from throughout the school system and organized for the purpose of critically reviewing and screening research proposals. We finally met before this committee and received an affirmative response and permission to proceed with gathering our research sample. Both teachers and principals in Richmond seemed most impressed with the collaborative nature of our research, our views of teachers as uniquely knowledgeable about classroom life, and our commitment to observations throughout the school year.

At the same time we were also beginning our negotiations in Conroy, a process that was initially more laborious and frustrating. After numerous attempts to contact various people in the central office of the school department, we finally arranged a visit with assistant superintendent Vance. Although cordial, his response to us was guarded as he asked a series of straightforward questions about the process, substance, and goals of our research. Having endured the wrath of teachers, parents, and children who had been overresearched for the past several years, he was particularly interested in the value of our study to the training of teachers and the education of children. Mr. Vance's questions were probing and tough, always taking the point of view of educational practitioners and consumers. Our proposed study, however, sounded "different" to him; our commitment to the practice of education seemed genuine. He agreed to support our research by contacting school principals who might be sympathetic to our efforts and whose student populations were appropriately heterogeneous. We were to follow his phone calls to principals with letters of introduction, short descriptions of our research, and requests for interviews with their teachers the following fall. Weeks of waiting for responses to phone calls and letters followed. Several of the principals expressed distrust or lack of interest, others claimed to be overwhelmed by year-end responsibilities, and a few expressed curiosity and interest and urged us to visit them in the early fall. Fortunately, after we presented our proposal, several teachers agreed to participate in the study, and the Inner School and the Outer School became the chosen sites. We preferred to conduct our research in Conroy because it seemed a more diverse, heterogeneous, and urban school system; Richmond's image was more precious and exclusive.

As we began our visits to Conroy and Richmond schools in September, we were joined by Gloria Chao, a student of anthropology and psychology who would serve as classroom observer and field coordinator. Our research team, composed of two black women professors and researchers and an Asian field coordinator, presented, we knew, an uncommon and often disconcerting image to an audience of typically white male administrators or white female teachers. We soon realized that our physical presence and style were a most important factor in our negotiations. Before entering the school setting we therefore discussed the roles each of us would play in the presentation of our research proposal. We thought it important first of all that the three of us be present during the initial sessions with administrators and teachers so that they would have a complete picture of who we were. Their reaction to us as people was likely to influence their decision to participate as much as the content of our message. We wanted to convey in person the nature of our commitment to the research, that each of us would be actively involved in the collection of the data, and that we would not introduce any new people into our research team during the course of the year. The intimate and long-term nature of the study demanded that we establish a trusting and comfortable relationship with teachers and that the teachers be able to anticipate our consistent presence and engage in continuous dialogue. It also seemed important that the teachers be able to watch the three of us interact, because our interactions offered another view of our personalities and professionalism. We were well aware that we would be observed and judged as individuals, and also that teachers would be interested in the relationships among us.

Although we thought it vital that we all participate in these initial interviews, we also sought to control the power of our collective presence by selecting a leader and spokesperson. I was chosen for this role because it required a degree of experience in school settings that I had gained in previous work. We felt that these initial interactions with teachers were critical moments in which we had to establish the subtle balance between assertiveness and restraint, between intimacy and distance, between humor and seriousness—a delicate balance that is partially learned through experience. With her considerable background in the subtleties of field research, Carew assumed the role of critical listener and observer. As I spoke she carefully watched the unfolding events and the reactions of the audience. When things were left unsaid, she would fill in the missing links. When people seemed confused or overwhelmed, she would simplify and clarify. When the mood became too heavy and serious, she would be light and humorous. Furthermore, Carew's listening role became important later to our analysis and understanding of the events as we looked at them retrospectively.

Chao played a deliberately peripheral role during the presentations. In part this was because she had had less experience in ethnographic and field research and was diffident about taking a central role; in part it was because we had decided that one of us should be responsible for documenting the content, mood, and interactions of various participants in these meetings, and Chao had had considerable relevant experience. Her role differed from Carew's in that she sought to record and describe rather than evaluate and intervene. She made no judgments of the quality of my statements nor was she interested in changing or improving the course of interaction. She remained relatively distant from the events so that her observations would be objective and descriptive. In addition, since Chao would be the main classroom observer, we thought it wise that she begin assuming a very low-key image in these initial meetings. It seemed important that teachers view her as quiet, nondisruptive, and potentially invisible in the classroom. Her noninteractive role during the presentations would begin to establish this image. Interestingly enough, the image that Chao sought to convey also matched most people's stereotype of the quiet, inscrutable Asian and may have helped to put our listeners at ease.

During my presentations I tried to be sensitive and responsive to the subtle dynamics of the environment and the people within it. Although my core message remained constant, the points of emphasis and elaboration shifted with each setting in order to present our ideas most persuasively to the audience.

First, I expressed our dissatisfaction with research about teachers and teaching. For the most part, the research literature portrays teachers as mindless beings who give very little deliberate thought to their actions and who are neither reflective about nor conscious of their decision-making process. Usually researchers come into classrooms with prescribed instruments that count specific teacher behaviors, and then those behaviors are correlated with student outcomes (achievement, self-image). Not only are the behavioral categories already determined but the observations are of minimal duration, capturing only a minute segment of daily classroom life.

We told teachers we hoped to create a research process that was substantially different. We regarded teachers as thoughtful, reflective beings who usually have sound reasons for what they do; hence one of our primary objectives was to understand the purpose, motivation, and rationale behind their behavior. Teachers, we claimed, were likely to be the real experts, the most experienced knowers about life in classrooms; consequently, their perceptions, feelings, and beliefs must be an integral part of our data. We talked about establishing a collaborative relationship with teachers and emphasized the reciprocal, participatory nature of the research task. I often mentioned our intention to carry out a retrospective interview designed to elicit the teachers' responses to the material we had collected over the course of the year, providing the opportunity for them to embellish, elaborate, and disagree with our interpretations. We spoke of the teachers as co-researchers.

Our presentation also stressed the fact that our research would be long-term rather than short-term. Although we were asking for more of their time (one year of observation) than is typical for classroom research, we would not be basing our findings on data that only reflected a small unrepresentative portion of classroom life. We described our research as generous in nature, allowing for change and adaptation and not dependent on the peculiar circumstances of a moment in time. So although we would be visiting their classrooms frequently and over a long time, our visits would be less intrusive and disruptive and our data more comprehensive and authentic.

In retrospect, the promises of collaboration were clearly the most persuasive aspect of our argument. In our discussions with the Richmond principals, for instance, the reciprocal, collaborative nature of our work was clearly the outstanding selling point. They were weary of high-powered researchers coming in and doing things *to* their teachers or making evaluative judgments. They thought of their teachers as highly skilled and intelligent people who should be an integral part of the research. Teachers not only responded to the implied intimacy of our message but also to the respect for teachers that we conveyed. We spoke of them as the true knowers and referred to ourselves as being able to listen, observe, and understand. In a real sense, we looked to them as authorities, as experts. This was clearly an effective and compelling strategy, and it was not dishonest, for we truly believed our words.

In one case, however, we realized to our dismay that our emphasis on collaboration, implying intimacy, closeness, and emotional support, might have been too seductive and compelling. The occasion was our very first interview with teachers in Conroy, at the Woods School. We arrived just after school when the teachers were visibly weary and worn from the hard day's work with their first graders. They knew well that their principal had given us a favorable response and probably felt some pressure to participate in the research. Ms. Smith, the more experienced and relaxed teacher, seemed mildly receptive, detached, and somewhat uninterested but willing to hear us out. Ms. Jones, a second-year teacher, seemed intense and somewhat defensive at first but became increasingly involved and committed to the research as the presentation unfolded and as I touched on the theme of collaboration in a common enterprise. By the end of the interview I recognized that we had not only probably won over both teachers but that Ms. Jones might be expecting too much of the research. Our enthusiastic portrayal of the research, our philosophy, our goals had sparked a fire in Ms. Jones that we had not anticipated and that was to become the source of great disappointment and conflict when we were not able to use her classroom in our study, for the reasons described below.

Although we often stated our interest in documenting life in classrooms where children were from many different and interesting backgrounds, we were never explicit about the ratio of blacks to whites that we required to implement our study. While we made our appreciation of variation and difference among children obvious, we did not make our criterion of a twenty percent black population known. In retrospect, I think we feared teachers and principals would be threatened by the explicit mention of race. We also felt that the presence of two black researchers was already threatening enough without our saying that race was a critical aspect of the research design. The decision to remain vague about this criterion for selecting classrooms led to many unanticipated ethical dilemmas. We were being dishonest in not emphasizing the relevance of race to our study, yet we feared that if we did so, teachers would not want to become involved, or, if they did, their behavior would be seriously distorted. We were convinced of the goodness of our goal, which was to understand and to help others understand how teachers ordinarily treat black and white children, but we worried whether it was honest or even necessary to conceal this purpose.

Our less than candid responses about the proportion of black children in the classroom got us into trouble in our relations with the teachers at the Woods School, who had apparently been very impressed by our presentation. In our initial conversation with the principal, Carew had asked about the number of minority children in each of the first-grade classrooms. We learned then that Ms. Jones' classroom did not have the appropriate proportion of minority children and therefore could not be used. Instead of being clear about our research criterion and avoiding any contacts with Ms. Jones, we proceeded to present our research study to *both* first-grade teachers and to seek their approval and participation. Both teachers were persuaded by our presentation and volunteered to participate in the study, and the teacher whose classroom we could not seriously consider became most committed to having us intimately involved with her classroom life.

Because we had not originally been candid about the sample criterion, we had to contrive one after the fact. We searched for one that would seem fair, research-oriented, and nonevaluative and decided that our professed reason for excluding Ms. Jones would be that we were selecting a relatively comparable group of teachers with several years of experience. Even though this decision was delivered gently to Ms. Jones as a tentative one requiring further discussion, she felt angry, excluded, and harshly judged. She would not have experienced the pain and anger she did had we been explicit from the beginning about our sample selection. Clearly our ad hoc criterion of teaching experience seemed contrived and arbitrary, and Ms. Jones was left feeling abused and cheated—an allegation that really stung us.

Our initial interviews with the teachers stressed the pragmatic value of our research and the links between our research and actual training materials for teachers. One of the ways we distinguished ourselves from other researchers was by our concern for the practical impact our work would have on the lives of teachers and children in the classrooms. We tried to make it very clear that we could not offer services, training, or consultation and that our classroom observations would not be of immediate benefit to their teaching. At the same time we emphasized to teachers the potential value of observation, reflection, and analysis. We spoke of our prior experience with teachers who claimed that the research process had given them the chance to pause and reflect on their behavior, to look self-critically at their pedagogical choices, and to ask themselves questions they were rarely forced to confront in the everyday experience of teaching. We hoped that they too would welcome the opportunity to look at their work in new ways and to have attentive and appreciative listeners.

We had very different experiences in the two schools that ultimately agreed to participate in our study. When we arrived at the Inner School, Mr. Hamilton, the principal, greeted us very warmly and invited us to sit in three chairs that had obviously been arranged, in a row to the right of his desk, in anticipation of our visit. He recognized Carew from a meeting they had both attended several months before and seemed to become even more relaxed and pleasant upon renewing their acquaintance. After a few minutes two first-grade teachers, Ms. Allen and Ms. Prima, appeared and sat on the couch facing Mr. Hamilton's desk. The principal introduced everyone. This was the first interview where we met initially with both principal and teachers simultaneously. The general pattern had been for us to talk first with the principal and gain his or her approval to speak with the teachers. But on this occasion the principal was with us during the entire interview and indeed seemed to play a prominent role throughout even while I made my presentation to the teachers. His presence seemed to work to our advantage. One had a sense that the teachers saw the principal as an authority, as the decision maker, yet that they had considerable respect and good feeling for one another. Mr. Hamilton seemed to proudly show off his two teachers as fine examples whom we might do well to include in our research.

As I presented our proposal I made a conscious decision to speak directly to the teachers. (Because of the seating arrangement, this required my facing away from the principal.) I wanted to indicate that teachers were the primary actors in our research and deserved the most careful and complete attention, for I had the sense that although Mr. Hamilton was prepared to invite us in, the teachers needed convincing. Ms. Allen and Ms. Prima listened dutifully but showed almost no reaction. When we asked the teachers if they had any questions about our research, they did not respond immediately, but then began to talk about the Inner School community. Ms. Allen spoke proudly of her long association with the school and her good feelings about the heterogeneous population of students: "You can't find nicer kids than the ones in this school." Many of these remarks seemed directed as much at Mr. Hamilton as at us. Ms. Prima made a few positive comments in the same spirit of admiration for the children and the school, but she was generally less open and expressive.

When we gently asked them whether they were interested in becoming involved in the research, they both indicated that they would participate. Their immediate affirmative response came as a welcome surprise but was clearly not the result solely of our attempts to persuade them. They seemed to have already been convinced before we arrived—probably by Mr. Hamilton. We left the Inner School feeling very pleased with the strong support and encouragement we had received from the principal, although we were also a bit baffled by it. It had been an extremely productive session and for the first time we began to believe there was a real chance of working in the Conroy Public Schools.

Our first visit to the Outer School was rushed and frustrating. Our appointment was scheduled during the teachers' lunch break, and by the time we all sat down to talk we had less than twenty minutes to make our presentation. Upon our arrival Mr. Barry, the principal, greeted us casually and tentatively and then went in search of his first-grade teachers. He returned alone and spent the next several minutes describing his school—the number of children, the neighborhoods they come from, the bussing patterns. Mr. Barry asked no questions about our research and was clearly not interested in becoming engaged in the process of deciding whether we would be welcome. It was obvious that he viewed his role as neutral and peripheral. He would deliver the teachers to us but he would neither support nor undermine our efforts. The decision seemed to belong completely with the teachers.

After our visit with the principal we went in search of the teachers, who seemed to have forgotten our appointment. The first one we found directed us to the teachers' room where the other two were rushing to get their lunch. Their minds were clearly on other things and we felt like intruders. Although they remembered the appointment after we appeared, none of them had anticipated our visit and Mr. Barry had been very vague about our purpose in being there. Apologizing for adding to their already burdensome day, we followed them into Ms. Ryan's room where we sat in children's chairs around a small table. My presentation of our research was rushed, almost breathless, as I hammered out our purposes, goals, and procedures.

The teachers ate their school lunches and listened. Children were already waiting at the classroom door to come in after lunch, and Ms. Ryan would get up intermittently to tell them to stop banging and wait more patiently. The whole atmosphere was pressured as I struggled against time to capture the interest of the teachers. But there was no time for elaboration or explanation, no time for us to get a sense of who they were, and no time for them to really respond with questions and comments.

Even under these circumstances, Ms. Ryan and Ms. Edwards showed their interest. Ms. Ryan expressed concern that we would be a source of disruption in her classroom. She said that she had very few visitors and was worried that the children would seek attention from us and demand that we interact with them. Her last year's class had been very unruly and caused her great anxiety; she did not intend to relive that experience or invite any threats to classroom order. To this Carew spoke briefly about our extensive experience as observers in classrooms and our ability to fade easily into the background. Ms. Edwards wondered whether we would be able to consult with them about children who seemed to be having difficulties learning and adjusting to school. I tried to make very clear that our roles would not be advisory or supportive, that we would not be offering professional consultation, and that we did not even claim to have the expertise to do so. We would be assuming an observational role, a nonevaluative function, but part of the research process would be sharing our conclusions with them at the end of the study.

This is a very important distinction. There is always a tendency for overworked teachers to seek additional support and resources and to ask for some immediate return on their efforts. And there is also a tendency on the part of researchers to promise more than they can or should give—partly out of empathy for the teacher's needs and partly as a way of gaining the teacher's approval and participation. The whole issue of roles and relationships is further complicated when one is seeking to develop interactional styles that are less distant and impersonal than those of "traditional" research. There appears to be a mixed and somewhat confusing message when the researcher says on the one hand that she will not serve in a consulting, advisory capacity, but on the other hand that she wants to establish a collaborative relationship. Ms. Edwards' question was the beginning of our attempts to strike the precarious balance between distant, objective researcher and caring, empathetic listener.

The conversation with the teachers ended abruptly as small children began to pour into the room. The teachers said they needed to consider our request and would call us within a week. We thanked them for their time, apologized once again for our jumbled words, and left feeling disheartened and discouraged. We decided to write them clear and precise letters about our research that might make our hasty presentation more understandable and acceptable. We felt we had truly entered the world of schools—a world that provides little space or time for elaboration or deliberation, a world of bells and buzzers, a world of schedules and deadlines. Because of the nature of our visit, we expected that the teachers would most likely turn us down.

One week later, when we had not yet heard from them, Chao called the Outer School and was informed that Ms. Ryan had agreed to participate and that Ms. Edwards had been sick for several days. We waited for Ms. Edwards' return to health, and Carew arranged to drop by her room after school one day for an informal chat. In this conversation Carew admitted our special interest in minority children and Ms. Edwards revealed her special willingness to cooperate with black researchers. She had never known any black researchers before; she wanted to help us because we were black; and further, the fact that we were black (and the impression she had gained of our personalities) had persuaded her that our intentions were good and that we could be trusted to use the research for altruistic rather than self-serving purposes. Carew also had the impression that Ms. Edwards simply felt more comfortable with the idea of being observed by non-whites and of developing a personal relationship with nonwhite professionals. She was the only one who directly alluded to our race in the many face-to-face conversations that we had in our long quest for a research sample.

4

The Social Context
of School and Community

Sara Lawrence Lightfoot

CLASSROOMS ARE NOT isolated and autonomous settings. Rather, each class
and its inhabitants are in constant interaction with the social contexts in
which they are embedded. The influences of family life, social class, ethnic
and racial history, political and social ideologies reach the school directly
each day through students and parents, teachers, and administrators. The
streets children negotiate to get to school, the people who live and work
along the way, the houses or apartments where families live, the nature and
quality of the social networks within the community are all important influences on the social, psychological, and educational forces at work in the
classroom. Classroom life, therefore, is very much shaped and constrained
by the norms, values, and traditions of the school, and likewise, the school
is an integral part of the community which surrounds it. Each of these social
systems—classroom, school, community—has its own structural arrangements, cultural idioms, and functional purposes, but each is also greatly influenced and sustained by the others.

The following brief description of the schools and communities surrounding the classrooms we studied will not attempt a comprehensive, ethnographic analysis of these environments but rather a selective account of
some of the sociocultural and economic realities of community life that we
perceived as highly significant to the identity and culture of the school. We
will also describe the school as a social setting with an organized life and
momentum of its own which becomes the most immediate, determining
force in the lives of teachers and children inside the classroom. This is not a
true community study of Conroy or of the two school districts in which we
worked, but is a crude map of the territory in each district, one that tells approximately where things are without attempting to explain or rationalize
them. It tends, if anything, to be an "official" map of the places described,

reflecting the perspectives and views of those in the city and school administration. The issues in each school and neighborhood may have many other important dimensions not discussed here. It is the existence of these complex issues, not the details of them, which is significant. Awareness of their critical importance helps to flesh out the background against which daily classroom activity takes place.

The City of Conroy

Conroy is a large city near one of the major inland industrial centers in the United States. Much of the city is populated by working-class families whose members work in the light manufacturing and service industries common in this area. Heavy truck routes crisscross the city, and most residential neighborhoods are characterized by large frame houses, usually built for three or more families. In some neighborhoods, these dwellings have been divided into smaller apartments for students or poorer families.

Conroy has a rich diversity of people from various ethnic, racial, and cultural backgrounds, and it is this diversity and distinctiveness of neighborhoods that most characterizes the city. Many people grow up and live in or near their old neighborhoods. They like to stay near family, neighbors, and childhood memories, much like the young receptionist at the Conroy Social Service Agency who told a friend that she was going to give up her job because it would require her to travel across city lines to an office in Fairfax which was only a few blocks away. "Nah," she said, "I don't want to do that—I'd have to go all the way out to Fairfax." Neighborhood boundaries are clearly defined and most people do not want to venture into unknown territories a few miles away. For the most part, neighborhood lines do not symbolize hostile or exclusive turfs; rather, they reflect cohesion, community, and a sense of familiarity and comfort.

Like the neighborhoods surrounding them, public schools in Conroy also have distinct identities known more or less to the local population. The Whitfield School is near one of the main campuses of the state university system, and many children of the university faculty attend Whitfield, giving the school an image of high intellectual exclusivity. Houses in this district are said to cost twice that of comparable houses in most other areas of the city. The Woods School, in a section of the city occupied by professional people and former college people, is said to attract parents with progressive and nontraditional political and social views. The Jordan School, on the south side of Conroy, is located near several low-income projects housing approximately two thousand school-age children mostly from poor and minority families. Although these schools are closely identified with the neighborhoods they are in, they also have distinct reputations, and like most knowledge that is "common" and "public," the reputations lag behind reality, often being only half-true and persisting long after the circumstances which created them have changed.

Among the districts in Conroy, the two chosen for this study are particularly varied in the races and classes of families who live within their boundaries. The Outer and Inner school districts are notable for the variety of families enrolled. In fact, there are few more varied social settings in the city than these two schools.

Conroy School Administration

Like most urban school districts, Conroy has an entire central administration staff devoted to primary education. The Supervisor of Elementary Education directs a staff of specialists for all subject areas such as reading, math, and social studies who plan curriculum and offer workshops for teachers. Other specialists rotate among the schools for the actual teaching of subjects like physical education, music, and art. The central administration establishes policies regarding enrollment, special programs, standardized testing, and the range of diagnostic and psychological services available through the city's Office of Student Services. The Office of Student Services also provides for guidance counselors (upper grades), school-adjustment counselors (primary grades), learning-disabilities specialists, speech therapists, physical-education teachers, and home-adjustment counselors who make home visits to students with special needs.

City legislation requires the frequent use of diagnostic tests for the detection of emotional and learning problems. These tests are referred to by parents and teachers as CASE evaluations and may be done in part or entirety. A child receives a full CASE evaluation when he is going to be absent from the classroom for more than twenty-five percent of the time as a result of his special needs, and it usually leads to a step-by-step individualized learning program involving at least one specialist on a regular basis. A full CASE includes five parts: a medical assessment by a doctor; a psychological assessment by a clinical psychologist; a home assessment by a social worker, guidance counselor, or nurse; a teacher assessment by the teacher who has worked most closely with the child in the past year; and an administrative assessment that includes a paper review of the cumulative school history of the child. A partial CASE follows the above procedure minus one of the five assessments and usually results in some individualized plan for the child followed by the classroom teacher, along with occasional work with outside specialists. Parents, teachers, and other school personnel can initiate a CASE evaluation by going to their principal and requesting one. If the principal is satisfied that everything available within the regular school program has been tried, he will begin the diagnostic and evaluative process. Principals, however, must respond to a parental request for a CASE evaluation.

The large increase in the number of specialists within Conroy schools and the number of children defined as having special needs has dramatically affected the quality of self-contained classrooms and the nature of the classroom teacher's function. Many teachers are frustrated by the continuous interruptions of children moving in and out and find it difficult to maintain an orderly structure and rhythm within the classroom. Some feel their "authority" as a teacher is undermined by the intervention of specialists, while others experience some relief at getting rid of the "troublemakers" who might disrupt a peaceful classroom. Both teachers and administrators recognize that sending children to sessions with specialists is a major procedural, structural, and political issue within the city's schools.

The Inner School

The Inner School neighborhood is bounded by a major trafficway, Grand Avenue. On one side of the school district is housing affiliated with the nearby university; on the other is a business district frequented by shoppers who appear to come from working-class or lower-class backgrounds. There is a mix of people here: old and young, black, white, and Hispanic. Influences from many directions meet in the Inner district, but there is a sense of a cohesive neighborhood. Though people are diverse in race, culture, and education, one can go to any part of the district and not feel out of place, out of the community.

Like most communities, this district is identified by residential landmarks. Redwood Estates is one of the city's oldest and most respected subsidized housing projects and the source of much community leadership. In recent years, Redwood Estates residents have complained of its "going downhill" and have been alarmed by evidence of drug traffic and crime within the buildings. Nearby is another housing complex, a part of the university's housing program, that is inhabited by families from all over the world.

Another border for the district is Commerce Boulevard, a street heavily traveled by trucks. During the 1940s and 50s this was a quieter avenue lined with trees and the homes of middle-class black families. Now it struggles to recover from being, in the words of a city housing official, "one of the city's major abandonment areas." It is beginning to look less neglected. Residents and housing staff are working to reduce truck traffic, and many damaged buildings have been or are being repaired.

Just off Commerce Boulevard the community is quiet though well-worn and densely crowded. Most of the streets are small and many are even too narrow for trees. What few yards exist are enclosed by hedges or chain-link fences. Some years ago several Conroy professionals and students bought and renovated houses at the edge of the district. A few left after break-ins occurred; others stayed. Mostly, however, people with children in the Inner School do not own their houses; property values are too high because the university is so close.

The Inner neighborhood, once familiar and safe, seems to be experiencing the beginning of deterioration. Teachers at the Inner school are starting to complain of senseless vandalism to school property; some have found their car tires slashed. Parents sometimes fear for the safety of their young children, who may be bullied or robbed of their lunch money by older children as they come and go to school.

Although the dangerous aspects of city life are evident, there is a vital community spirit in this neighborhood. There is a lot of life on the streets and much of it happens near the school. There are clusters of young kids sitting on stoops, playing tag in the street, making up games, and watching passersby. Usually there are groups of older brothers or sisters or neighbors nearby who keep an eye on the younger ones. Near the university housing, people on the streets are often small family groups: mothers and children or fathers and children from India, Korea, South America, and other countries. For young people there are two additional centers of activity. One is the Conroy Community Center located in a newly painted and renovated house on a quiet street. A new playground for younger children is outside; inside, the center offers activity and group projects that attract many neighborhood adolescents and young adults. In addition, the Conroy Community School program, using the Inner School after school hours and weekends, offers facilities for athletics and classes in topics from homemaking and health to parenting.

In this neighborhood many of the established community and school leaders are black and many continuing relationships between the Inner School and the community are maintained by black families living in and around Redwood Estates. Occasionally, because some of these parents are outspoken and represent more radical views on community participation in schools and politics, they are looked on by some as troublemakers. Yet the city and district administrators speak of these parents as a positive influence on community-school relations.

Since it was built more than twenty years ago, Redwood Estates has been a relatively stable community. In describing the project, one housing official emphasized that families stay in these apartments, that many members of families are regularly employed, that families are eager to move in, that few problems with residents and maintenance are reported here, and that residents are active in tenant organizations and involved in community affairs. The community image of Redwood Estates is slightly more tarnished than the offical perception of the housing authority. There are frequent complaints from residents of vandalism, drug traffic, and crime within the buildings. By Conroy housing-project standards, Redwood Estates is small. Partly because of the number of working people in these apartments, rents are slightly higher, on the average, than those for other projects. The relatively high rent paid by some tenants not only reflects the employment there but seems most directly related to the generally very low turnover—a rate that is among the lowest for subsidized housing in the city.

Rents in the university housing project, on the other hand, run much higher. Although parents from this complex are often quite vocal and visible while their children are in school, as graduate students they are considered by school staff and other community people to be basically elitist, transient, and unattached to the community. The Inner School's principal says that he can count on the university community to supply about fifty children every year but that these children are always concentrated in the lower grades. Being students, he explains, the parents are not usually old enough to have children in the upper grades; by the time the children have reached the upper grades, the family has moved on.

The Inner School's principal has his own perspective on the district community. He grew up there. Now middle-aged, Steven Hamilton has been at the Inner School for many years. He recalls living "just down the street" from the present site in a cold-water flat with his widowed mother and brothers and sisters. The neighborhood was always diverse, he recalls, and full of hard-working people. Many were not far from being poor then, as now, but basically he sees the community as a "family neighborhood." While Hamilton remembers earlier days in Conroy as seeming simpler, he is firmly planted in the present. It's sometimes difficult to get parents into the school, he says, unless there's something they don't like; but once in school, he believes that he shares with them a basic objective: the "best possible" education and environment for their children.

Mr. Hamilton wants visitors to appreciate the complexity of the school and of the children and parents who live nearby. As a white administrator in this neighborhood where much parent leadership is black, he has talked and disagreed with, listened to and accepted criticism from, the more outspoken parents in the district. During one of our visits to his office, Steven Hamilton interrupted the discussion to take a call from a mother of a former student at the Inner School. It was October and she was calling to ask where her child should be enrolled.

"Did you call the Eastman School Department?" he asks.

"Did you get the transfer card you need from us?" and then, not unkindly, "Where has he been the last six weeks? He should be in school."

While visitors wait, he searches the telephone directory for the number of the appropriate office of the Eastman School Department. "You call this number," he says, "and do what they tell you to enroll him. If you have any trouble, call me back at this number." He is patient, clear, and direct. He gives an impression of fatherliness that is a welcome stereotype: firm and decisive, sentimental at times, and very intent on being fair although this does not mean to him that everything is equally valuable.

Mr. Hamilton is proud of the school but concerned that it is a big and pretty complicated environment for an elementary school child to comprehend and negotiate. Having recounted a long list of the school's facilities, he suddenly shrugged and said, "Why, we've got a whole city here." The Inner School's enrollment remains fairly steady from year to year at about 650; of the thirty regular homerooms, eight are classes for children with special needs. Like other Conroy schools, this one has facilities for music, art, lunch, physical education, and the services of many specialists.

From the outside, the Inner School does not look that big. Its warm rust color minimizes the size, and several windows look out onto the street. Around the central stairway there are large color paintings made by children to show where they came from. They extend all around the hallway; Africa and India are prominent.

Two rooms of Head Start classes meet every morning and another two rooms make up the day-care center. Since last year, the Inner School has also housed a separately funded and primarily parent-governed school-within-a-school: the "Alternative School." Its five nontraditional classrooms serve children from kindergarten through third grade. Its presence has allowed parents to see and choose different learning arrangements and be involved in a greater degree of parent participation. It has also raised a number of questions for teachers, administrators, and parents about how to best educate children, run schools, and develop new solutions to problems in education.

Because of the Alternative School and its impact on the regular school during its first year, the recent history of the Inner School as a social organization points more than usual to the role of parents. One might, in fact, overemphasize the importance of the new Alternative School and its five classrooms on the remainder of the school. The majority of classrooms are regular ones; that is, they are flexibly arranged by seating and daily routine to reflect the style of the teacher and the age of the children. Most of these teachers are not committed to the open-classroom model—their philosophies of education, modes of presentation, and classroom social structures reflect a wide range of pedagogical approaches. It was in these regular classrooms that our observations of teachers and children were done. Although detailed analysis of the impact of the Alternative School on life at the Inner

School is not appropriate here, it is important to recognize that these two school cultures were not always in equilibrium, and were sometimes in conflict. The presence of these five open-structured classrooms created a sphere of influence which surrounded classroom teachers, children, and, less directly, parents during the year of observation.

The divisions and tensions between the "progressive" and "regular" classrooms were not the only pedagogical differences recognized by parents and teachers at the Inner School. People who know the school well also made distinctions between the quality and styles of education in the lower school (kindergarten through third grades) and upper school (fourth through eighth grades). The primary grades are generally regarded as educational settings of superior quality. During the past few years, first-grade reading scores at the school have been the best in the city. The upper grades, however, have not enjoyed such a high reputation. As children move into the upper grades, their test scores decline, the classroom environments become more rigidly traditional, and the teachers seem concerned primarily with maintaining discipline and order. The primary teachers, often proud of the talent they have nurtured in their young charges, worry that their hard work will be undone as the children continue through school. Parents often express concern about the general deterioration of educational quality and standards as their children grow older.

In recent years one major problem has been that of pulling kids out from the classroom to work with specialists; teachers felt that this was a major disruption to classroom scheduling and a significant disadvantage to the children whose school day was being severely fragmented. Steven Hamilton not only expressed concern about the confusion and fragmentation for "special needs" children but also thought that in general there was too much movement from place to place for young children to become "rooted" and comfortable in the environment. During a typical week, for instance, even primary classrooms would go as a whole to the gymnasium, to the library, to the art room, and to the cafeteria each day.

The use of testing and school records was another issue of contention among teachers. Although Hamilton maintained that teachers liked the standardized tests for children because they helped assess how well both child and teacher were doing, there was clearly no consensus among teachers about the worth and appropriateness of tests. Some teachers trusted their own experience and diagnostic judgment of children's skills and aptitudes more than the "objective" evidence of evaluations and tests. Others complained that the labeling of "special needs" children was providing an easy excuse for lazy teachers who did not want to solve their own problems within the classroom. And there were those who feared the potential damage to children whose school records branded them with negative and pejorative labels they might never be able to break away from.

Testing became a source of tension between the teachers in the Alternative School and the regular classrooms because the former were generally opposed to standardized tests and grading. Therefore, teachers who inherited children from the Alternative School were often presented with incomplete and inconsistent records, and some felt at a loss about how to judge and evaluate these children's previous experience. Interestingly enough, few parents who enrolled children in an experimental, open-style classroom in the Inner School continued it for their child's third-grade year. After two years (first and second grades) of the humanistic-expressive mode for their children, these middle-class parents seemed to want to return to the more traditional, time-honored models of education. So the tensions between the Alternative School and the regular classrooms were not solely based on struggles over physical space, unequal resources and facilities, or different administrative policies. The tensions were more deeply enmeshed in the subtle clashes between the educational philosophies and goals that each setting offered and symbolized. The "sides" and boundaries of these philosophical and curricular approaches were not clearly drawn. In fact, a sharp distinction between the Alternative School and regular classrooms might have made their coexistence easier. Parents and teachers on both sides seemed to feel some ambivalence, and this lack of certainty led to greater defensiveness and distrust.

Steven Hamilton was greatly concerned about whether the alternative and regular classrooms would ever be able to coexist comfortably. He always enjoyed the "family feeling" in his school, and the rapid change and disruption that the Alternative School brought with it have been distracting to the sense of togetherness. He values roots and continuity—both strong themes in the Inner neighborhood and school—and he hopes that the fragmenting effects of the school-within-a-school, the CASE evaluations and testing, the overscheduling and movement of children, will not jeopardize the "family" tradition. The vice-principal at the Inner School, a young and energetic black man, did not comment on the changes in the school, but in his assessment of the community he concurred with Steven Hamilton. He grew up here, too, and said, "It's pretty much the same here. No, not much has changed in this neighborhood for years."

The Outer School

The Outer School District occupies a much larger territory than the Inner School District, though enrollment at the Outer School is only greater by about a hundred children. Unlike the Inner District, the Outer is much too expansive to be considered a single community. From a glance at the city map, it appears to be the largest district in Conroy. Size is one important reason why this district is not a clearly defined or cohesive community; the other is the history and diversity of its residents.

There are three readily identifiable groups in this district, and their neighborhoods run into each other. The largest and closest to the school is the middle group—in income, type of occupation, property—all those things people mean when they say this is "a middle- and working-class neighborhood." A few in this neighborhood are college and graduate students, but most are people in civil service, public utilities, small businesses, and other blue- and white-collar positions. They are Catholic and Protestant, black and white, and most have lived here for many years, some for generations.

Farther from the school geographically and fewer in number are the upper-middle-class, well-educated, professional families. Most of these are white and live in large, expansive houses surrounded by beautiful gardens.

At the opposite and poorer end of the district are residents who live in and around the Lakeside Terrace housing development. Most of these families are black and working-class and some receive welfare. A number have moved from the ghettos of other cities in hopes of finding better housing and a healthier environment for their children. Not only are these families generally poorer and more transient than others in the Outer District, but they are also identifiable as a group by their relative isolation from the rest of the district's population. There is no inner-city ghetto at this end of Conroy, but within several blocks of each other are three medium- to large-sized housing projects with relatively large minority and lower-class populations. They are not, by any standards, considered the worst projects in Conroy; yet the neighborhood in which Lakeside Terrace, Grant Plaza, and Skyline Apartments are located is clearly set apart from the more "respectable" residential parts of the district.

There has been a good deal of change and some turmoil within the Outer District during the past four years. Administrators at the Outer School and in the central Conroy administration, however, believe that the school has gone a long way toward resolving problems arising from rapid growth and relocation in the district. But the Outer School's image in the rest of the city has remained tarnished, as people cling to memories of a more chaotic and disorganized period. While some of the problems associated with rapid institutional transformations contributed to its mediocre reputation, the school's progress in solving such problems has not yet improved its public image. In one recent year, the rate of student transfers from the Outer School was higher than for any other city school, but this movement of students cannot be attributed solely to changes in district population. The transfers also reflect its relatively large size, its diverse population, and the presence of many other schools, both public and private, near the district's borders.

Prior to the seventies the Outer School District was called the Glenwood School District, and the school building was located nearer to the more affluent area around Rutherford Square. Part of the Glenwood School's image derived from its proximity to wealth and professionalism. Most of these parents were financially able to enroll their children in one of several nearby private schools. Their decision to send them to Glenwood School therefore tended to be a deliberate choice based on philosophical, political, and educational notions. Once having opted for public schooling, they became a vocal, fairly aggressive force in the district and were most often perceived by teachers and administrators as powerful and threatening. Their homes in the Rutherford Square section exude affluence. This part of the district is relatively quiet, stately, and peaceful. Although many families live here, it seems like an adult environment, undisturbed by the sounds and sight of children. There is no active street life, and children's games, jump-rope, and bicycles do not have to be contended with by drivers, as is the case on some streets nearer the Outer School.

With increasing enrollments in the district the Glenwood School became too small, so the Outer School was built. The new school was located deeper in the heart of the district's largest constituency, the working- and middle-class people who had lived in the area for generations. This area resembles the other working-class neighborhoods of Conroy. As one nears the school, the number of two- and three-family apartment houses increases. These houses are well-kept but have been harder used by families over the years. They are lively in appearance, painted in yellows, blues, and greens. The yards are smaller, filled with trees and decorative flower beds. Homeowners and long-time renters take pride in their sturdy dwellings and spend a great deal of energy on household maintenance and neighborhood cleanliness. There is a lot of life in these streets. Neighbors know one another well and engage in friendly chatter; children romp and play street games, and older people swing on their porches or sit quietly watching the activities of the young. There is a visible sense of extended families and of several generations under one roof.

The Outer School is located in the heart of this lively neighborhood, but traffic patterns make it easier to see than to reach unless one knows how to get there. Most passersby see it from behind as they travel along Magnolia Street. North of Magnolia Street, the three-family frame houses continue and upkeep is good, but one begins to reach open spaces. A couple of ball fields and playgrounds are well kept and well used. Along the street is the new Lakeside Terrace project built by a private developer for low- and moderate-income families. It is a long stretch of repetitious apartments. There are few trees and little greenery around—the feeling is one of great expanses of modular concrete.

Despite the open spaces and playgrounds nearby, the houses hug the streets with little extra room for yards or garages. At present, most families in Lakeside Terrace are black. Although it is relatively new and in decent repair, Lakeside Terrace projects the image of potentially rapid decay, and it is located closer to the older and more neglected projects than to the affluent sections of the Outer District. Just over the district line, for instance, is Grant Plaza. Although its appearance and maintenance have improved in recent years, it still has the look of housing whose residents struggle against the great odds of poverty and overcrowding. Also nearby are the Skyline Apartments, high-rise buildings for low- and moderate-income inhabitants. A number of young black professionals and families live here as well as a relatively large proportion of white families. Flowering shrubs bloom at the edge of the parking lot in spring, but the buildings look cold, no matter what the season.

From this side of the district, it seems miles to the Outer School. In fact, it is perhaps fifteen blocks away, but two busy streets are in between and the psychological distance feels vast. For safety purposes, children from Lakeside Terrace are bussed back and forth to school. The bus ride increases the feeling of distance and isolation from the life of the school. Most other children independently negotiate the path from home to school, or their parents deliver and pick them up. Even those who live just as far away in the direction of the university are able to walk to school because of the absence of heavy traffic and major highways. The black children from Lakeside Terrace probably do not experience the Outer School as a close and friendly neighborhood school, but as a far-away place that can only be reached by bus.

The geographical isolation of the Lakeside Terrace area probably exaggerated the difficulty for many parents in becoming part of this newly constructed school community. According to school administrators, many of the Lakeside Terrace families with children starting at the Outer School that first year had come from other cities in and out of the state. These newly transplanted parents not only experienced isolation from the Outer School but also had to endure the turmoil and dislocation within their housing development. Originally built for low- and moderate-income families, Lakeside Terrace soon had more than enough applicants to fill the apartments, but not the proportion of moderate-income residents that developers had anticipated for a "balanced" environment. Because they had only seventeen subsidized units in the project, the Conroy Housing Commission had little interest in becoming involved in the administration of the project.

Rather than turn away applicants and allow the building to remain empty, the developers agreed to permit tenants to move in at lower rents than they had originally stipulated and planned for. Disputes seemed inevitable, and trouble collecting rents followed. A few, some say very few, evictions were made, and after an initial period of crisis and tension, the project is said to be more settled now. School administrators who are acquainted with Lakeside Terrace families believe that some parents are beginning to emerge as leaders within the development and that, in general, it is beginning to stabilize as a small community.

On first appearance the Outer School seems to be one in which people must work to humanize the somewhat imposing physical structure. Like many modern schools, it is heavy on cement and seems to have few windows through which to look in or out. Inside, a central entranceway is dominated by long carpeted stairs and open space of brick floors and concrete pillars. A sign eight feet up on the wall welcomes visitors; a second sign just below advises them to check in at the principal's office. As one walks toward the principal's office and the hallway leading to classrooms, a scattering of other bright, neatly lettered signs indicate that this is a school for children. For the most part, however, the sounds of children are not heard, and very few children are even seen, except at lunch, recess, and school's end.

The principal's response to comments about the physical scale of the Outer School is to open a classroom door. Immediately the sense of structure falls away; inside is a warm, carpeted, and busily decorated room. There is a lot going on behind the classroom door. Nooks and corners are arranged to make individual spaces or to display papers and projects. Children's papers are hung in profusion and desks and tables are movable. In this room, at least, there is not a single "eyes front" focus in the arrangement of furniture. So the life of children and teachers at the Outer School seems to be very different inside the classroom from that suggested by the hallway and external building structure.

Mr. Barry, the principal, is a slight, middle-aged man who speaks in the language and style of an administrator who has been through many wars— his words are measured, his statements are carefully calculated, and he avoids disruptive and controversial issues. In our first meeting with him before our study began, he limited his discussion of the school to some very general statements about bussing patterns, school population, and daily schedules. Although he was willing to introduce us to his first-grade teachers, he did not want to take sides about whether they should agree to participate in our study. He assumed a very noncommital, neutral role and left the decision entirely up to the teachers. Although his stance might be viewed as a reflection of a democratic and responsive administrative style, it became evident over time that his general approach to decision making within the school was noncommittal, nondirective, and often left people wondering about "where he was coming from."

Most teachers we spoke to claimed he was a "nice enough guy" who, because he wished to avoid offending anyone, rarely took decisive stands. Teachers who had experienced conflict with parents commented that he was not their advocate and did not protect them from the intrusions and verbal assaults of overly aggressive parents. And parents also remarked about the lack of strong administrative support and guidance.

In our last conversation with him, Mr. Barry was much more open and responsive than he had been initially; he talked at great length about the overwhelming size and diversity of the school population. He was especially strained by the minority of professional, affluent, and well-educated parents who were aggressive, assertive, and "influential with the central administration." He seemed to fear their power and thought it best to avoid contacts with them. Mr. Barry spoke nostalgically about his positive administrative experiences before coming to the Outer School. For several years he had been principal at the nearby Whitney School, "truly a neighborhood school," which has a much smaller, more homogeneous population. The Whitney School was absorbed into the Outer School, and Mr. Barry misses the comfortable, familiar atmosphere in which parents trusted his judgment and children were more controllable and mannerly.

In the absence of strong leadership from the principal, the teachers look to Mike O'Connor, the assistant principal, for administrative strength, support, and protection. Mr. O'Connor seems to know the school inside out and has played an important part in maintaining contact between parents and the school. He gives the impression of having come up through the political ranks of the Conroy School Department and of knowing both its teaching and administrative ends.

Mike O'Connor's neighborhood experience goes back a long way; he grew up in the district, not far from the school's present site. He recalls that, when he was a child, the space where the Outer School now stands was fascinating woodlands, just right for exploring with friends. His recollections of the area are unsentimental but not unfeeling.

O'Connor claims that eighty percent of the district's families are educationally conservative: "They believe in pulling yourself up by your boot straps and hard work." They have faith in the traditional skills, training, and intellectual focus of schooling. The remaining twenty percent, he feels, are families whose intellectual expectations are high, intelligence above average, and who consider creative and affective processes to be part of the "basis" of an integrated and comprehensive education.

Teachers seem to think highly of O'Connor and to consider him the leader. Outside of faculty, his importance in the district has most likely been due to his willingness to initiate and maintain contact with parents. "I've been to houses in this district and I've been to projects," he says, "so that they know who I am." Especially with families new to the district, he says, "I try to make sure I still call some of those families . . . especially when there's something good to say about a kid. Just so they know that every time the school calls, it doesn't mean trouble."

In this school there are a myriad of people and issues to keep track of. Like the Inner School, the Outer is a big operation. It has over thirty regular homerooms and five homerooms for children with special needs. Among the sixty-five teachers are a number of specialists in the areas of learning disabilities, media, physical education, reading, remedial education, resource centers, and music. The school has a gymnasium, a cafeteria, auditorium space, a woodworking shop, and music and art facilities. A Community School program offers activities for many different age groups, including senior citizens.

Historically, the school's enrollment grew in two convulsive leaps. The first came when the Outer School was built and faculty and students moved from the old Glenwood School. They were joined that first year by the seventh and eighth grades from the increasingly crowded Whitney School. Two years later, the Outer opened in September with two hundred new students from Lakeside Terrace. During that period the strains and tensions within the school were easy to recognize, but the causes were complex. The near-double enrollment meant increasing the faculty by fifty percent in two short years. Not only were experienced teachers trying to make sense and working order out of the new school's structure, but they were also trying to establish relationships with a very large number of colleagues, many of them in their first year of teaching.

With the sudden explosion in student enrollment, some parents grew increasingly concerned that rapid growth would bring deterioration in the high quality of education at the Outer School. Some were eager for new teachers to maintain high academic standards, while others were more concerned that teachers focus on helping new children from other cities and schools accommodate to the school and that a comfortable learning environment be created and sustained. Although many of the new families were black, the basic issue, according to the principal and other school administrators, was not racial but one of "adjustment to change." Some parents, long accustomed to speaking out about "their" school, were eager to become involved and actively participate in decision making, while the newcomers, many of them minorities, did not yet feel comfortable about establishing an aggressive presence in the school and did not relate to the Outer as "their" school.

During our year of research, therefore, we saw a school that was beginning to recover from the fragmentation of rapid institutional transformation. The recently hired teachers, many of whom were new and inexperienced, had not had the opportunity to build supportive and productive relationships with colleagues, and they often felt alone and isolated against the intrusions of frustrated and aggressive parents. The principal's approach had been one of noninterference, a laissez-faire position that provided neither leadership and protection for teachers nor structure and receptivity for parents.

Not only had the population of the district increased enormously in the last few years, but the school had also brought together divergent groups from various social class, racial, ethnic, and educational backgrounds. The geographical distances and territorial boundaries *within* the district had intensified feelings of threat and discomfort among the various parent groups and had made it difficult for them to get to know one another. The more affluent, well-educated families from the relatively homogeneous and neighborly Glenwood School felt entitled to make demands of teachers and administrators and were perceived as the most powerful and feared group; the frequently black, lower- and working-class residents of Lakeside Terrace were mostly isolated from school life and often felt demeaned and excluded by teachers and upper-middle-class parents.

In the midst of all these divergent forces, it was impressive that in many of the classrooms, teachers were able to build supportive and productive learning environments. Children and teachers must have experienced the stresses of transition and change, but the daily life of school went forward; and in the process of work and play, children and teachers within the classrooms created livable communities.

5

Observing Teachers and Children in Classrooms

Jean V. Carew

A MAJOR THEME of this book is the need for research on teaching to adopt broader, more varied approaches employing a number of convergent methodologies. We argue that in order to provide a balanced analysis of schools as a significant source of experiences in the lives of children, teachers, and parents, many types of data must be gathered and integrated. These include information on the social, political, and physical aspects of the school and surrounding community; empirical data on what actually goes on within the classroom including observations of teacher and child behavior and the social structure in which these transactions are embedded; and the broad array of information needed to arrive at some understanding of the character, personality, motives, and perceptions of the principal actors in the classroom drama—teachers and children.

To obtain these data we used several complementary research strategies, the primary ones being repeated observations of both teachers and children in their classrooms and interviews with teachers, children, parents, and school administrators. Because of their relatively technical nature, these data are presented here somewhat in isolation from the interview data. Later, in the case studies, they will be introduced again as we attempt to synthesize all the information collected in this study and to construct more complete, multidimensional portrayals of each teacher.

The need for research on teaching to document the actual transactions between teachers and children in classrooms is now recognized. Studies in which students are merely tested or evaluated at the beginning and end of the year or before and after a new curriculum, program, or intervention is introduced are no longer considered adequate. Now more than ever before researchers and evaluators realize the need to record what goes on between teachers and children in the interim in order to understand their results. Al-

though they have a long history and many advances have been made, observational studies on classroom processes still seem to be struggling to overcome some basic conceptual and methodological problems. Three problems
are strikingly apparent. First, the lack of a longitudinal perspective. In
many research studies, classroom observations span only a short period of
time (days or weeks). Yet we know that major changes in relationships between teachers and children take place over the course of the school year as
teachers and children develop skills and understandings and have an impact
on and adapt to one another.

The second problem is the lack of interest in variation of treatment within
classrooms. Few studies attempt to record the interaction of teachers with
identifiable individual children. Yet research and informal observation suggest that the experiences of different children in the same setting typically
vary dramatically, and this variation may have major consequences for student achievement and development (Brophy and Good 1974). To characterize a teacher's behavior solely by averaging her interactions with all of her
pupils is not only to misrepresent classroom realities but hardly does justice
to the intentions and skills of those teachers who consciously strive to indi-
vidualize their treatment of children in response to their differing needs,
abilities, and temperaments. The particular dimensions along which the
teacher differentiates her treatment and the individual and ascribed status
characteristics of children who receive exceptional attention from her can
also tell us much about the teacher's basic personality structure—her values
and prejudices, the things that motivate and reinforce her, and those that
threaten and alienate her. Such an analysis is essential if we wish to distinguish between the discriminating and the discriminatory teacher, the one
who acts out of sensitivity and respect for individual differences and the one
who acts out of prejudice and dislike of the social class, race, or sex of the
children.

The third major drawback in observational research on classrooms is the
lack of a focus on the behavior and characteristics of children independently from their interactions with the teacher. Most studies focus exclusively on
the teacher as a target of observation and the transactions he chooses to engage in with students. Yet we know that only a small part of a child's day at
school is spent directly interacting with the teacher. (In a class of twenty or
more children it could hardly be otherwise.) Indirectly the teacher may continue to control the child's behavior by assigning work, supervising activities, and requiring the observance of classroom protocol. But a teacher cannot control all of the children all of the time, nor do most teachers wish to
do so. Many prefer to give children wide latitude to pursue their own activities; others are simply unable to prevent children from doing so, given the
large number of students and the rapid pace of classroom events. Whether

by design or default, the result is that children are often the makers of their classroom experiences, and we cannot know what their lives there are like unless we observe them apart from as well as with the teacher.

Child-focused observations are also critical to understanding the bases on which the teacher forms perceptions, expectations, and judgments about children. Judgments about students' abilities and personalities are normal, ubiquitous, and necessary to effective thinking. But teachers vary greatly in how they arrive at these evaluations (the sources of evidence they use, the personality and status characteristics of the child that appear salient, the accuracy of their perceptions, their openness to change) and how these judgments influence their behavior. By providing a view of the child that subsumes but goes beyond his interactions with the teacher, child-focused observations can tell us much about the child and also much about the teacher. Are his perceptions consistent with the observer's picture of the child? Are they sufficiently differentiated and responsive to changes in the child over time? Do they take into account social and emotional aspects of development as well as cognitive and academic ones? Do they seem to be affected by the child's social class, race, or sex? How important is it to the teacher that children do their work, observe classroom rules, enjoy themselves, get to know each other, learn to work out interpersonal problems? What characteristics and behaviors seem to make a teacher become attached to one child, concerned about another, indifferent to a third, rejecting of a fourth? By providing an independent view of the child, child-focused observations can tell us much about the teacher's understanding of children, of how they develop and how their development can be influenced, of how they differ and what aspects of diversity the teacher values.

Observation Methods

With these considerations in mind we included in this exploratory study three types of classroom observations: repeated longitudinal observations of the teacher's interactions with individual children, in groups or singly, in the context of various classroom activities (teacher-focused observations); repeated, longitudinal observations of selected individual children in the context of seatwork or play in which the teacher was infrequently involved (child-focused observations); and repeated longitudinal observations of the classroom social structure, including the assignment of children to hierarchically ranked reading groups and to various seating arrangements.

Each classroom was visited nineteen or twenty times over the course of the school year. Observations began with an initial orientation period followed by four phases of data collection in the four quarters of the school year. In the orientation period one observer visited the school to explain the research procedures, to obtain class lists and information on the teacher's weekly schedule and convenient times for visits, and to familiarize herself with the setting, seating patterns, and identities of children. Each classroom was then visited by one of two observers approximately once per week for five to six weeks in each quarter of the school year. Each visit typically lasted about two hours, with observations evenly distributed as far as possible across days of the week and times of day. However, visits seldom took place on Fridays (notoriously a bad day for teachers), nor did we observe activities that took place outside the classroom with someone other than the main teacher, such as art, music, gym, recess, and lunch, nor the private tutoring sessions that several children regularly had with specialists.

The main purpose of the classroom observations in the first half of the school year was to observe the behavior of teachers in their interactions with children. In contrast, the chief aim of the visits scheduled for the second half of the school year was to record the behavior of selected individual children when they were not interacting with or being attended to by the teacher. Table 1 shows the observation schedule and amount of coded observation time per visit.

Teacher-Focused Observations   Two observational schemes, the *Structured Interaction* (SI) and *Unstructured Interaction* (UI) systems, were developed to record and code interactions between teachers and children. The SI system was freely adapted from the Brophy-Good System (1970a). To gather these data the observer, equipped with stopwatch and the Structured Interaction coding form, focused her attention on the teacher, watching her behavior and that of children with whom she interacted during the first thirty seconds of each minute, then coding or recording these communications in the next thirty seconds. Whether or not the observed interactions were coded immediately on the Structured Interaction coding form or described and coded later on the Unstructured Interaction form depended on the kinds of behavior that actually ensued. Most behaviors occurring in question and answer sessions, reading and math groups, evaluations of seatwork, and the like could be coded on the spot in terms of the categories of the Structured Interaction system. Behaviors that did not fit into these categories and all behaviors initiated by children were described in a comment section of the SI and coded later in terms of the complementary coding scheme, the Unstructured Interaction system. The UI was designed to capture the less predictable behaviors occurring in structured academic activities and also the much wider range of behaviors taking place in interactions concerned with nonacademic topics, procedure, and behavior control.

Table 2 lists the main variables that enter into the quantitative analyses. Several variables included in the complete SI and UI systems do not appear

Table 1. Classroom observation schedule.

Observation	Month	Allen	Prima	Edwards	Ryan
Teacher-focused		*Coded observation time (minutes)*[1]			
Scheduling visit[2]	October	0	0	0	0
Orientation observation[2]	October	0	0	0	0
Observation 1	October	42.0	53.5	33.5	25.0
Observation 2	October	21.0	46.5	41.0	36.0
Observation 3	November	59.0	43.5	15.0	67.0
Observation 4	November	25.5	28.5	25.5	62.5
Observation 5	November	52.0	68.0	25.5	54.5
Observation 6	November	51.5	57.5	61.5	34.5
Observation 7	January	53.0	36.5	47.5	53.5
Observation 8	January	59.0	55.5	55.5	52.5
Observation 9	January	37.5	57.0	54.5	79.5
Observation 10	February	55.0	54.5	63.0	83.5
Observation 11	February	58.5	56.0	50.5	—
		514.0	557.0	473.0	548.5
	(hours)	8.6	9.3	7.9	9.1
Child-focused[3]					
1-3 visits	March	147.0	134.5	98.0	119.0
0-2 visits	April	45.5	—	61.0	—
1-2 visits	May	86.5	28.5	48.0	66.0
1-2 visits	June	49.5	95.0	79.0	87.0
		329.0	258.0	286.0	272.0
	(hours)	5.5	4.3	4.8	4.5
		Total visits per teacher			
		7	7	7	7

1. Refers to the amount of time spent actually observing the teacher's behavior. Thirty seconds of each minute the observer was working in the classroom was spent observing behavior and thirty seconds was spent coding or describing it. Thus, the coded observation time is equal to half the actual visit time.

2. Not coded.

3. Four children in each classroom were observed during each of 7 visits for which they were present.

Table 2. Teacher-focused observation variables.

Variable	Definition
Overall context variable	
Activity context	
(a) Academic	Includes subject matter lesson; reading and phonics; math; penmanship; work recitation; seatwork; paperwork review.
(b) Nonacademic	Includes nonacademic activities that are typically structured by the teacher (e.g., storytelling, Simon Says) and nonacademic activities in which the teacher usually does not participate (e.g., play with toys and games).
(c) Other	Includes class routines and transition periods between organized activity.
Number of children involved	Whole class versus subgroup.
Child participants	Identity of each child involved in the activity.
Rank of subgroup	Rank of reading or math group.
Structured interaction (SI) variable	
Recipient	Identity of child.
Teacher-child interaction topic	May coincide with the overall activity context (e.g., in a reading activity context, T teaches reading) or diverge from it (e.g., in a reading activity context T asks C to count); only academic interaction topics are coded in the SI, as defined for activity context (a) above.
Teacher behavior	
Makes open vs. direct demands	*Open:* T asks C to answer a question or perform a task after waiting for sign that C wants to do so (e.g., handraising). *Direct:* T directs question to C or directs C to do a task without waiting for sign C wants to do so.
Asks free vs. process vs. product question	*Free:* T asks question with no right or wrong answer. *Process:* T asks question that requires C to think through answer or figure out solution; T provides information demonstrating thinking-through/problem-solving process.

Table 2 (*cont.*)

Variable	Definition
	Product: T asks question or makes work demand having a single right answer; T provides single right answer.
Provides assessment vs. no assessment	*Assessment:* T provides feedback to C as to whether C's response/work is correct/complete or incorrect/incomplete.
	No assessment: T does not provide such feedback.
Gives positive vs. negative evaluation/reinforcement	*Positive:* T praises C's response/work/behavior.
	Negative: T criticizes C's response/work/behavior.
Sustains interest by asking new question vs. repeating question or giving a clue	*New question:* T sustains C's interest in task by asking new question.
	Repeat or clue: T urges C to respond by repeating question or giving a clue.

Unstructured interaction (UI) variable

Initiator	Identity.
Recipient	Identity.
Teacher-child interaction topic	
(a) Academic	Same as for activity context (a).
(b) Nonacademic	Same as for activity context (b).
(c) Other	Same as for activity context (c).
(d) Privilege	T grants C special favor or privilege (e.g., T selects C to run an errand) or C requests a privilege.
(e) Appropriate child behavior	T explicitly recognizes child's "good" or appropriate behavior (e.g., when C seeks opportunity to perform or helps others).
(f) Inappropriate child behavior	T calls attention to child's "bad" or inappropriate behavior (e.g., when C annoys or disrupts other children or is inattentive to his work).
(g) Health, distress	T responds to child's physical health, distress, discomfort, or fear.
Teacher behavior	
Gives positive vs. negative reinforcement	*Positive:* T praises C's response/work/behavior; T offers positive incentive.
	Negative: T criticizes C's response/work/behavior; T inhibits, reprimands, threatens punishment.

(*cont.*)

Table 2 (*cont.*)

Variable	Definition
Grants vs. rejects C's request	*Grants:* T provides information, help, permission at C's request.
	Rejects: T refuses, defers information, help, permission at C's request.
Provides academic vs. procedural information	T instructs, explains academic vs. procedural aspects of a task.
Directs	T directs C to do a task.
Converses, plays, jokes	T engages in conversation, play, humor with C.
Child behavior	
Appropriate	C engages in appropriate school behavior (e.g., seeks evaluation of work or performance).
Expressive	C expresses opinion, makes comment, jokes.
Dependent	C asks for direction, information, help, materials, or permission from T.
Inappropriate	C engages in inappropriate behavior (e.g., annoys or disrupts other children or is inattentive to work).

in table 2 because they occurred too infrequently to warrant separate statistical treatment. These variables were either combined to form conceptually reasonable composites or eliminated from the data analysis. The complete SI and UI coding systems, including behavior definitions and examples and the procedures for combining and analyzing variables, are described in appendices A and C.

Each interaction between the teacher and an individual child that occurred in a thirty-second observation interval was coded in terms of either the SI or UI dimensions listed in table 2. The number of behaviors of a particular type was then calculated separately for each teacher, as a percentage of the total number of SI or UI interactions observed in her classroom over the ten or eleven teacher-focused observations. This procedure allows us to compare teachers in terms of the relative percentage of time spent on different activities or on different types of behavior.

An important purpose of this study was to assess the extent to which teachers treated individual children differently, as individuals or as blacks or whites, or boys or girls. To accomplish this objective, the observer identified the specific child participating in each interaction with the teacher (for example, the child whom the teacher asks to read; the child who asks the teacher for help). First, in the data analysis the number of interactions in which each child was a participant was calculated as a percentage of the total number of interactions for which he was present and in which, theoretically, he might have participated. Next, the number of interactions dealing with a specific topic or characterized by a particular child or teacher behavior listed in table 2 was calculated for each child as a percentage of the total number of interactions of that type in which, theoretically, he might have participated. To illustrate, suppose we were interested in knowing whether Ms. Smith treated children differently so far as the number of academic questions she asked them in class was concerned. Ms. Smith's class consists of eight children, four boys and four girls, and during our morning's visit we observe each of the following activities:

Activity	Children included
Subject-matter lesson	All 8 children
Show and Tell	All 8 children
Reading group 1	4 girls
Reading group 2	4 boys
Math group 1	2 girls, 2 boys
Math group 2	2 girls, 2 boys

We record each time Ms. Smith asks a child an academic question in the context of these activities and find her questions are distributed among children as follows:

Activity	Girls				Boys			
	A	B	C	D	E	F	G	H
Lesson	2	2	0	0	0	0	0	0
Show and Tell	3	3	0	0	0	0	0	0
Reading group 1	10	10	5	5	—	—	—	—
Reading group 2	—	—	—	—	5	5	0	0
Math group 1	5	5	—	—	0	0	—	—
Math group 2	—	—	5	5	—	—	5	5
Actual questions	20	20	10	10	5	5	5	5
% actual/maximum (=80)	25	25	12.5	12.5	6.25	6.25	6.25	6.25

Ignoring the fact that girls and boys are not always included in the same activities, we see that the maximum number of questions any one child might have been asked is eighty. If Ms. Smith treated individual children equally, then the number of questions each girl and boy received should be ten, or 12.5 percent of the total. We find, however, that girls A and B were each asked twenty questions, twice as many as they should have, girls C and D received ten questions, exactly as many as they should have, and boys E, F, G, and H received only five questions each, half as many as they should have. If asking more questions is a form of favoritism, then Ms. Smith clearly seems to favor girls A and B, and her favoritism is evident in all activities that were observed, including subject-matter lessons, Show and Tell, and reading.

These hypothetical data can also be used to illustrate how one might determine whether or not Ms. Smith favored the girls in her class as a group compared to the boys, in addition to favoring individual girls over other children. Comparing the average percentage of questions addressed to girls and boys, we are struck by the large difference: 18.75 percent go to girls versus 6.25 percent to boys. This discrepancy can be statistically tested and, if significant, provides presumptive evidence that Ms. Smith discriminates among children in her class on the basis of sex. If Ms. Smith's class included black and white children, or middle- and working-class children, we could determine in a similar way whether she discriminated on the basis of social class or race.

Child-Focused Observations   One limitation of teacher-focused observations is that the child's behavior is not observed except when he is interacting with his teacher. But the teacher's view of the child is influenced by more than his interactive behavior with her; she may observe him at seatwork or in social interactions with other children, for example. Hence to understand the teacher's behavior toward the child, we must observe the child in other contexts. It also seems important to know to what extent the child's behavior in the classroom corresponds to the teacher's description and warrants any exceptional treatment that he may receive. If Ms. Smith often criticizes and scolds John, is this because John more often misbehaves than other children whom she treats more positively? If Ms. Smith sees Mary as a sweet, helpful child, is Mary truly so or is she really a brat when the teacher is out of sight?

With these ideas in mind we selected four children from each classroom for intensive individual observation. Children were chosen on the basis of preliminary classroom observations and teachers' comments in the course of the first two interviews. Overall we tried to sample roughly equal numbers of boys and girls, and black and white students. However, particular children were singled out for observation not so much because of their race or sex but because their relationship with the teacher seemed to illustrate some significant aspect of her personality, values, beliefs, or style.

These child-focused observations took place during our bi-weekly visits in the second half of the school year and were conducted when the children were engaged in individual seatwork or free play in the classroom rather than in a teacher-structured activity such as reading or math. During each visit the observer focused on each child twice for fifteen minutes at a time, using a time-sampling procedure in which she observed the child's behavior for thirty seconds and described it in the next thirty seconds. The observed behaviors were then coded in terms of the variables listed in table 3 and appendix B. Some of these behaviors (for example, "appropriate" and "inappropriate" behavior) are defined in much the same way as the corresponding child behaviors in the teacher-focused observation system (the UI codes) and permit us to compare the child's actions when he is or is not directly interacting with the teacher.

Classroom Structure Toward the end of the first quarter of the school year information was obtained from teachers as to the ranking and composition of reading and math groups and when and on what basis children had been assigned to different groups. The actual composition of reading groups was recorded whenever they were called during our observations in the classroom. Similarly, teachers were asked to describe the seating arrangements in their classrooms and their reasons for using particular patterns and placements. The actual location of each child's desk in the classroom was noted and the overall seating arrangement recorded on each visit to the classroom.

Results

In the following discussion we shall often be comparing and contrasting teachers, classes, and schools, but with a sample of only four teachers and two schools, we obviously cannot use customary statistical procedures to test the significance of reported differences. Only in cases where we compare the experiences of groups of children within a class (for example, in table 11) are statistical tests feasible and appropriate. The reader is therefore cautioned that when we contrast teachers and schools, most of the time we are simply pointing to differences that seem large and meaningful in a descriptive sense rather than to statistically significant ones.

The only criteria used for selecting the four first-grade classrooms used in this research were that they should be "regular" classes belonging to the same public school system and that they contain a cross section of students

Table 3. Child-focused observation variables.

Variable	Definition
Interaction	Whether the focus child interacted verbally or nonverbally with another person or persons or was not interactive.
Verbalization	Whether the focus child spoke to another person or persons, or to himself, or was silent.
Exhibition of appropriate or inappropriate behavior	Whether the child exhibited appropriate (e.g., helping), inappropriate (e.g., teasing), or neutral behavior, usually in interaction with others.
Reception of appropriate or inappropriate behavior	Whether the child received appropriate, inappropriate, or neutral behavior from other children, or received positive or negative reinforcement from the teacher.
Child activities	The predominant activity or event in which the child was engaged.
	Work: any academic task or quiet, constructive activity; includes paperwork, reading, drawing, and class rituals.
	Play: any concentrated free-time activity such as playing with toys and games, make-believe, and role playing.
	Talk: conversation, social chitchat, comments other than about work.
	Self-care: attending to personal needs such as going to the bathroom, dressing/undressing, getting a drink of water.
	Idling: off-task, unfocused, restless, or daydreaming activity.
	Wild/disorderly: clearly disruptive, unruly, or aggressive activity.
	No code: ambiguous, transitional, and all other activities or events not clearly codable in terms of the definitions above.

in terms of social class and race, including at least 20 percent black children. No attempt was made beforehand to find out about the teachers' teaching methods, pedagogical objectives, or personal characteristics, nor would such knowledge have affected their eligibility for the study. As it turned out, however, the two schools (Inner and Outer) and four teachers who took part in this research (Allen, Prima, Edwards, and Ryan) could hardly have been better chosen if we had deliberately set out to find contrasting first-grade classrooms. Imagine two dimensions, the first having to do with the academic substance of the curriculum, the regularity of schedules, and the efficiency of classroom management, and the second referring to the quality of teacher-child relationships. The major similarities and differences that were revealed in the quantitative analysis of the observation data can then be summarized succinctly as follows:

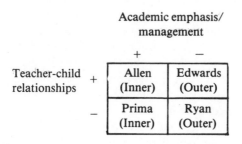

		Academic emphasis/ management	
		+	−
Teacher-child relationships	+	Allen (Inner)	Edwards (Outer)
	−	Prima (Inner)	Ryan (Outer)

The first dimension distinguishes schools; the second cuts across schools. On academic input and management efficiency, Mses. Allen and Prima, the two teachers in the Inner School, are relatively high compared to Mses. Edwards and Ryan of the Outer School, whereas on the quality of teacher-child interactions, Ms. Allen of the Inner School and Ms. Edwards of the Outer School are high compared to Mses. Prima and Ryan.

Academic Emphasis and Management Efficiency In Mses. Allen's and Prima's classes in the Inner School there clearly was such a thing as a typical day. In fact, virtually every day was typical. A set routine was adhered to, activities followed each other smoothly with minimum time spent in transition, and even leisure time was predictably scheduled. Starting at about 9:00 a.m., the first activity observed in both classes was always one in which the whole class was involved, focusing generally on reading and language arts. Mses. Allen and Prima might lead a phonics game ("Tell me a word that has the same sound as 'moose' ") or pose riddles ("What word beginning with 'ch' is the name of a little red fruit?") or conduct a writing or spelling drill (two teams compete to spell "at" words). Typically this fast-paced whole-class activity lasted a brief ten to fifteen minutes and was immediately followed by the calling up of reading groups, one after the other until lunch at 11 a.m. After lunch the curriculum became more varied. Now we were more likely to see whole-class or small-group activities focused on math or penmanship, individual reading, seatwork, and paperwork review, and in the last half hour of the day some creative or "fun" activity such as storytelling, making holiday collages, or acting out television stories.

By contrast, the agenda of activities observed in Mses. Edwards' and Ryan's classes was more irregular, the differences being most marked in

Ms. Edwards' room. Reading-related activities usually took place in the morning and math in the afternoon, but these were most often conducted on a whole-class or individual basis, and time spent on these activities varied considerably from one visit to another. In general, activities in Ms. Edwards' class were much less crisply demarcated, and transition time from one to the other often struck an observer as excessively high. (It should be noted, however, that at Ms. Edwards' request visits to her class did not begin before 10:00 a.m. Thus, the activity schedule constructed from our observations may not be an accurate representation of her typical routine.) Ms. Ryan, the other teacher in the Outer School, also seemed to have a more flexible schedule than the teachers in the Inner School, although not quite so loose as Ms. Edwards'. However, transition periods in Ms. Ryan's class were even longer than in Ms. Edwards' (five minutes on the average, as long as eleven minutes on one occasion), and Ms. Ryan was also the only teacher to incorporate regular rest periods in her curriculum. Typical daily schedules for the four classes are given in table 4.

Complementing the information of table 4 are the data of table 5, which show more precisely the various activity contexts that were observed and the proportion of time they absorbed. A complete listing of the frequency of occurrence of each variable included in the SI and UI coding systems and each combination of variables used in the computer analyses is given in appendix C. One salient feature of table 5 is the difference between the classes in the Inner and Outer schools in the academic content of their curricula. Mses. Allen and Prima devoted 85 and 90 percent of their time to teaching reading, writing, math, subject-matter lessons, work recitations, and seatwork and paperwork review. In contrast, Mses. Edwards and Ryan spent, respectively, 29 and 48 percent of their time on reading, 17 and 22 percent on math, and 74 and 68 percent overall on academic topics. Activities with less of an academic focus such as Show and Tell, art projects, games, and rest took up 17 and 11 percent of their time, and morning rituals and transitional activities such as passing out and collecting papers absorbed the remaining 9 and 21 percent.

Table 5 provides some other intriguing comparisons among the four classes. The two teachers in the Inner School allocated much more of their time to activities involving small groups of two to seven children than their counterparts in the Outer School (66 and 61 percent versus 22 and 44 percent), and correspondingly much less time to activities involving larger groups or the whole class. The reason, of course, is that the first pair of teachers devoted a large proportion of their time to teaching reading to small, clearly organized reading groups.

One other interesting set of differences is evident in table 5. This has to do with the length of activities and is the only aspect of scheduling on which the

Table 4. Typical daily teacher schedules.

Teacher	Morning (before lunch)		Afternoon	
Allen	9:00-9:15	Whole-class language arts and reading	11:30-12:00	After lunch "choosing" and play
	9:15-11:00	Reading groups, one after the other; groups often met twice in this period; occasional 5-minute subject matter lesson or class game (e.g., Freeze).	12:00-2:00	Whole-class activities including math, penmanship, paperwork review; also individual help, math groups, class fun activity (e.g., singing); activities lasted 5-15 minutes each.
			2:00-end	"Choosing."
Prima	9:00-9:20	Reading and language arts class activity, game, or drill.	11:30-12:00	Not observed.
			12:00-12:45	Whole-class math lesson.
	9:20-11:00	Reading groups, approximately one-half hour each, in order from low to high rank; after groups finished, children worked on papers, T gave individual reading help.	12:50-1:00	Penmanship.
			1:00-1:30	Library, gym—not observed.
			1:30-1:40	Math paperwork.
			1:40-2:15	Class activity: word riddles, collages, TV story.
Edwards	9:00-10:00	Not observed.	11:50-12:40	Paperwork, whole-class math, math paperwork (sometimes until 1:00).
	10:00-11:00	Reading groups, class paperwork and review, penmanship practice, reading and language instruction, individual help, transition periods (e.g., storytime, cleanup).	12:40-1:00	Show and Tell, Weekly Reader, TV story.
			1:00-2:25	Whole-class math, smaller-group math, math paperwork; late afternoon fun activities (making calendars, life-size paper dolls).
Ryan	8:30-9:00	Morning routine, free play, and transition.	11:50-12:10	Rest period after lunch, sometimes followed by storytime.
	9:00-11:00	Reading groups, whole-class reading and paperwork, seatwork; reading groups often met twice; occasional Show and Tell, library period.	12:10-1:00 or 12:30-1:30	Whole-class math lesson (35-45 minutes), math group, math papers.
				Occasional long rest period, fun activity (making paper leaves).
			1:15-2:20	Class math, math paper, math group while others play; T reads to class, plays word games.

Table 5. Activity contexts.

Activity context	Allen	Prima	Edwards	Ryan
	Proportion of teacher's time spent[1]			
Subject-matter lesson	0%	0%	2.3%	1.7%
Reading/phonics	75.3	77.3	28.7	47.5
Math	6.6	4.5	17.2	11.9
Penmanship	1.0	2.3	2.3	0
Other academic activities	0	0	4.6	1.7
Seatwork, paperwork review	2.0	5.7	18.4	5.1
All academic activities	84.8	89.8	73.6	67.8
Nonacademic activities	3.5	3.4	17.1	6.7
Rest and recreation	0.5	0	0	4.2
Transitions	11.1	6.8	9.2	11.9
Morning routine[2]	0	0	0	9.3
Activities involving 1 child	5.1	2.3	4.6	0
Activities involving 2-7 children[3]	65.6	61.3	21.8	44.1
Activities involving more than 7 children	29.3	36.4	73.6	56.9
	Median number of children in all activities			
	6.1	6.6	12.9	17.8
	Mean activity length (minutes)			
	9.8	24.0	19.8	15.5
	Total number of activity contexts			
	198	88	87	118
	Total number of observations			
	11	11	11	10

1. Entries are percentages of all interactions coded in the SI and UI observation systems combined. An activity context is coded for each interaction.

2. Except in the case of Ms. Ryan, observations were not made during the first half hour of the day (8:30-9:00 a.m.), when morning routine activities typically occurred.

3. Organized reading groups in the four classes nearly always had between 2 and 7 members, and nearly all interactions involving 2-7 children occurred in the context of reading. Math or other academic subjects usually involved a larger group or the whole class.

two teachers in the Inner School differ substantially. Activities in Ms. Allen's class typically took no more than ten minutes, whereas those in Ms. Prima's class lasted twenty-four minutes, more than twice as long. Both teachers ran very tight ships, and activities and groups followed one another smoothly and swiftly like clockwork. But Ms. Allen believed in the short session. By mid-year, the four reading groups in her class were each called *twice* in a morning for ten minutes at a time. Each of Ms. Prima's reading groups also met with her every day, but only once and for twice as much time per session.

The classroom activities and groupings of children that we have discussed so far establish the overall contexts in which interactions between teacher and children take place. In a given activity context some proportion of interactions between teacher and children may be directly concerned with the ostensible activity topic, and some proportion may not. For example, suppose the teacher calls up a reading group. Reading as an activity context might start when the first child is asked to read and end when the last child has his turn and the group is dismissed. Within this context, however, some proportion of the teacher's interactions with children may have little to do with reading per se. She may occasionally engage the children in chitchat, she may spend a fair amount of time explaining procedures (for example, "Turn to page 3; read the sentence in your head; keep your book flat on the table"), and, almost inevitably, she will make some remarks about behavior ("John, you're not paying attention! Mary, stop that silly giggling!"). In our classroom observations, therefore, both the overall activity context and the topic of the teacher's specific interactions with children were recorded. The latter data are presented in table 6.

One general index of the teacher's concern with academic matters is simply the percentage of total interactions that the observer was able to categorize in terms of the Structured Interaction coding system, since only those behaviors that had an obvious academic focus and followed clearly structured, well-routinized sequences (question/answer/assessment/evaluation) were accommodated in this coding framework. Table 6 shows a large discrepancy between the Inner School and Outer School teachers on this index. Between 45 and 49 percent of all interactions and behaviors in Ms. Allen's and Ms. Prima's classes were coded in terms of the SI system, as compared to 34 and 25 percent for the other two teachers.

Comparing the figures for activity contexts in table 5 and for interaction topics in table 6, we note three important changes. Time spent on academic subjects has dropped by 15 to 25 percent, time absorbed by procedural matters has increased by 7 to 22 percent, and an important new topic of teacher-child interaction, namely "inappropriate child behavior," now accounts for 5 to 12 percent of observed interactions. These changes all reflect the extent

Table 6. Teacher-child interaction topics.

Interaction topic	Allen	Prima	Edwards	Ryan
	Percentage of all dyadic interactions[1]			
Academic	69.6%	65.3%	51.0%	43.4%
Nonacademic	3.8	4.7	7.3	8.0
Procedure	18.4	15.3	31.3	32.2
Privilege	1.5	1.4	2.8	4.3
Appropriate child behavior	0.3	0.5	0.3	0.2
Inappropriate child behavior	5.5	12.1	6.7	11.2
Health, distress	0.9	0.7	0.6	0.8
	Percentage of total interactions coded in SI			
	54.8%	49.0%	33.5%	24.9%
	Total number of interactions			
	2,564	3,038	2,162	2,253

1. Coded in either the SI or UI.

to which teachers and children became involved with something other than the actual teaching or learning of the subject implied by the overall activity context as they actually interacted with each other. Again, we note substantial differences between the teachers in the Inner and Outer schools in the proportion of interaction time spent on academic subjects (70 and 65 percent versus 55 and 46 percent) and, conversely, on class management (18 and 15 percent versus 31 and 32 percent).

The data of table 6, however, are not without surprises. For the first time we see a contrast among teachers that cuts across schools. The variable in question is "inappropriate child behavior" (disruptiveness, inattentiveness, aggression) which the teacher chooses to call attention to or make an issue of. Now, instead of the familiar Inner School versus Outer School dichotomy, we find an interesting new alignment: Ms. Allen of the Inner School and Ms. Edwards of the Outer School versus Mses. Prima and Ryan. The latter pair evidently were much more likely than the former to make a child's inappropriate classroom behavior the focus of their interaction with him (Mses. Allen and Edwards, 6 and 7 percent, versus Mses. Prima and Ryan, 12 and 11 percent).

In sum, regardless of the kind of analysis used, whether we examine schedules, activity contexts, or interaction topics, it is clear that Mses. Allen and Prima, the two Inner School teachers, emphasized academic affairs and managed their classes more efficiently than Mses. Edwards and Ryan, their counterparts at the Outer School. But, as we shall see, this contrast, which is as much between schools as between these pairs of teachers, does not go much beyond these particular variables. On the second major dimension distinguishing classrooms in this research—the quality of teacher-child relationships—differences between schools seem to vanish and a completely new alignment of teachers emerges. This new pattern cuts across schools, linking Mses. Allen and Edwards on one side and Mses. Prima and Ryan on the other.

Quality of Teacher-Child Relationships Specific teacher behaviors that seem to us to refer to the quality of the teacher's relationship to her pupils are listed in table 7. The following aspects of teacher behavior, recorded in either the Structured or Unstructured Interaction coding systems, are of particular interest: the use of an "open" versus a direct mode of questioning children; the asking of questions allowing "free" responses; positive versus negative evaluation and reinforcement; positive versus negative responses to children's requests; and the teacher's participation in casual conversation, play, or humor with children. These behaviors seem to us to reflect a "child-centered" orientation on the part of teachers, greater willingness to give children latitude in responding, and more tolerance and approval of their behavior. Table 7 shows that the trend of results for many of these variables favors Mses. Allen and Edwards. These two teachers are clearly more likely to use an open mode of questioning children, in which the child was called on only if he had signaled his desire to answer (25 and 17 percent versus 10 and 8 percent) and to give positive evaluation of children's responses (17 and 19 percent versus 7 and 5 percent). Conversely, they are less likely to reject children's requests (3 and 2 percent versus 4 and 4 percent) or to negatively reinforce them. The difference between the two pairs of teachers in the use of negative reinforcement is particularly striking. Mses. Allen and Edwards are much less likely to criticize, restrict, scold, and punish their first graders than Mses. Prima and Ryan (15 and 18 percent versus 34 and 23 percent).

What of the behavior of the children themselves? Table 8 summarizes observed child behavior in terms of four categories: appropriate behavior (typified by achievement-oriented behavior such as seeking evaluation of one's performance), expressive behavior (for example, child expresses his opinions, engages in conversation with the teacher), dependent behavior (for example, child requests information, help, permission), and inappropriate behavior (child annoys others, disrupts others at work, or is inattentive to his own work). Again, the pattern of results is unequivocal. Children in Mses. Allen's and Edwards' classes more often engage in appropriate actions (20

Table 7. Quality of teacher-child relationships.

Teacher behavior	Allen	Prima	Edwards	Ryan
	Percentage of all dyadic interactions coded in SI			
Question/demand mode				
open	24.7%	10.1%	17.2%	8.0%
direct	74.1	86.3	74.2	86.4
other	1.2	3.6	8.4	5.5
Question/demand type				
free	4.3	0.5	5.7	4.3
process	4.9	18.7	11.7	6.3
product	90.8	80.6	82.5	89.5
Evaluation				
positive	16.9	7.1	19.2	5.0
negative/mixed	0.4	0.6	0.4	0.0
	Total number of interactions coded in SI			
	1,405	1,488	725	560
	Percentage of all teacher behaviors coded in UI			
Reinforcement				
positive	5.5%	6.5%	5.2%	3.5%
negative	15.4	33.5	17.5	22.6
Response to child request				
grants	12.6	9.1	9.3	9.8
rejects	2.7	4.1	2.4	3.7
Converses, plays, jokes	7.2	7.0	5.3	3.7
	Total teacher behaviors coded in UI			
	1,234	1,654	1,552	1,813

and 27 percent versus 16 and 13 percent) and expressive behaviors (27 and 26 percent versus 18 and 18 percent) and less often exhibit dependent behavior (30 and 27 percent versus 36 and 40 percent) and inappropriate actions (23 and 20 percent versus 30 and 29 percent) than children in Mses. Prima's and Ryan's classes.

The concept of individuation refers to the teacher's interest in perceiving individual differences, changes, and needs in children and to her ability to act appropriately regarding these differences. There is an obvious conceptual affinity between this idea and the interpersonal behaviors that we have just discussed. However, the concept of individuation requires two other types of data in addition to the recording of teacher-child interactions: in-

Table 8. Child behaviors.

Child behavior[1]	Allen	Prima	Edwards	Ryan
	Percentage of total child behaviors			
Appropriate	19.7%	16.4%	27.1%	13.2%
Expressive	27.2	17.5	26.3	18.0
Dependent	30.0	35.7	26.7	39.8
Inappropriate	23.1	30.3	19.9	29.0
	Total child behaviors			
	320	736	532	711

1. As coded in UI.

formation on the teacher's perceptions of the needs and characteristics of individual children and data on the correspondence between these perceptions and the "objective" characteristics of the children in question. In this study these data were obtained from interviews with teachers and from observations specifically focused on individual children in contexts in which the teacher's influence was less likely to be dominant than in our teacher-focused observations. These findings will not be discussed here since they lend themselves most appropriately to the case-study approach adopted in the second half of this book. Instead, we shall examine certain quantitative aspects of individuation that are apparent in the teacher-focused observations and which seem to be associated also with positive teacher-child relationships.

The main analysis centers on the degree or pattern of variation in the teacher's behavior toward individual children. Do the quantity and quality of her interactions with individuals vary greatly? Do some children receive much more than their "fair share" of her attention and some children far less? If so, in what ways is her treatment of these children different from that encountered by the average child? Which teacher is likely to show more variation in her treatment of children, the one whose behavior is characteristically more positive or more negative?

Table 9 shows the degree of variation in quantity and quality of interactions with their teacher that individual children experienced in each class. In these analyses the data for each variable are computed as a percentage of each child's total number of interactions with his teacher. A profile displaying different types of teacher and child behavior is thus generated for each child. This procedure controls for the wide variation across children in quantity of teacher-child interaction which may be affected by situational

Table 9. Individual variation in children's interactions with teachers.[1]

Variable	$\overline{X}$	Min.	Max.	L	H	$\overline{X}$	Min.	Max.	L	H
Interaction topic		*Allen (n = 22)*					*Prima (n = 20)*			
Academic	69.8%	58.7%	81.2%	0	0	66.9%	48.4%	89.0%	0	0
Nonacademic	3.8	0	11.0	5	2	4.4	0	8.7	3	0
Procedural	18.3	11.8	28.6	0	0	15.0	5.5	28.9	1	0
Privilege	1.5	0	4.5	9	4	1.5	0	3.8	7	3
Appropriate C behavior	0.2	0	1.0	17	5	0.4	0	2.1	9	3
Inappropriate C behavior	5.4	0	9.6	4	0	11.2	1.8	23.3	3	1
Health, distress	1.0	0	3.1	10	5	0.5	0	2.6	11	4
Specific child and teacher behaviors										
Appropriate C behavior	2.4	0	5.3	16	3	3.9	0	7.7	4	0
Positive T reinforcement	13.0	3.8	25.9	2	0	7.0	3.1	12.0	2	0
Expressive C behavior	3.5	0	8.7	7	3	4.0	0	8.0	5	0
T humor, conversation	3.3	0	9.8	7	3	3.6	0	9.3	3	1
Dependent C behavior	3.7	0	8.6	5	1	8.8	1.0	15.3	3	0
T grants request	6.2	1.8	11.5	2	0	4.6	1.0	11.3	4	1
T rejects request	1.1	0	5.1	11	5	2.2	0	5.5	3	2
Inappropriate C behavior	2.9	0	6.3	6	2	6.9	0	14.7	6	2
Negative T reinforcement	7.3	0	12.5	5	0	17.6	3.7	33.3	4	0
T open/free question	17.5	2.6	29.5	5	0	5.6	0.6	12.1	4	2
T process question	3.1	0	7.1	7	3	10.2	5.7	19.4	0	0
T product question	54.2	38.5	66.3	0	0	43.6	27.9	64.9	0	0
T does not assess response	27.5	19.1	41.9	0	0	16.3	6.2	32.2	2	0
T assesses response	31.9	19.3	44.7	0	0	37.2	18.4	51.4	1	0
T gives directive	63.2	49.6	79.5	0	0	56.8	39.0	77.2	0	0
T procedural behavior	2.8	0	5.5	4	0	4.9	1.7	9.0	4	0
Total interactions	5.0	3.3	8.8	0	1	5.4	3.0	8.9	4	2

1. Unless otherwise noted, entries are percentages of all interactions between the teacher and an individual child in which the behavior specified on the left of table occurred. Several of the variables listed in this and subsequent tables are composites derived from the SI and/or UI coding systems as

Table 9 (*cont.*)

Variable	X̄	Min.	Max.	L	H	X̄	Min.	Max.	L	H
Interaction topic		Edwards (*n = 17*)					Ryan (*n = 21*)			
Academic	53.7%	41.9%	64.0%	0	0	44.9%	27.0%	82.1%	0	0
Nonacademic	3.8	0.7	7.6	4	0	5.7	1.1	10.3	4	0
Procedural	32.2	25.8	43.6	0	0	30.6	7.7	42.0	3	0
Privilege	3.2	0	9.7	3	1	4.7	1.0	16.3	3	1
Appropriate C behavior	0.2	0	1.9	13	4	0.04	0	0.9	18	3
Inappropriate C behavior	6.2	0	12.2	3	0	10.3	0	25.2	5	2
Health, distress	0.6	0	3.0	9	3	0.6	0	3.4	12	4
Specific child and teacher behavior										
Appropriate C behavior	7.4	3.6	11.8	0	0	4.2	0	7.3	4	0
Positive T reinforcement	11.3	6.6	17.6	0	0	4.0	0	8.2	3	1
Expressive C behavior	7.1	2.8	12.3	2	0	6.2	1.3	13.4	1	1
T humor, conversation	4.1	1.4	10.6	2	1	3.0	0	6.8	4	2
Dependent C behavior	7.3	2.6	14.3	1	0	12.6	0	23.3	4	0
T grants request	7.9	3.4	17.3	2	2	8.4	0	17.3	4	1
T rejects request	2.0	0	8.0	6	3	2.7	0	7.4	7	3
Inappropriate C behavior	5.1	0	10.6	3	2	9.4	0	24.0	4	2
Negative T reinforcement	12.8	6.5	26.8	0	1	16.9	2.2	40.9	6	3
T open/free question	8.3	3.1	14.6	5	0	3.2	0	8.0	4	2
T process question	4.5	0	11.8	7	2	2.5	0	6.7	6	2
T product question	29.3	19.1	42.4	0	0	29.6	3.1	78.6	2	1
T does not assess response	6.5	0	11.0	3	0	11.9	0.6	23.2	5	0
T assesses response	34.2	22.7	41.9	0	0	24.4	8.8	53.6	1	1
T gives directive	50.6	37.5	62.4	0	0	50.4	25.8	83.9	0	0
T procedural behavior	8.5	3.2	15.5	1	0	11.2	1.8	19.0	4	0
Total interactions	7.3	5.3	11.7	0	2	5.0	2.2	9.1	1	4

described in table 2 and in appendix C. X̄ represents the mean; *Min.* refers to lowest percentage; *Max.* refers to highest percentage; *L* refers to the number of children whose percentage was less than half the mean; *H* refers to the number of children whose percentage was more than twice the mean.

factors such as absences from school and also by characteristics of the teacher and child. Table 9 presents the mean, the lowest and highest percentages, and the number of children whose percentages are more than twice or less than half the average for each variable.

Clearly, the quantity and quality of teacher-child interaction differ greatly in the four classes. Consider first the range in the sheer quantity of encounters. In Ms. Allen's class one child receives 8.8 percent of all interactions, another receives 3.3 percent. The highest and lowest percentages in the other three classes are: Ms. Prima, 8.9 and 3.0 percent; Ms. Edwards, 11.7 and 5.3 percent; Ms. Ryan, 9.1 and 2.2 percent. The quality of teacher-child transactions also varies dramatically from child to child. On many variables the highest percentage is several times larger than the lowest, and often enough the percentages for several children are more than twice or less than half the figure for the average child. To cite two specific examples: positive reinforcement ranges from 3.8 to 25.9 percent for the children at the two extremes in Ms. Allen's class, from 3.1 to 12.0 percent in Ms. Prima's, from 6.6 to 17.6 percent in Ms. Edwards', and from 0 to 8.2 percent in Ms. Ryan's. Conversely, negative teacher reinforcement oscillates between 0 and 12.5 percent in Ms. Allen's class, between 3.7 and 33.3 percent in Ms. Prima's, between 6.5 and 26.8 percent in Ms. Edwards', and between 2.2 and 40.9 percent in Ms. Ryan's. If these findings are representative of individual children's entire experience in a classroom, then some children may receive no positive or negative reinforcement at all, while others may experience such reinforcement in a quarter, one-third, or even two-fifths of their interchanges with the teacher. These data underscore the folly of describing classroom experiences solely in terms of averages, as if teachers and students behave uniformly. In fact, striking variation rather than standardization may be typical. It should be noted that this differentiation applies to the behavior of students no less than teachers. Inappropriate child behavior, for example, ranged from 0 in all classes to a maximum of 6.3 percent in Ms. Allen's class, 14.7 percent in Ms. Prima's, 10.6 percent in Ms. Edwards', and 24.0 percent in Ms. Ryan's.

We also focused on those children who received a great deal more or less than the average share of attention from their teachers. Here we use a simple index, namely the number of children in each class who received 50 percent more or less than the number of interactions due to the average child if the teacher's attention were equally distributed among all pupils. The outstanding result is the difference between Mses. Allen and Edwards on the one hand and Mses. Prima and Ryan on the other. In the first two classes far fewer children received exceptional amounts of attention than in the last two classrooms: in Ms. Allen's class one child received a high amount of attention, none low; in Ms. Edwards' class two children received high amounts of attention, none low; in Ms. Prima's class two were high, four were low; in Ms. Ryan's class four were high, one low. This finding suggests that the more child-centered and positive the teacher's behavior toward children in general, the less likely she is to discriminate among them in the sense of giving very much more or less attention to some than to others.

What now of the quality of the teacher's interactions with these exceptional children? Do they behave very differently from other children? If so, are they likely to attract a particular kind of attention from their teachers? To answer this question we have plotted in table 10 profiles of teacher and child behavior for the nine children who received a disproportionately high amount of attention in the four classes. To construct these profiles, we computed each type of behavior as a percentage of the individual child's total interactions with his teacher and we compared the percentage to the corre-

Table 10. Children receiving disproportionately high amounts of attention.

Child	Inappropriate		Dependent		Expressive	
	Inapprop. C behavior	Neg. T reinf.	C depend. behavior	T rejects requests	C comments	T humor, play, talk
Allen						
Simone	4.3%	9.0%	7.1%[1]	3.8%[1]	7.1%[1]	6.7%[1]
Average C	2.9	7.3	3.7	1.1	3.5	3.3
Prima						
Dennis	11.7[1]	28.5[1]	13.3	2.0	3.9	3.5
Charles	14.7[1]	33.3[1]	7.8	3.1	3.9	3.1
Average C	6.9	17.6	8.8	2.2	4.0	3.6
Edwards						
Judy	5.4	26.8[1]	14.3[1]	8.0[1]	6.3	2.7
Daniel	6.7	18.5	6.7	1.0	12.3[1]	6.7[1]
Average C	5.1	12.8	7.3	2.0	7.1	4.1
Ryan						
Lydia	10.7	18.3	19.8[1]	5.3[1]	8.4	3.8
Madeline	10.8	17.0	20.5[1]	7.4[1]	5.1	3.4
Vanessa	16.2[1]	34.6[1]	10.6	2.8	8.4	3.9
Kenneth	23.3[1]	40.9[1]	13.2	6.3[1]	5.7	4.4
Average C	9.4	16.9	12.6	2.7	6.2	3.0

1. The child displayed or received the behavior specified in the column head at least 50% more often than the average child in his class.

sponding figure for the average child in the class. Table 10 includes only those teacher and child behaviors on which at least two high-attention children deviated by 50 percent or more from the average child. Two patterns are clearly evident. The first pattern characterizes children who display conspicuously higher than average levels of inappropriate behavior. This kind of behavior becomes an issue with the teacher, and consequently the child receives more than an average share of negative reinforcement. The second pattern applies to children who exhibit relatively high levels of dependent behavior. These children frequently ask the teacher for help and direction and have their requests rejected more often than average. Two inferences can be drawn from these findings: first, children who obtain excessive amounts of attention overall from the teacher receive disproportionately more negative attention; and second, their actual behavior seems superficially to warrant this kind of disapproving reaction on the teacher's part. Although high-attention children in the four classes tend to fall into one or the other of these two categories, it is interesting to note how the two patterns are modulated in Mses. Allen's and Edwards' cases. Of the nine children, only two, Simone in Ms. Allen's class and Daniel in Ms. Edwards', also enjoyed more than an average amount of light-hearted conversation, play, and humor with their teachers. In their cases the teacher's frequent negative reactions to their behavior seem to be offset by friendly, easygoing exchanges that indicate acceptance and delight in these two children.

The rapidity with which the teacher forms reading groups, the criteria she uses in assigning children to them, the degree of movement she permits from one to the other, and the way she composes, perceives, and ranks them are all factors that are likely to be related to the dimension of interpersonal behavior. An examination of the pertinent information on reading groups collected in this study shows the now familiar pattern of Mses. Allen and Edwards linked on one side and Mses. Prima and Ryan juxtaposed on the other. For example, although all four teachers reportedly relied primarily on personal observations of the individual child's reading skill in making assignments to reading groups, Mses. Allen and Edwards apparently gave more serious consideration to personality and motivational factors in making these decisions. Both teachers regarded reading groups as important contexts for socioemotional as well as academic development and spoke of deliberately teaming the shy and the confident, the more and less skilled, so that the latter could inspire and help the former. They both worried about the effects of relegating children to meritocratic structures defined solely by academic skill, but the solutions they adopted were rather different. Ms. Edwards' strategy was simply not to use reading groups very much, and when she did, to form one large group of ten to eleven children of mixed ability plus two other small groups of two to three much more or much less advanced children. With most children placed in a large, heterogeneous, intermediate group, Ms. Edwards was less pressed to promote or demote individuals and in fact, after the first few weeks of school, no children changed groups in her class. Ms. Allen adopted virtually the opposite tactic. She was by far the most flexible of the four teachers in permitting children to move from one reading group to another. Thus, by the end of the second quarter of the school year, seven of twenty-two children in Ms. Allen's class had either been promoted to or read frequently with a higher reading group in addition to their core group, and only one child had been demoted. By contrast, after a brief experimentation period, all children in Ms. Prima's class kept their initial placements and moved neither up nor down. Similarly, only two children in Ms. Ryan's class changed assignments, both moving down to a lower group. Ms. Allen was also the only teacher who did not entirely relegate to a separate reading group those children in her class who received remedial tutoring from the school specialist. In the other three classes these children formed the bottom ability group and read only with each other. In Ms. Allen's class there was such a "specialist" group that met separately but the children in it were also regularly invited to read with other groups composed of children who had not been singled out for remedial help. Ms. Allen vigorously opposed the automatic use of specialists for children having reading difficulties, arguing that the harm inflicted on the child by being cut off from his classmates, labeled, and made to feel different more often than not outweighed the benefits of special tutoring. Unsuccessful in her efforts to have the four "specialist" children in her class mainstreamed, she went out of her way to include them in as wide a cross section as possible of the reading activities going on in her classroom.

Like reading groups, classroom seating patterns often reflect the teacher's basic attitudes toward children. Two aspects of seating arrangements struck us as important: the frequency with which desks are rearranged and the use of isolation as a technique for controlling disruptive or distractible children. On the first variable, Ms. Allen again stands out. In her classroom not only was there no typical seating arrangement, in fact desks were rearranged and most children had different neighbors on every one of our visits. Clearly, as with her reading groups, these changes were made by design, not by happenstance. Thus Ms. Allen deliberately used large groupings of six to ten adjoining desks as well as smaller ones and changed these so frequently that the average child in her class of twenty-two could become acquainted with as many as eleven or twelve different desk neighbors. In contrast with Ms. Allen, the other three teachers tended to settle on fixed arrangements after a short period of experimentation in the first few months of school.

These teachers also favored small groupings of two to four children so that most children encountered the same few neighbors most days, or an average of six to seven different neighbors over the course of the year.

Discrimination   We have found that the four teachers differed substantially in the emphasis they gave to academic matters, the efficiency with which they ran their classrooms, and their attitudes and behavior toward their students. In substantiating these conclusions, we have concentrated for the most part on the teacher's typical behavior as indicated by her treatment of the average child. But because the data we have gathered records the teacher's interactions with individual children, it is also eminently suitable to answering another kind of question which so far we have hardly broached. Given that the four teachers differed from each other in their typical patterns of behavior, did they vary also in their treatment of children of different races and sexes? In the section on individuation we noted that one pair of teachers, Mses. Prima and Ryan, were more likely than the other to treat individual children very differently from others. Were these two teachers also more likely to discriminate between blacks and whites and boys and girls?

To answer these questions two sets of data were constructed and analyzed. First, each child's interactions with his teacher were isolated in the teacher-focused classroom observations, then profiles of teacher and child behavior were computed for each individual and averaged for children of a given race and sex. The assumption guiding this analysis was that if boys and girls and black and white children behaved similarly and were treated similarly, then no significant differences should be found in these profiles when scores for individuals are averaged. The second set of data concerned the composition of reading groups and seating patterns in the classroom. Again, our assumption was that if groups were equitably treated, there should be no evidence of systematic differences in these assignments. Specifically, the proportion of blacks and whites and of boys and girls in higher and lower reading groups should correspond to their proportions in the class, and similarly with respect to favored and less favored seating arrangements.

Table 11 shows the average proportion of various types of behavior received or emitted by black and white girls and boys within each of the four classes. In the statistical analysis an arc sine transformation was applied to the proportions and the between-group differences tested by means of analysis of variance. In the following discussion only those differences between race and sex groups that reached the $p \leqslant 0.10$ level of significance will be considered. Significant statistical interactions between race and sex are indicated in table 11, but these will not be interpreted because the small number of children in the data cells made any conclusions as to interactions between these two factors highly dubious.

The most compelling feature of the results is the *lack* of significant differences either for race or sex groups except in one class, Ms. Prima's. In the other three classes there are few differences either in the behavior of children of different races and sexes or in the behavior of teachers toward them.

Of the twenty variables analyzed only one difference in Ms. Allen's behavior was found for race and none for sex groups. Ms. Allen more often positively reinforced black children, but this may well be explained by the concomitant finding that black children in her class behaved more appropriately than whites. There were no differences that were clearly a function solely of race in Ms. Edwards' class and only one notable difference between the sexes, namely, boys were more likely to engage in inappropriate behavior than girls. There were two significant differences for race groups in Ms. Ryan's class, but these went in opposite directions. Ms. Ryan more often failed to give academic feedback to white than to black children, but she more frequently engaged in academic activities with whites than with blacks.

Only in Ms. Prima's class was there an unequivocal pattern of differences in the teacher's treatment of black and white children. In every case it is black children who were favored over whites. Specifically, Ms. Prima provided more positive reinforcement to black children and more positive responses to their requests. She more frequently asked them "open" questions, more often gave them feedback on their accomplishments, and more often engaged with them in conversational, playful, or humorous interchanges and in nonacademic activities. Correspondingly, black children in Ms. Prima's class were more likely than whites to come to Ms. Prima with requests for information and help. One might characterize Ms. Prima's differential treatment of black and white children in her class by saying that, in general, her relationship with black children was more positive and child-centered than with white children. Although overall her style of interaction with children was *less* positive and child-centered than was the case for Mses. Allen and Edwards, this difference was less marked with respect to the blacks in her class. Possible reasons for these findings are discussed in the case studies of the teachers in the next section.

The race and sex composition of reading groups at the end of the second quarter of the school year (when our teacher-focused classroom observations ended) are given in table 12. As was true for the behavior observation data, there seems to be little evidence of race or sex discrimination in three of the four classes. The exception is Ms. Ryan's classroom at the Outer School, which stands out in terms of the preponderance of whites and girls in her top reading group. Although 29 percent of the children in her class

Table 11. Race and sex differences in behavior. BG = black girl, WG = white girl, and so on. [1]

Variable[2]	Allen				Prima				Edward				Ryan				Effect[3]		
	BG	BB	WG	WB	BG	BB	WG	WB	BG	BB	WG	WB	BG	BB	WG	WB	Race	Sex	RXS
Interaction topic																			
Academic	.25	.22	.21	.21	.25	.27	.24	.22	.27	.27	.25	.30	.22	.22	.22	.25	R**		
Nonacademic	.23	.16	.16	.27	.25	.35	.21	.19	.28	.28	.26	.29	.27	.21	.21	.19	P**		A**
Procedural	.22	.24	.21	.22	.21	.32	.27	.21	.27	.28	.26	.29	.21	.24	.21	.22			P**
Inappropriate C behavior	.23	.21	.17	.24	.19	.36	.26	.21	.23	.28	.21	.34	.18	.25	.16	.26			P**
Specific child and teacher behavior																			
Appropriate C behavior	.26	.23	.12	.18	.23	.30	.19	.20	.20	.28	.26	.30	.24	.22	.17	.25	A*		
Positive T reinforcement	.25	.24	.18	.21	.26	.30	.19	.21	.25	.28	.26	.28	.23	.20	.21	.19	A**P**		
Expressive C behavior	.20	.20	.17	.23	.24	.33	.30	.18	.29	.26	.28	.24	.25	.20	.21	.21			
T humor, conversation	.20	.17	.18	.25	.29	.32	.21	.18	.27	.25	.30	.23	.26	.13	.21	.16	P*		
Dependent C behavior	.22	.20	.17	.22	.27	.28	.13	.21	.23	.26	.29	.29	.13	.15	.21	.26	P*		
T grants request	.22	.22	.20	.21	.29	.29	.19	.18	.27	.28	.28	.22	.21	.24	.20	.20	P**		
T rejects request	.19	.14	.04	.21	.24	.31	.18	.19	.25	.21	.27	.21	.14	.17	.21	.18			
Inappropriate C behavior	.24	.18	.14	.22	.18	.38	.25	.18	.10	.27	.22	.36	.24	.23	.18	.21		E**	P**
Negative T reinforcement	.23	.23	.18	.22	.16	.34	.27	.21	.20	.28	.26	.28	.26	.24	.18	.23			P**
T open/free question	.25	.21	.22	.21	.23	.35	.14	.20	.32	.25	.26	.25	.22	.16	.22	.28	P**	P**	
T process question	.24	.21	.24	.20	.23	.28	.25	.24	.17	.17	.26	.30	.27	.15	.18	.22			
T product question	.24	.22	.22	.21	.26	.25	.24	.22	.31	.27	.24	.31	.22	.19	.22	.25			
T does not assess response	.24	.21	.24	.20	.24	.21	.23	.24	.20	.28	.19	.33	.17	.17	.25	.23	R**		

T assesses response	.25	.23	.20	.22	.26	.28	.24	.21	.29	.26	.26	.30	.25	.21	.21	.25	P*
T gives directive	.23	.21	.22	.21	.24	.26	.25	.22	.27	.27	.26	.30	.23	.22	.22	.24	
T procedural behavior	.21	.24	.15	.21	.18	.28	.27	.24	.35	.29	.22	.32	.11	.25	.19	.26	R* P*E**
Expected interactions[4]	.30	.21	.18	.31	.23	.11	.11	.55	.07	.52	.49	.16	.10	.19	.59	.16	
Actual interactions[4]	.34	.20	.18	.28	.23	.16	.12	.48	.07	.52	.48	.17	.11	.22	.55	.17	
n[5]	6	4	4	6	4	2	2	10	1	7	7	2	2	4	12	3	

1. In this analysis, the total number of a specific type of interaction (e.g., positive teacher reinforcement) for which the child was present and was a potential recipient was first calculated for each child. The proportion of these interactions in which the child was involved as a participant was then computed. These individual proportions were then transformed to arc sines, and averages for race/sex cells calculated. A separate analysis of variance testing the between-group differences was performed for each class.

2. These items are derived from the SI and/or UI coding systems as described in table 2 and in appendix C. Three interaction topics (privilege, appropriate C behavior, and health/distress) were excluded from the table because their low frequencies made statistical analysis invalid.

3. Teacher initials A (Allen), P (Prima), E (Edwards), and R (Ryan) refer to a significant effect for the particular teacher/class.

*p < .10. **p < .05.

4. Entries are proportions of total interactions going to each race/sex group after student absences were taken into account.

5. Four children were excluded in the analyses of Mses. Allen's and Prima's classes. The two boys (Ms. Allen's class) and two girls (Ms. Prima's class) were foreigners learning to speak English as a second language and were difficult to classify as either black or white.

Table 12. Race and sex composition of reading groups.

Rank of group		Allen[1]		Prima[1]		Edwards		Ryan	
	Race:	B	W	B	W	B	W	B	W
1(top)		2	6	2	5	1	1	0	6
2		4	1	2	4	4	4	2	5
3		2	2	2	3	2	3	4	3
4		2	1	—	—	—	—	—	—
Total		10	10	6	12	7	8	6	14
	Sex:	G	B	G	B	G	B	G	B
1 (top)		4	4	2	5	1	1	5	1
2		3	2	3	3	4	4	5	2
3		2	2	1	4	2	3	3	4
4		2	1	—	—	—	—	—	—
Total		11	9	6	12	7	8	13	7

1. Four children are excluded from the table for Mses. Allen's and Prima's classes. See Table 11, n.5.

were black and 33 percent were boys, no black children and only one boy was included in the seven children belonging to her top reading group. Conversely, of the seven children in her bottom reading groups, four were black and four were boys. In contrast, the distribution of blacks and whites and boys and girls in the reading groups in the other three classes was much more in keeping with their representation in the classrooms as a whole. In fact, in Mses. Prima's and Edwards' classes, the race and sex breakdown of each reading group almost precisely paralleled their overall class distribution.

Table 13 on seating patterns in the classroom shows no evidence of racial differences in the use of isolation, defined as the seating of a child apart from his classmates for at least one third of our observations. The same, however, cannot be said for sex discrimination. All eight children isolated in the four classes were boys! Seating patterns were also examined for evidence of race or sex segregation. The question here was whether, say, white children were more likely to be seated next to whites, or boys next to boys, thus limiting their opportunities to become acquainted with children of a different race or sex. For this analysis we first counted the number of neighbors each child had during our observations, noting the race and sex of each child and of his neighbors (where neighbor is defined as a child seated at a desk adjoining the focus child's). For each child the proportion of black

Table 13. Race and sex of seat neighbors and isolates.

Neighbors	Allen			Prima			Edwards		Ryan	
Race:	B	W	F[1]	B	W	F[1]	B	W	B	W
All neighbors (%)	39	53	8	36	57	7	49	51	30	70
White children (%)	43	51	6	37	55	8	58	42	28	72
Black children(%)	36	50	14	26	67	7	37	63	37	63
Isolates (*n*)	1	0		1	2		2	2	0	0
Sex:	G	B		G	B		G	B	G	B
All neighbors (%)	51	49		39	61		55	45	64	36
Girls (%)	47	53		24	76		48	52	59	41
Boys (%)	57	43		48	52		64	36	75	25
Isolates (*n*)	0	1		0	3		0	4	0	0

1. F refers to "Foreign." See Table 11, n.5.

and white neighbors and male and female neighbors was then computed and averaged for children of the two race and sex groups. These proportions were then compared to the corresponding proportions of black and white and male and female neighbors in the class as a whole, the assumption being that if there was no systematic bias in seating patterns then the proportions for each subgroup should roughly parallel the overall proportions for the class.

As shown in table 13, we found no evidence of segregation in seating patterns. Rather, there is considerable evidence of deliberate attempts by teachers to "integrate" their classes across race and sex. Thus, in the two classes (Mses. Prima's and Edwards') in which the proportions of black and white neighbors for race subgroups diverge conspicuously from the proportions for the class as a whole, the bias is in the direction of overcompensation. For example, in Ms. Edwards' room, the proportions of white and black neighbors in the class as a whole were 51 and 49 percent. On the average, however, 58 percent of neighbors for white children in her class were black, and 63 percent of neighbors for black children in her class were white. This teacher thus seems to have gone out of her way to ensure that children of different races had opportunities to come to know each other as seat neighbors. Overcompensation in seat assignments is even more apparent in table 13 with respect to sex. In each of the four classes girls had a lower proportion of female neighbors than theoretically expected and the same was true for boys and male neighbors.

In our discussion of individuation we noted that fourteen children in the

four classes were given either exceptionally high or low amounts of attention by the teacher and that eleven of these fourteen children were either in
Ms. Prima's or Ms. Ryan's class. We also found that the behavior profiles
of the "high-attention" children indicated one of two patterns—a high level
of inappropriate child behavior accompanied by high levels of negative
teacher reinforcement, or a high level of dependent child behavior accompanied by a high level of teacher rejection of the child's requests. We note
that four of the five children whose profiles indicated the "inappropriate
behavior" pattern were boys and all were black, whereas all four of those
showing the "dependent" pattern were girls and only one was black.

TWO DIMENSIONS clearly seem to distinguish the four teachers participating
in this research. In the first dimension—the academic substance of the curriculum, the regularity of schedules, and the efficiency of classroom management—the two teachers in the Inner School, Mses. Allen and Prima,
contrasted strongly with the two teachers of the Outer School. They adhered
to more regular schedules and devoted much more class time to teaching
children in small organized groups and substantially less time to procedural matters. In the second dimension—the quality of interpersonal behavior—differences among teachers cut across schools, with Ms. Allen of the
Inner School and Ms. Edwards of the Outer School aligned on one side, and
Mses. Prima and Ryan on the other. The first pair of teachers gave children
more scope to express themselves, were more responsive to children's requests, and more approving and less critical of their performance and behavior. Concomitantly, the children in these two classes more often engaged
in appropriate and self-expressive behaviors and less often displayed dependent and inappropriate behaviors than their counterparts in the other two
classes. These contrasts in interpersonal behavior were also related to differences in the structure of reading groups and seating patterns in the four
classes, where Mses. Allen and Edwards showed relatively more interest in
socioemotional considerations and more flexibility in their arrangement of
groups and seating patterns than did Mses. Prima and Ryan.

   On the issue of race and sex discrimination in the four classes, no consistent evidence of differential treatment of blacks and whites or boys and girls
was found, although one teacher, Ms. Prima, clearly favored black children
in her day-to-day interactions, and another, Ms. Ryan, seemed to favor
whites and girls in the structuring of her reading groups. These results were
not unexpected in view of the fact that the teachers had agreed to have their
classrooms scrutinized by minority researchers. Nevertheless, the lack of
evidence of race or sex discrimination in the very detailed, longitudinal data
gathered in this research is a testimony to these four teachers.

PART TWO

Introduction

Jean V. Carew

BEHAVIOR OBSERVATIONS by themselves do not explain why people act the way they do. Motives, intentions, feelings, reasons for action are not unambiguously evident in overt behavior, and an observer's interpretation may often be at odds with the actor's. To understand a teacher's behavior in more than a superficial sense, one needs to know something about his upbringing, cultural background, values, and ideology; the social context of the school and community that constrain his actions; his pedagogical objectives, skills, and experience; his perceptions of the needs of individual children and how he sees himself as meeting those needs; his views of the racial, cultural, social class, and sex groups to which children belong; and the reasons why he might like or dislike, be interested in or indifferent to particular children in his classroom.

Teachers, after all, are people—unique, individual, multidimensional human beings. They have personal histories that significantly influence their professional role; they bring different values and objectives, temperamental qualities and personal predilections into school; they feel proud and ashamed, committed to or unconcerned about different aspects of teaching; and most important, they are insightful knowers of their classrooms, who reflect upon, justify, and critique what goes on there, and whose understanding of themselves and of their students is as interesting and valuable as that of an outsider.

How does one get to know the teacher as an individual? One might start, quite simply, by talking with her. Not, as is often done, in a context where the researcher is clearly the authority and the teacher's role is to supply answers to questions the researcher deems important; but rather in a context where the teacher is encouraged to reflect on, analyze, and articulate her own ideas and to view herself as the authority on the meaning of her behavior.

This objective was uppermost in our minds as we embarked on a series of interviews with each teacher—lengthy affairs spread out over the school year and absorbing as much as twenty hours per teacher. The transcripts of these discussions read like dialogues between friendly colleagues. Like conversations, their form and substance vary in rich and unpredictable ways. Sometimes rambling, imprecise, incoherent, occasionally contentious, passionate, eloquent, most often low-keyed, down-to-earth, and to the point. Little wonder, then, that we felt at the end of most of these interviews that we had engaged in an amicable, candid dialogue with a seasoned expert who had much to say and was seldom reluctant to say it.

From the outset we stressed that our interest was in the teacher as an individual and that her perceptions of children in her class, of parents, administrators, school, community, her reflections on her motives, intentions, objectives, beliefs, values, and behavior were what we wished to learn about. General topics and certain specific questions were worked out in advance for each session, but the essence of our approach was to encourage the teacher to feel free to engage or avoid any issue she wished. We relied on intuition and our previous experience to tell us when we were "turning on" or "turning off" our respondent. When a topic seemed to stimulate a teacher's interest, we pursued it although it might seem tangential or trivial to us at the time. Conversely, when an issue sparked little response or seemed to touch a raw nerve, we trod more delicately. In such instances, we might rephrase the question more tactfully, or postpone it to a more opportune moment, or drop it altogether. We did not feel constrained to follow exactly the same line of questions or style of communicating with each teacher but rather sought to establish a comfortable context for her to express her own opinions, a relationship whose terms, for the most part, the teacher was free to set.

Interviews with teachers took place in the school, typically immediately after class was dismissed, and were tape-recorded with the teacher's permission. The teachers were given the option to meet elsewhere—at our homes or offices, at their homes, in a restaurant over a cup of coffee, wherever they preferred—but all chose their own classrooms after school as the most convenient time and place. All interviews with Mses. Allen and Ryan were conducted by Carew and those with Mses. Prima and Edwards by Lightfoot. Chao, the third researcher, sometimes accompanied us but mostly played the role of nonparticipant observer. This allocation of responsibilities met a practical need to divide up the work, but it also sprang from our strong desire to establish a familiar, continuous, trusting relationship between the teacher and one of us and to distinguish the roles of the classroom observer and interviewer. Complete separation of these roles was neither feasible nor desirable. Although Chao was the principal classroom observer, we each spent many hours observing the classrooms; similarly, although Carew and Lightfoot were their chief interviewers, Chao had many informal conversations with teachers when she visited the schools.

The first interview (December) concerned the criteria the teacher used in organizing children into reading and math groups. The teacher was also asked to describe each child according to the social and cognitive dimensions she viewed as important. The second interview (April) was conducted after we had observed a few individual children in each classroom. The teacher was asked to talk about several children in depth (including those whom we had observed), their progress, and her relationships with them. The third interview (May) asked the teacher to describe how her own experiences and background might have influenced her educational philosophy, goals, and methods. In this interview we were particularly interested in exploring her motives for becoming a teacher and the importance of teaching in her life.

The fourth interview (May/June) asked the teacher to describe her colleagues, the school, its administrators, and the community. The fifth interview was conducted just after the end of the school year (June). The teacher was asked to trace each child's progress and development over the course of the year.

The last interview (the following October) was scheduled to fulfill our commitment to share our findings and interpretations with the teachers and, if necessary, to revise our report in the light of their reactions. Accordingly, the opening chapters of this book plus her own case study were sent to each teacher with a request that she read and critically react to them either in writing or by meeting with us personally. Only two of the four teachers, Mses. Allen and Ryan, responded. Having ascertained that the other two teachers had received the material, we renewed our invitation to meet, but still receiving no reply, we pressed them no further. In the sixth interview Ms. Allen expressed great satisfaction with her case study while Ms. Ryan voiced great dissatisfaction. In fairness to her, therefore, an account of the sixth interview closes our study of Ms. Ryan.

In addition to the teacher interviews, discussions were held with the focal children whom we had selected for individual classroom observation, with their mothers, and with the two school principals and assistant principals. Interviews with children were conducted by Chao in a private room at the school and typically took a brief fifteen minutes. Our main interest here was in finding out how the child felt about his school, classmates, and teacher and whether he saw himself as especially liked or disliked by his teacher. Interviews with mothers took between one and two hours and were carried out informally in their homes. The main purpose of these conversations was to obtain each mother's views of the school, teacher, and child and to note the points of correspondence and discord between her account and that of the teacher. Interviews with school administrators were carried out by Lightfoot and Carew in their offices and lasted one to two hours. Administrators were encouraged to talk about the history of the school, its structure and organization, its image in the eyes of the community, current problems, and future directions.

Each case study is divided into two sections. In the first section we present a portrait of the teacher based solely on the interview material. In the second section we compare and integrate this portrayal with one derived primarily from the more objective observation data. Section 2 ends with a depiction of the teacher's "special" relationship with one child in her class, a relationship that seemed to us to exemplify and illuminate the most salient aspects of the teacher's personality and approach to teaching.

It was quickly decided that the person who had conducted the interviews with a teacher should be responsible for their analysis and interpretation in the opening section of each case study. To do otherwise simply was not sensible, given that only one of us was in a position to know a particular teacher well. At the same time we were acutely aware of the risk of personal bias and of possible differences between us as researchers and writers in what we might consider important, valuable, and appealing. We therefore worked out in advance certain basic ground rules for analyzing the interview material and for reviewing each other's work. Each of us read the interview transcripts of all four teachers independently, listed the important themes and their supporting evidence, and discussed these with the other. These discussions resulted in a rough outline of each case study that we both agreed upon. When the first draft of a case study was completed, we then critiqued each other's writing, focusing particularly on points that seemed inadequately substantiated by the transcripts. In short, although the writer of the case study is responsible for the final version presented here, this interpretation was informed by numerous interchanges and criticisms based on independent readings of the raw material.

Our approach to interpreting the interview data is best characterized as a thematic analysis, unique to each teacher. We read and reread the material several times in a search for salient themes that expressed what the individual teacher cared about most and that seemed to us most revealing of her character, personality, teaching style, values, and beliefs. Specific issues and concerns were often demarcated by the teachers' varied responses to common questions we had posed to all of them, but frequently they sprang from topics that the teacher had spontaneously introduced in the course of the interview and on which we had encouraged her to reflect and elaborate.

In searching for themes, we deliberately avoided comparing one teacher with another either explicitly or implicitly by reference to a preset, organizing framework. Just as in the interviews themselves, we sought to allow each teacher to speak for herself, to define what was important to *her,* so in the analysis of the interview data we sought to present each teacher as an individual, to capture the personality and character she revealed to us in her manner of self-presentation and in the form and content of her remarks.

The man purposes of the second section of each case study are to bring together the several different types of data collected on each teacher and to compare the more subjective portrayal based on the interview material with the more objective one derived from the observation data. To accomplish this purpose, we adopt a relatively uniform, standardized approach to organizing the material from teacher to teacher. In contrast to the first section, here the main themes around which the discussion revolves are the *common* dimensions on which we compared teachers in the quantitative analysis of the observation data reported in chapter 5. Characteristics of each teacher are systematically considered under headings such as academic orientation, management efficiency, quality of teacher-child relationships, discipline, and fairness. The picture of each teacher derived from the quantitative analysis is fleshed out as we go along by verbatim descriptions of her actual interactions with children (excerpts from the behavior observations) and is compared with the more personal, subjective interpretation based on the interview material. Each case study ends with an account of the teacher's "special" relationship with one child in her class. This child was one of four whose interactions with the teacher were isolated in the quantitative analysis of the teacher-focused observations, whom we individually observed over a period of months in the child-focused observations, whom we interviewed and whose mother we also met and talked with. These quantitative and qualitative data are brought together at the culmination of each case study as another way of synthesizing the diverse perspectives from which we viewed each teacher.

Ms. Allen

Interpretation   *Jean V. Carew*

INTERVIEWER: How would you describe yourself as a teacher?
Ms. ALLEN: I love teaching.
INTERVIEWER: You love it?
Ms. ALLEN: I really do . . . I love children . . . I just feel a warmth toward
               them . . . I think I am sensitive to what they need . . . and I
               hope I am fair to all of them.

THE SHEER SIMPLICITY of Ms. Allen's words took my breath away. How many teachers would have the confidence to say these words to someone who had observed and analyzed their classroom behavior for many months? Coming from one less modest, less straightforward, less genuine, these words would have seemed boastful or self-serving, but in Ms. Allen's case they struck me as no more or less than the truth. Our descriptions of ourselves seldom are plainly that.

I thought of Ms. Allen's growing-up years and wondered what it was about her childhood and schooling that might have enabled her to say what she did. She was born just across the street from the school in which she now teaches. Both sets of grandparents immigrated from Ireland and both parents lived most of their lives in Conroy. Ms. Allen was their only child, but numerous cousins played the roles of brothers and sisters and she remembers a happy, sociable childhood filled with love and laughter.

Ms. Allen's parents sent her to parochial rather than public schools because "it was the Catholic way" and her father was devout. She became a favorite of the nuns and virtually "lived with the sisters," running errands for them and fervently imbibing their values and lifestyle. On graduating from high school, she and a dozen of her friends joined the convent. No one pressured or proselytized; it was the natural and expected thing to do. Six years later, half of the original group of a dozen girls had left the order, Ms. Allen among them. It took her that long to realize that if she had a calling, it was not to a convent but to some other place. After a year of working in business to repay some money she owed the convent, Ms. Allen became a regular substitute teacher, obtained accreditation at a local university, and after two years was appointed to a school in Conroy, the predecessor of the Inner School. Twenty years later she is now the senior first-grade teacher at the Inner School. She has been there since it opened.

Ms. Allen talks about the Inner School with a curious mixture of love, pride, and reproachfulness. Often she sounds as if she were describing a student in her class whose parents, basically loving, providing, protective, and sensible, are nevertheless sometimes neglectful, shortsighted, and even cruel. With some justice, she censures certain members of the School Committee for their dangerous neglect of the physical plant of the Inner School: "Some of them . . . they just don't care about children. The air conditioning in this building works in December and the heat works in May . . . Last winter, I would say there was at least one month that we sat with our coats and gloves on. Something was wrong with the heating system and the pipes could have burst. It's amazing to think how they deal with children's lives." Later she continues: "Our school is four years old and we've never had a dedication. We're only four years old and I don't know whether you've noticed the appearance of the building. It's disgusting. The doors are broken and they haven't been fixed . . . We have a woodworking room and it isn't open yet. We have two gyms. One was vandalized three years ago and it's still inoperable. The two gym teachers have to share the one gym . . . it becomes personal . . . people get at each other . . . and the children suffer."

In Ms. Allen's eyes, the Inner School should be first and foremost a community school, a school built to serve the mixed black/white, rich/poor neighborhood in which it is located. She is proud of the live-and-let-live spirit that has imbued this community, one of the few stable, truly heterogeneous and integrated localities in the area. She is a fierce defender of *this* community's right of first access to the Inner School because the community itself is socially and racially mixed.

The recent installation of alternative open classrooms at the Inner School ostensibly to achieve racial balance by attracting white students from outside the community is a case in point. Ms. Allen sees this move as a naked grab for power and resources by middle-class whites.

It's a group of vocal parents in the city that wanted something and were able to go after it . . . I resent it because it's an elitist kind of approach . . . If they're going to have [such a school] they should give every child a chance who wants to go into it. But they're very select. If the child seems the least bit undisciplined they don't want that . . . But this is a public school. The Inner School for the Inner School neighborhood. Parents waited a long time for this school and if some want their children in the open school, why aren't their needs met before the needs of this other group?

Ms. Allen empathizes with the community parents who resent the patronizing approach of the middle-class intruders. She describes a recent meeting in which a representative of the Alternative School referred to their coming in to "help out you people at the Inner School." This remark enraged a black parent who retorted, "We don't need you. We've done very well, long before you came!" "I really think the parent had a right to say that," remarks Ms. Allen quietly.

The inequity of the situation also rankles.

Why do they have aides but the regular classroom teachers don't? Why do they have two weeks at the beginning of the year to prepare and the regular teachers don't? Why do we have to test our children and they don't? How come they can exclude children who they say are undisciplined or have problems and we can't?

If they are within a public school, I think they should go along with the same policies that we do . . . If our children want to be in those classes then I think they have a right to be in there . . . I don't think they should force any of our black children to move out and go to other schools.

It is something of a surprise to hear a white teacher turn the desegregation argument around and argue for the right of the black community to predominate in and have first access to a neighborhood school. As I hear Ms. Allen's words I cannot help wondering what she would say if this were a school in an all-white neighborhood under court order to desegregate. She clearly puts the safety and happiness of children so far before other considerations that I cannot be sure what her reactions would then be.

It is indeed through the eyes of little children that Ms. Allen evaluates most school policy. She is first and foremost a child advocate, a worker in the children's crusade, and it is part of her mission to speak out boldly and passionately on their behalf. In our interview she cited several examples of bureaucratic insensitivity to children's needs. First a recent, perhaps trivial, but nevertheless revealing incident:

Now last week we had a circus for the kids. [An upper-grade teacher] puts it on and they give them popcorn, potato chips and everything. They got us there at 10:15 but they didn't start the performance until 10:30. Then we had to rush the kids out in the middle of it just to run them over to lunch at 10:50 . . . everything's set around a lunch program. There's no idea of what it's going to do to the kids . . . We get downstairs and the kids are excited and they drop their lunch trays and they have people in the kitchen yelling at them. They're screaming and crying, they won't eat anything . . . It's all because *no one bothers to think how it will affect little kids.*

The last phrase is one that Ms. Allen often uses in her critique of bureaucrats and teachers. Regulations are made, schedules arranged, assignments set by people who have had no experience of actually teaching young children and who are impervious to their needs. A case in point that incenses Ms. Allen is the blind application of the city regulation referring children for special tutoring solely on the basis of test scores and regardless of the evidence that the tests may not be valid nor the remedies appropriate. She points to several children in her class who automatically had to attend remedial tutoring because of their initially low test scores despite compelling evidence that they now either had no reading problem, or, if so, that some condition other than a learning disability was its cause. "Bonnie, she's a fantastic girl. She came out really low on the test, really low. Now she can read almost anything I hand her. Yet she has to go to the reading specialist because of her score on that test . . . I had to *fight* to keep Paul out. There is a problem with his sight . . . I knew there must be something because he held his book so unusual . . . You have to look for all of the reasons why a child may be slow . . . before they're labeled a learning problem, I'd like to see what is the matter."

Ironically, it is relatively easy under the regulation to get a child retested if the teacher suspects a new problem but almost impossible to do so if she believes he does *not* in fact have any special learning difficulty. Once a child is tested and a reading problem is discovered, the child is automatically sent to a specialist for tutoring whether the diagnosis and the remedy are valid or not.

Ms. Allen opposes the frequent use of reading specialists in the primary grades on several other grounds. In the first place she feels that teachers often use tutors as a "cop-out," to escape having to teach problem children. "I'm not against the specialists themselves because I do think that some children need the help. But *too many* children are going. Out of one class of 22, 13 are going! Now something is wrong . . . I think that when a child presents a discipline problem he is immediately labeled that way [as a learning problem], so they can get rid of him. Put him out."

Just as detrimental is the fact that the children themselves resent being made to feel different, inferior, or excluded from regular classroom life. When, in addition, the tutor uses methods and materials that conflict with the classroom teacher's, more is likely to be lost than gained from such a remedial program. It is for these reasons that Ms. Allen has worked closely with the primary reading specialist at the Inner School to develop a curriculum that complements and reinforces the classroom teacher's approach, takes the latter's recommendations as to individual needs seriously into account, and is open to all children, both advanced and slow, so that those for whom attendance is mandated are not thereby stigmatized. This particular reading program has apparently been outstandingly successful. Reading scores in the primary grades at the Inner School are now the highest in Conroy and are attributable in part to the tutoring strategies that Ms. Allen helped to develop.

Tests are used in the Inner School to diagnose mental, emotional, and behavior problems as well as specific reading disabilities. City regulations require that a series of psychological tests—a CASE evaluation—be carried out on any child whose screening test scores indicate serious risk of school failure. Ms. Allen does not totally disapprove of such tests any more than she entirely opposes the use of reading tutors, but she is acutely aware of their potential danger. Test results are frequently invalid, the remedies suggested are often inappropriate, and the tests encourage facile labeling of children with terms that may permanently bias others' perceptions of them. Ms. Allen notes that it is not uncommon for the child himself to collaborate in having himself thought of as a problem because this designation at least attracts attention. The child or parent may not understand that, ironically, the fact of receiving help as a result of such an evaluation may be permanently damaging. "I would rather see the parents work out of the school to get help for their child than through the school, because it gets on the child's records . . . The minute the teachers think that a child is getting any sort of help, that's it. He's labeled as different. I've seen children's spirits broken. It breaks your heart."

On the usefulness and validity of the IQ tests given in first grade, Ms. Allen is even more skeptical. With wry humor she describes the administration of such a test to her class: "Their pencils broke . . . They got upset. They might have marked two answers . . . Or the mark didn't get inside the little box . . . A couple of them got panic-stricken and started crying, but by then they've lost the whole idea. They don't know what it's all about. They feel they should know all the answers. They don't understand that they can't get them all."

Discussing the particular result for each child in her class, she disputes at least one third of the scores. If IQ measures intelligence, then many children are considerably brighter than their scores indicate. Reasons for low IQs may be poor motor skills, anxiety, perfectionist standards, and so on. "I have been known to spill coffee all over the test scores," Ms. Allen remarks conspiratorially.

Just as she resents the glib labeling of children, so Ms. Allen rejects the stereotyping of teachers and classrooms as traditional versus progressive, structured versus open, and the like. In her words it is "the teacher who makes the philosophy,'' not the other way around. Ms. Allen describes her own teaching as more ''teacher-directed, more structured at the beginning of the year, then gradually becoming more open, free and flexible'' as the year progresses. She is the only one of the four teachers to have actually experimented with truly ''open'' methods and with team teaching. Ms. Allen was not altogether satisfied with the results of her experiment and has come back to her own eclectic approach, which provides most structure and clarity in the early months, when children are more at a loss behaviorally and academically, and more freedom and individuation at a later stage, when they have learned the ground rules and are more motivated and self-monitoring. Different methods work best for different teachers. She has returned to her own blend because she simply feels more comfortable with it personally and has confidence that it works for her.

The main item on Ms. Allen's classroom agenda is the teaching of reading. Ms. Allen loves to teach the subject and believes that any normal child can learn to read. ''I think all children can be taught to read. I really believe that. I think there're a lot of cop-outs in teaching and one of them is sending children off to tutors.''

For the young child, learning to read can be a momentous achievement, a source of pride and sense of competence. In Ms. Allen's view, success depends largely on building confidence. Consequently, from the beginning the child's feeling of being able to read something, no matter how simple, should be reinforced. Her eyes sparkle as she describes the thrill of mastery, the dawn of the magic day. ''They come in and they can't read and they go out and they can! Like with Deidre. Something all of a sudden is clicking. And you sense it. You can feel that with her. It's a magic day. Sometimes I'm more excited than any of them!''

In forming her initial reading groups Ms. Allen pays no attention to readiness scores, relying instead on her own observation of each child's reading ability and work habits in the first few weeks of school. ''I viewed the children first and observed their work habits and ability. One group, the Apples, came out almost immediately, and the next group followed along very closely. The other children started off in the third group but before you know it they'll be moving up. They just need to develop that confidence.''

Ms. Allen often speaks of children ''moving themselves'' into a reading group, as if it were entirely up to the child to decide which group to join. ''Tanya has put herself in this group, you just can't keep her back. . . Bonnie might soon move herself over here . . . Imani was in this group but she didn't want to be away from her friend Cara, so she put herself back here.'' Although the decision in fact rests with the teacher, not the child, the images of choice, movement, flexibility, and self-direction aptly convey the open, hospitable nature of Ms. Allen's reading groups. Not only are children promoted from one reading group to another, but Ms. Allen deliberately blurs the boundaries between them by not totally segregating children who receive remedial tutoring from others, by having borderline children belong simultaneously to two groups, by permitting any child to listen in on a reading group's activity from his desk, and most important, by using many other criteria in addition to skill in forming and reforming the reading groups. These criteria involve myriad personality and social considerations: whether a child is comfortable with other members of the group; whether he has a particular friend there; whether he is ready for independent work or needs to socialize a bit longer; whether he is likely to be challenged or frustrated by the material; whether he will gather or lose confidence by observing the progress of others. "Certain children can be of help and inspiration [to other children in a reading group]. They bring the others out by talking to them, sharing ideas with them. I've had this happen so many times. Deidre is pulling Kevin along. Ernie is very withdrawn and depends very much on Tom. He wants the assurance that he's doing what Tom is doing."

Ms. Allen applies these generous, multiple criteria to seating arrangements in her classroom as well. She changes these arrangements almost every week. "That's why I don't keep my room set up the same way. I like them to see who they work best with. Some children have personality conflicts just as adults have personality conflicts. So you don't sit them near to one another. But then there are other children who work really well together . . . Tom is a very calming influence on Lawrence. Naomi is a child who loves to talk and I sit her with children to bring them out."

Clearly, one of Ms. Allen's outstanding characteristics as a teacher is her interest in, knowledge of, and skill in responding to the individual temperaments, abilities, and needs of children. Within the comfortable structure of her calm and smoothly humming classroom, Ms. Allen seems to allow each child optimum space, time, and context to develop and display his interest and personality. The discernment and development of uniqueness in children is of the very highest value to her. "I think that the worst thing you can try to do is to make the child a carbon copy of what you are. I don't want to take their personalities away in trying to have them meet the school situation. I think that each child has his own personality to be developed and that you should channel that personality."

Ms. Allen almost never spontaneously refers to an individual child as a member of a racial, ethnic, or social-class group or even as a member of a basic skill group in her class. She seems to think of children completely as individuals with highly differentiated and complex personalities requiring careful nurturance. Asked to talk about the children in her class, she describes them in rich detail and with subtle analysis of their strengths and weaknesses. She is sensitive both to transient swings of mood and to more pervasive affective dispositions, for, in her view, a critical aspect of effective teaching is the ability to distinguish which things ought to be noticed and which are best ignored. "If a person is short or curt with you, it might not be because of you, it might be because of a series of events that happened before. So you don't hold it against them. You have to think about this with children too."

For example, Ms. Allen judiciously ignores some of Simone's moods— her pouts and sulks—which she knows are displayed to get her attention. She knows the difference between these staged behaviors and the real feelings of anxiety, rage, and confusion Simone experiences when her estranged father visits and makes his extravagant, empty promises. Similarly, Ms. Allen senses Ernie's insecurity and disorientation, expressed in alternating fits of hyperactivity and daydreaming. She traces this state to an influx of visitors at home, drastic change in basic routines, and his parents' temporary preoccupations. She recounts also Mona's strange behavior over a two-week period. "You can tell when they're going to be sick. You can tell when something's bothering them. You really get that feeling when something's wrong and they want to tell you but they don't know how to tell you about it . . . It's like a sixth sense that you get that something's wrong and you don't exactly know what it is. So finally yesterday about 2 o'clock she says, 'I'm not coming back, I'm never coming back,' and then a flood of tears." It turns out that Mona's parents are leaving town in a hurry the next morning, and the child was threatened with punishment if she let on.

Ms. Allen is alert to signs of physical problems that may interfere with the child's functioning in the classroom. She suspects that Paul needs glasses because he holds his book so strangely and immediately brings this condition to his parents' attention. In two other cases she wonders whether the children are getting the proper food and enough rest: one child seems constantly tired, lethargic, and pale, the other hyperactive and tense. She gently questions the children about how late they watch television, who cooks the supper, and so on but takes the matter no further since in both cases she thinks the parents are likely to retaliate against the child for telling.

There are several children in Ms. Allen's class whose condition poses an ethical dilemma for her. She is both a fervent advocate of children's rights and a strong supporter of parents vis-à-vis school officialdom. But what is she to do when the parent seems to be the cause of a serious problem in a child, not the school? Discreetly she mentions a case of suspected child abuse. Jesse is so nervous and tense that he literally shrinks and pulls back from the slightest physical contact. "I have a feeling that there's a lot of yelling in the house. Because of the way he acts. Jumpy. You can't even go near him. He pulls back, as though he does get hit." He comes to school with cuts, bruises, and even broken bones suspiciously often. When his mother comes to pick him up, he immediately starts to cry and tremble. Once, hearing that her son had been scolded by the vice-principal, she collared him in the cafeteria and hit him hard across the ears in front of everyone. Now whenever Jesse does something wrong, his first tremulous words to Ms. Allen are: "You going to tell my mother?"

The harshness of Jesse's mother goes beyond issues of discipline. Ms. Allen remembers once when Jesse proudly took a book home to show his mother how well he could read and she brusquely returned it with the message that she didn't have the time to waste. Jesse's mother was not always quite this surly. A new husband and a new baby in the house may be partly responsible for her apparent disgust with her son and, in turn, for Jesse's behavior problems. In class Jesse can be mean, slyly looking for opportunities to kick, hit, or trip other children, spoil their papers, disrupt their games. He is extremely distractible, has great difficulty completing even short tasks, and needs constant supervision and encouragement to try.

Ms. Allen's account of the strategies she is using to help Jesse overcome his problems is instructive. Her first aim is to inspire trust—trust in adults, and trust in himself. She has to help Jesse realize that he can depend on her to like and protect him. She will not tell tales to his mother; she will not automatically side with school officials or other children against him; she will not hit or yell at him. Ms. Allen also has to help Jesse understand that he can be successful at school work and be liked instead of hated by other children. Ms. Allen plans her tactics carefully. She begins by seating Jesse apart from the other children then very gradually places him closer to a few of the calmer, kinder ones who can tolerate his restlessness and handle his aggressive outbursts. Ms. Allen herself spends brief but regular amounts of time with Jesse, sitting close to him, playing a game or chatting, simply trying to make him feel important, liked, and respected. She invites him to read in two different reading groups and also sends him to the reading tutor for extra, individualized teaching. She breaks up his seatwork assignments into small bits that he can finish quickly and be rewarded for. In general, she tries to positively reinforce his good behavior and ignore his misbehavior as far as possible. She notes some progress. By the end of the year Jesse is reading above grade level, he is not quite so tense and jumpy, and his behavior is noticeably more controlled. Jesse's home situation, however, has not improved. His mother still seems to regard Jesse as a nuisance and Ms. Allen as too patient and indulgent a teacher. "With Jesse's mother it's 'I don't know what to do with him. I can't stand him at home either. He'll try you. He'll push you against the wall. You've got to let him know who's boss!'" Ms. Allen judges that she can accomplish little by collaborating with this parent. The best she can do for Jesse's future is to ensure that he gets a sympathetic teacher next year and the reputation as an unloved and unlovable child that followed him from kindergarten to first grade does not continue to haunt him ever after. Nevertheless, Jesse is one of the few cases in which she thinks it would be useful to request a CASE evaluation, if only to change the mother's perception of Jesse from a child in need of punishment to a child in need of understanding and help.

Ms. Allen describes several other children whose problems concern her deeply. First Mona, a little waif of a girl, much smaller than she should be for her age, always pale, listless, slurring, and hesitant in her speech, "as if she were not allowed to say too much at home." At the same time Mona seems to be burdened down with adult responsibilities. Her few references to home life usually describe chores: "I had to finish the ironing," "I had to do the shopping." These are clearly not fabrications since, from time to time, Mona has come in with burns from an iron on her arm and is sometimes seen trundling heavy grocery bags down Main Street all by herself. In class she often seems preoccupied and anxious, as if weighed down with cares. All the verve, playfulness, and vitality of childhood seem to have been snuffed out. Quietly, sadly, not daring to participate, she lingers always on the periphery of the classroom scene.

Ms. Allen worries about Mona. She suspects she is not getting adequate food, rest, and physical care and there may be a medical problem. She has the school nurse check the child, but nothing serious is detected. Ms. Allen invites Mona's mother in for a conference, but she evades and procrastinates. It is up to Ms. Allen to do what she can in class to help Mona enjoy a little of her childhood. Again her strategy is deliberate. She seats Mona next to talkative, gregarious children who "will help bring her out." She finds time as often as possible to sit with her and chat about this or that. She encourages her to leave her unfinished seatwork and take extra play breaks. She sends home a report card that emphasizes her strengths rather than her deficiencies although, in truth, there are many more of the latter. Slowly Mona seems to be gaining confidence and a measure of vitality. But Ms. Allen can do only so much without the parent's cooperation. How limited is her ability to effect change in Mona's life is sadly underscored when in the spring her parents remove Mona from school without warning or explanation to go and live with an invalid grandfather. Ms. Allen envisions Mona struggling down the streets of New York City, once more weighed down by cumbersome shopping bags and the heavy burden of adult responsibilities. She hopes Mona will be cheered by the brief, relatively carefree interlude that she tried to create for her at the Inner School.

There are other children in her class who stand in need of and receive Ms. Allen's classroom therapy. And there are still others who have no problems to speak of but are pure sources of delight and wonder. Ms. Allen describes both kinds of children articulately, touching on many dimensions of personality and of academic and social development in each child. An impressive aspect of her descriptions is the absence of stereotypic assumptions about the links between the child's home background and his success in school. As our vignettes of Jesse and Mona illustrate, Ms. Allen is very likely to trace the origins of a child's problems in school to difficulties in the home, but Ms. Allen's interest is always primarily in parental behaviors— how the parent actually treats the child—not in social characteristics such as race, social class, family structure, and the like. In fact, whenever she mentions these, it is usually in order to challenge a stereotype. "Wade's mother is unmarried and expecting another child. She takes excellent care of him and it hasn't hurt him at all not to have a father. Simone's mother is black, separated from her husband and on welfare. She knows Simone very well and is extremely interested in her education and development."

Eschewing easy generalization, glib labels, and clichés, Ms. Allen tries to get to know as many parents as possible personally. She is a very active member of the Parent-Teacher Association, which she helped start, and learns as much as she can about the families of students by listening to and supporting the efforts of parents in that context. Her classroom is open to visits from parents at any time, and she often takes the initiative to contact parents and work out collaborative strategies with them for handling problems the child may be having. Her basic judgments of parents seem to rest on whether or not they truly care for and are interested in helping the child rather than in simply asserting their power over him. Thus, before she invites a parent to work with her she first satisfies herself that the parent is not likely to retaliate against the child for exposing any deficiencies of the home. In such cases Ms. Allen's reaction is to shield the child by handling any problem that arises in the confines of the classroom. However, when Ms. Allen judges that the parent is really interested in helping the child, she goes to great lengths to involve him in analyzing what is wrong and what might be done. For example, she refers to the case of Deidre. Didi is very often late for school and often arrives in tears. One cold day she came in wearing only her panties under a thin, half-buttoned coat. On other occasions Ms. Allen found her skulking in the hall, unwashed and unkempt, too embarrassed to come into class. Deidre is a very nervous child who easily dissolves in tears when teased or criticized. Ms. Allen surmises that her mother, very young and inexperienced, has unrealistically high expectations for her (for example, expecting her to get ready for school with no help and expecting her to learn to read after a few lessons at home). She also suspects a problem with drugs or alcohol. She undertakes a series of conferences with Didi's mother, in which they work out various strategies for working with Didi and explore the possibility of a CASE evaluation for the child and psychological counseling for the mother. They agree on this as a last resort if the remedies they have worked out fail.

Ms. Allen gives similar accounts of collaborating with other parents in a child's behalf. She strongly believes in working with parents first, and turns to counseling services within the school system only when the parents are obdurate or desperately in need of help themselves. She notes with dismay, however, that nowadays parents are less and less able or willing to invest time and effort on behalf of their children. "You can't buy a child's respect or a child's love, or his good behavior. That's what happens with a lot of parents today. I think they've given the children so much in the material sense but not of themselves and the kids feel it."

For many years Ms. Allen has had few discipline problems in her class. Teachers swap stories about her famous "look," a quiet, penetrating stare that evidently quells the savage beast in any child. Ms. Allen recounts how once a teacher burst in on her class with the urgent request: "Ms. Allen, please come and just *look* at them for me!" Ms. Allen does not know exactly what it is about this look of hers that calms the noisiest, the most disruptive of children, but she is sure it is not just a look. It is a consistent way of behaving that children can understand and depend on. She seldom raises her voice, she seldom threatens, she seldom loses her temper, she seldom nags, she seldom disparages or ridicules, she is nearly always scrupulously fair.

The essence of Ms. Allen's approach is summed up in the advice one of her own teachers gave her and which she has tried to follow ever since: "*See* but don't *notice* everything." Ms. Allen believes that it is a serious mistake to criticize a child for every misdemeanor, attaching blame and exacting guilt for every transgression. "I don't believe in getting *on* a child at all. I really try to work from the personality and get them to function. And I don't ever like to make a spectacle of a child . . . holding him up to ridicule . . . I don't think that's teaching."

When a teacher does so it is often the case that she wants each child to measure up to some unrealistic image of the "good child" within herself, an image that is often a projection of her own feelings of shame and guilt. She may try to impose an idealized personality on the child instead of "working from the child's real personality outwards." To such a teacher only a relatively narrow range of behaviors, traits, and characteristics of children are acceptable, and excessive time and effort must be spent in control and disciplining the many who deviate from her norms. Thus, the teacher creates the problem by defining it to be so. As an example, Ms. Allen refers to a student teacher whom we had observed working in her classroom. "Ms. Ames and Simone just didn't click. Ms. Ames didn't click with lots of children. It seems as though a child is a threat to her. She forgets the child is only six years old. [In such a case] we don't meet the child's personality, we meet our own personality."

Ms. Allen recalls that from time to time she has acted like that herself, expecting too much of a child, insisting on correcting every inadequacy, taking the child's misbehavior as a personal affront. "I'm not going to say it doesn't happen . . . it's happened to me time and again . . . but I do feel that if you're having a hard time every year and a hard time communicating with parents also, then I think one should start looking at the teacher and not blaming the children all the time."

Ms. Allen is no paragon of virtue and I know she would hate to see herself described that way. She has made her mistakes and she has not always had the success she enjoys this year. But Ms. Allen has devoted all her energies these last twenty years to understanding children, to learning to be sensitive, to be fair, to inspire their confidence and respect, to love them. She is justifiably, admirably proud of what she and other teachers at the Inner School and in the Conroy school system can show to researchers, to educators, to community parents about what is going on in their supposedly very ordinary public-school classrooms. Asked what were the real reasons for joining our research project, Ms. Allen summed it up with characteristic candor. "We felt it was about time that we not let only those who could do all the verbalization and not have the experience have their say . . . I've seen what some of them have done to kids and then they've got the nerve to get up and give their opinions . . . and I start thinking about the people who really care about children . . . I'm not a show-off, not an exhibitionist . . . but we felt we had really sat back long enough and said nothing, and it's not right because there's a lot of good going on."

Once more I marveled at the simple confidence inspiring these remarks. How could she be sure that our observations would bear her out? Ms. Allen did not know what aspects of her behavior we had scrutinized week after week, how we had interpreted what we saw, what values and beliefs might inform our assessment, what we had heard about her from children and parents. Yet she was willing to take the risk, put herself on the line and deliver her classroom to the judgment of outsiders. This I knew to be true for the other three teachers as well. I saw both their vulnerability and their courage and hoped that our research would meet the challenge of describing honestly the good and the not so good in these four very complex classrooms.

Synthesis   *Jean V. Carew*

As it turned out, we need not have had many qualms in Ms. Allen's case concerning the suitability and sensitivity of our observation procedures for capturing the style and substance of her classroom behavior. The findings of the qualitative analysis of our observations in her classroom proved to be extraordinarily congruent with Ms. Allen's characterizations of herself in our interviews with her. Similarly, our observations of individual children in her classroom were uncannily consistent with her portrayals of them.

Academic Orientation and Management Efficiency The two teachers at the Inner School clearly placed significantly more emphasis on academic instruction and were more efficient managers of their classrooms than their counterparts in the Outer School. Ms. Allen's was in fact the easiest of the four classrooms to observe. A set agenda was adhered to, activities followed one another smoothly with minimum time spent in transition, and even play breaks were predictably scheduled. Starting at about 9:00 a.m., the first episode observed was generally a whole-class activity focused on language arts instruction. Typically, this activity was immediately followed by the calling up of reading groups, one after the other, each group twice for ten to fifteen minutes at a time. After lunch at 11 o'clock came a half-hour play break ("choosing time") followed by whole-class academic activities, individual seatwork review, or occasionally, arts and crafts or other "fun" projects.

Given this typical day's routine, it is not surprising to find that 85 percent of Ms. Allen's interactions with her first graders took place in academic contexts, 75 percent specifically in reading-activity contexts, and 66 percent in small reading groups. The academic orientation of Ms. Allen's class and her management efficiency are also indicated by the finding that 70 percent of her interactions with individual children had an academic task as their topic and only 18 percent were focused on procedural matters. Finally, we note that 55 percent of all behaviors in Ms. Allen's class (the highest percentage of the four classes) was coded in terms of the Structured Interaction coding system. The latter provides a useful index of the academic orientation and smooth management of a classroom, since only those behaviors that were obviously focused on academic matters and followed a clearly-structured, well-routinized sequence (question/answer/assessment/evaluation) were accommodated in the Structured Interaction observation protocol.

The data just presented are very similar to the corresponding figures for Ms. Prima, Ms. Allen's co-teacher at the Inner School, and are considerably different from those for the two teachers at the Outer School. They are also entirely consistent with Ms. Allen's own account of her classroom agenda and her objectives as a teacher. Many times in our interviews Ms. Allen emphasized her belief that children need and want to learn basic reading skills, that the mastery of such skills was intimately connected with their feelings of competence and worth, and that reading groups afforded an excellent context for the development of confidence and verbal expressiveness.

This point is nicely illustrated in the following two excerpts describing

Ms. Allen's interactions with the Peaches, her third reading group. Throughout she encourages the children to associate the reading material with people, places, and events in their own lives and thereby to express their personal ideas and opinions.

TEACHER: I'm thinking about three words [pointing to cards with the words "street," "house," and "step"]. Which one of these words tells me about this picture? [Rhonda frames the word "street."] Good. Now let's talk about this other word. What is it?
LAWRENCE: House.
TEACHER: Okay. Now, let me tell you about my house. My house is painted gray. It's made of wood. It has a red door and windows in the front. Please describe your house, Deidre.
DEIDRE: My house has red bricks.
TEACHER: Anything else?
DEIDRE: No.
TEACHER: What's your house like, Rhonda? [Rhonda delays.] Is your house made of brick? wood? concrete?
RHONDA: Wood.
TEACHER: What color is the house next to yours, Odette?
ODETTE: Same color as mine, but it has a round thing that sticks up!
TEACHER: [To Rhonda] What about your house?
RHONDA: I don't know.
TEACHER: [Goes to desk and gives out pictures of houses which the children had drawn earlier.] Who lives at Elm Street? [Gives picture to Rhonda.] See, that's a picture of your house, Rhonda.

Two weeks later we see the same strategy.

TEACHER: We've been reading about where people work. Let's talk about where they work. Naomi, where do people work?
NAOMI: They work for the city.
TEACHER: [Writes this on the board.] Do you know anyone who works for the city?
NAOMI: A mailman.
TEACHER: Good! You gave me a new word! Now read the sentence you made.
NAOMI: "A mailman works for the city."
TEACHER: Now Deidre?
DEIDRE: People work in a school.
TEACHER: Very good. That's true. [Writes the sentence.] Now Rhonda?

RHONDA: [Delays.] People work in restaurants.

TEACHER: [Writes.] Is there a special name for people who work in restaurants? [Rhonda shakes her head.] Some are called waiters and waitresses.

LAWRENCE: [Excitedly] I have one!

TEACHER: Okay.

LAWRENCE: People work in a doctor place.

TEACHER: What's that?

LAWRENCE: In a hospital!

TEACHER: [Substitutes the children's names for "people" in the sentences on the board.] Now Deidre, read your sentence again.

DEIDRE: [Reads] Deidre was in a school.

TEACHER: That was good because it does start with "w" but the word is "works," not "was." Where do you work in this sentence, Rhonda? [Rhonda says nothing.] Where did you tell me people work?

RHONDA: A restaurant.

TEACHER: Right. In this sentence you work in a restaurant. See how I made the change for you?

These last two observations suggest some important differences between Ms. Allen and Ms. Prima, her co-teacher at the Inner School. Both teachers ran efficient, highly academically oriented classrooms and for both the teaching of reading was the primary item on the day's agenda. In Ms. Allen's case, however, management efficiency and academic orientation were complemented by extraordinary skill at interpersonal relationships and interest in the individual needs of children. This unique combination of qualities is clearly demonstrated by the quantitative data describing the quality of Ms. Allen's interactions with individual children.

Certain types of teacher behavior seem to denote "child-centeredness" and the teacher's interest in and responsiveness to children's individual needs. These variables include the use of "open" or "free" rather than direct modes of questioning which allow children little latitude in whether to respond or how to respond; positive versus negative reinforcement/evaluation; and positive versus negative responses to children's requests. On all these variables Ms. Allen ranked first or second among the four teachers, her behavior being similar to Ms. Edwards' in the Outer School and conspicuously different from her co-teacher, Ms. Prima's at the Inner School. Thus, in Ms. Allen's class, the percentage of "open" questions was 25 percent (compared to 10 percent for Ms. Prima); the percentage of "free" questions was 4 percent (versus 1 percent); the percentage of positive evaluations of children's responses was 17 percent (versus 7 percent); and the percentages of positive and negative reinforcement of children's behavior were 6 percent and 15 percent (versus 7 percent and 34 percent).

Further evidence of Ms. Allen's skill as a teacher of young children comes from our observations of their behavior in their interactions with her. In the data analysis, child behavior was divided into four major categories: appropriate behavior (including achievement-oriented behavior and prosocial behavior such as helping and sharing); expressive behavior (expresses opinions, comments); dependent behavior (asks for help, materials); and inappropriate behavior (including disrupting and annoying others and inattentiveness to one's work). It comes as no surprise to find that the children in Ms. Allen's class ranked first or second on appropriate and expressive behavior and third or fourth on dependent and inappropriate behavior. Again Ms. Allen's classroom closely resembles Ms. Edwards' and significantly contrasts with Ms. Prima's, her co-teacher at the Inner School.

These cold statistics hardly do justice to Ms. Allen's teaching style and personal manner, which are much more vividly conveyed by observations showing her in action. In the next excerpt Ms. Allen is once more working with the Peaches.

TEACHER: Okay, Deidre, I'd like you to read this for me. [Deidre reads]. What are the people doing?

DEIDRE: Going up.

TEACHER: Okay. Which sentence tells you they are going up?

DEIDRE: This one.

TEACHER: Okay, did the picture help you, Deidre? [Deidre nods and continues reading. Teacher helps Deidre as she stumbles. Deidre reads.] That was very good, Deidre. You knew every single word on that page! [Teacher asks Odette to read. Odette makes an error.] Odette, you had some trouble with that yesterday, so I'll help you. [Teacher helps Odette sound out several words.] Now it's your turn, Kevin. You may have some trouble but don't worry about it. Give it a try. [Kevin reads. Lawrence has trouble finding his place in the book.] Larry, we always start from the top, then go down. See, here, then here. Which word should you underline, Deidre? [Deidre underlines a word.] Now, pretend the word is here and read the sentence with the word in it. [Deidre reads.] What is that word?

DEIDRE: One.

TEACHER: Which word sounds best? People *on* the street or people *one* the street?

DEIDRE: One.

TEACHER: Does that sound right to you?

DEIDRE: No, "on."
TEACHER: So which word do you underline? [Deidre underlines "on."]
         Right! Very good!

In this excerpt we consistently see certain qualities that are characteristic of Ms. Allen: her patience, her helpfulness, her liberal use of praise, her sparing and gentle use of correction and criticism.

This brings us back again to the question of discipline and behavior control. In a class of twenty-two children one expects to find the teacher spending a fair amount of time redirecting children to their work, correcting misbehavior, arbitrating arguments, and so on. But Ms. Allen seldom seems to need to do this. The children clearly know what they are supposed to do and how they should behave and one is only surprised at how willingly they do it. They nearly always seem busy and productive yet relaxed and enjoying themselves, as if school was a very pleasant place to be. Typically, two-thirds of the children are at their desks working on papers or else reading or playing a game in the "choosing" area while Ms. Allen is in a corner of the room with a small group clustered around her taking reading turns. While so engaged Ms. Allen seems to pay full attention to the reading group yet somehow she is monitoring all the children in the class, since from time to time we witness the famous look—a gentle, penetrating stare across the room at some child who is just beginning to overstep the limits. Usually the look is enough, but sometimes she adds a polite reminder: "Excuse me! Lawrence, please!" "Odette, thank you!" "Deidre, are you forgetting something?" "Bonnie, would you please sit down and do what I asked?" One is amazed that she almost never seems to raise her voice or speak harshly. Combing through the observations the harshest reprimands we came across were on the order: "Sit up, Simone. You're not going to act so silly"; "Wade, I don't want to hear your voice that loud again"; "Ernie, I don't need you to count after me and disturb the others. That's what makes people unhappy with you." Each of these reproaches is delivered in a matter-of-fact, quiet way, with no hint of threat or ridicule. As Ms. Allen once explained when talking about Simone, "For me to get on Simone would be the worst thing in the world for that child. To pick on everything she does wrong would devastate her. I have to be sensitive to when she needs me to come in and when she does not."

Finally, let us consider the issue of fairness. Ms. Allen hoped she was fair to all children, by which she meant that she gave equal amounts of positive attention to individual children regardless of their ability or personal characteristics. "I want to be sure that all children get an equal amount of my attention. I feel that even if a child has the ability to go on, I still want him to feel I'm going to give him time. There are children who demand time and want extra attention, but I just don't feel I should take it away from those that are good and don't bother you at all."

How fair was Ms. Allen in practice? Once more we find that Ms. Allen's perceptions of herself were indeed highly congruent with our observations. The data analysis presented in table 10 shows that Ms. Allen was the teacher most likely to distribute her attention equally among individual children and least likely to single out any one child for exceptional treatment. Only one child in her class, Simone, attracted notably more than an average share of her attention, an exception which Ms. Allen also unabashedly acknowledged many times in our interviews.

Another form of discrimination occurs when teachers treat groups of children differently. The teacher may not be aware that she is responding, say, to black children differently than to whites, or to girls differently than to boys, but analysis of her interactions with children belonging to these groups and their assignment to reading groups and to seating arrangements may nevertheless show this to be so. In this study we were particularly interested in the issue of prejudicial discrimination and went to some lengths to examine the data for each classroom in this light. In Ms. Allen's case, as shown in table 11, there was little or no evidence of race or sex discrimination. Of the twenty variables analyzed, only one difference in teacher behavior was found for race and none for sex. Ms. Allen positively reinforced black children more often than whites but, at the same time, black children in her class more often behaved appropriately than whites, which may well have accounted for her different responses to the two groups. There was also no evidence of discrimination in Ms. Allen's assignment of children to reading groups or seating arrangements. Of the ten white and ten black children in her class, seven whites and six blacks were assigned to the top two reading groups; and of the eleven girls and nine boys in her class, seven girls and six boys were assigned to the top groups. The findings for seating patterns were also unimpeachable. Black children and white children sat next to black and white children equally often, and boys had approximately equal proportions of boys and girls as seat neighbors. We note finally that only one child, Jesse, a black boy, was regularly seated apart from the other children. The technique of physical isolation is often used by teachers to control distractible, disruptive, or aggressive children and Jesse was certainly such a child. But in this case it was Jesse's nervousness and fear of physical contact that compelled Ms. Allen to isolate him, since this was not a form of control that she normally used. Over the course of the year it was interesting to see how she gradually incorporated Jesse into the class, seating him closer and closer to some of the calmer and quieter children with whom he might learn to modulate his own nervous, restless, and aggressive behavior.

The many themes that we have touched on so far in our portrait of Ms. Allen come together best when we think of her in relation to individual children, and to one child in particular, Simone. Simone was one of the four children in Ms. Allen's class whom we observed individually over a period of months during seatwork and other independent activities. We selected Simone for individual study because Ms. Allen's remarks about her in our interviews and our observations of her interactions with her clearly suggested that this was a child for whom Ms. Allen had a very special feeling and who at the same time presented an extraordinary challenge to and test of Ms. Allen's skills as a teacher.

Simone is a seven-year-old black girl, the only child of a divorced mother. Simone and her mother live in a small apartment in a two-family house close to the school in a not unpleasant street filled higgledy-piggledy with small, charming houses struggling against deterioration and decay. Simone's mother has left her job to return to school to get her college degree, and their income now comes mostly from welfare. Simone's mother is a large, extremely articulate woman. She radiates pride in Simone. Beaming, she shows the interviewer Simone's report card replete with As, a large stack of her intricate drawings, and Simone's self-made workbooks from which she assigns herself additional homework. Simone and her mother sometimes study together, visit the library together, watch the same television programs. They are both determined to go far through brains and application. Several times Ms. Allen refers to the help and reinforcement that Simone's mother gives her at home: "She works with her a lot in reading and praising her and helping her with her math." And Simone herself also proudly acknowledges her mother's role.

TEACHER: Your mother must have been so excited when she heard [about Simone's promotion to a higher reading group].

SIMONE: Yep, she was yapping about it all night to her friends on the phone!

Simone's mother has a very close relationship with Ms. Allen—the closest of any mother with the teachers in this study. The two women talk on the telephone almost every week and make no secret of it from Simone. The relationship between them began when Simone's mother raised concerns about her daughter's aggressive and taunting behavior toward other children at a neighborhood community center. They discussed this and her similar behavior toward one of her classmates and agreed that "Simone is the kind of child you have to be firm with. You can't give in to her moods or emotions. She's going to try to get attention . . . in whatever way she can. The more that you acknowledge her when she's like that, the worse she gets."

She takes a lot of patience.'' Their solution was for Simone's mother to keep Simone out of the community center and for Ms. Allen to separate Simone as far as possible from the classmate she was victimizing. Simone's aggressive behavior improved markedly as a result but her attention-seeking continued to be a problem, symptomized now by sulks and pouts when she did not get her way.

Ms. Allen's tactic for dealing with Simone's moodiness is generally to ignore it. She laughingly describes an episode in which Simone "did everything" to get her attention including ripping her workbook. "She drew her Queen X on me, but I just ignored her . . . and she punished herself by going into the corner.'' Later in the year she recounts a similar incident in which Simone had made an elaborate bid for attention by dropping her pencils, standing up, sitting down, dozens of times. Simone finally punished herself by huddling in the corner, but Ms. Allen surprised her by calling on her to do an errand. Simone: "How come you're letting me do this, when I've been bad?'' Teacher: "Because you know you've been bad and now you want to do something good.'' In Ms. Allen's words, "You just don't carry it over. You correct her when she needs it . . . but then you praise her and explain to her . . . so that she realizes that I'm not acting against her.''

Simone indeed does require a lot of patience and understanding. Both teacher and mother know she is "a real little actress,'' adept at manipulating adults. "She knows how to work around you. If she can get the best of you, then she'll get the best of you. But if you just work around her and work toward what you want her to do then she'll do it.'' One of the more difficult judgments Ms. Allen must make is to distinguish Simone's manipulative attention seeking from deeper psychological states brought on usually by visits from her estranged father. Apparently he promises her "the sun, the moon, and the stars,'' gets her all worked up in anticipation, then as often as not fails to follow through. Simone "goes into a mood'' after each such visit. She cannot concentrate on her work, picks on other children, uses every means to attract Ms. Allen's attention. We saw this state build up in one of our observations and witnessed Ms. Allen's sensitive and sensible reaction: Ms. Allen goes across the room and says, "Simone, what's the matter?'' Simone does not answer, but walks around, not looking at Ms. Allen. Ms. Allen says, "C'mon, give me a big smile . . . is it a deal?'' Ms. Allen urges her again. Simone finally gives her the smile, and they shake hands.

This delicate balance of affection, concern, and firm guidance is the essence of Ms. Allen's relationship with Simone. Simone openly shows affection for and interest in her teacher with hugs, whispered confidences, and personal comments. Similarly, Ms. Allen unrestrainedly acknowledges her special feeling for Simone. "She's a fantastic child. I really love her!'' And it is true that despite her moods, her manipulativeness, and her occasional aggressiveness, Simone is a compelling, charismatic person. She is the sort of child who easily stands out in a crowd, whom an observer cannot help noticing. To everything she does she adds a certain style, verve, vivacity— singing to herself as she works, tapping her foot to a rhythm, dancing as she moves around the room. In a group sing-along, for example, it is Simone who takes the lead, for she invariably knows the words and the tune and pipes out confidently in a loud, clear voice. Her style and talent as a per- former draw other children toward her like a magnet. She has "personality plus . . . a tremendous sense of humor and a great imagination." Ms. Allen tells how once, when Simone was asked to think of a word with an "f" sound, she volunteered "faggot" and sweetly reminded her teacher to put it up on the board along with "fat," "fine," and "Phillip." Simone is quick and observant. One afternoon she sat staring at Ms. Allen for a long time: "You look different. You don't look the same as when you went downstairs to lunch," she said, puzzled. "I guess you combed your hair!" Simone is also very intelligent and verbally expressive. When asked to interpret a pic- ture in the book her group is reading, she often launches into long, compli- cated, imaginative descriptions that rivet everyone's attention. She is a clas- sic "high achiever." Starting off at the beginning of the year in the second reading group, she "moved herself" up to the top group as she gathered confidence and the basic skills. By the end of the year Simone was reading at high third-grade level according to her test scores. But Simone is not merely skilled at reading, she genuinely loves to read. She is one of the very few children whom we actually heard make remarks like "It's nice to read . . . When are we going to read a harder book? . . . I wish I could read all of this by myself." She is very proud of her progress and not a little boastful. In our interview with her Simone talked about how far she was in advance of one of her rivals. "Deidre thinks she's smarter than me, but I'm in the highest group and she's in the lowest group. She's gotta show off like *she's* in the highest and *I'm* in the lowest. First we was on *Around the City* and she was on nothing! Then she was on *Around the City* and we was on the book about the *Houses*. Then she got to the *Houses* and we was on *Uptown/ Downtown*. Now she's on *Uptown/Downtown* and we have *Under the Apple Tree!*"

Competitiveness is clearly one of Simone's less endearing traits. She is a natural leader and she plays to win. During one "choosing" period when children were allowed to select their own activities, Simone and Rhonda chose a board game. Simone quickly defines the game and declares the rules. "Choose the number pieces to fit and place them on the board," she says and plunges in. Soon the two girls notice that Odette is playing the same game but has only a few number chips. Simone locates a chip for her and shows Odette where it goes. With the introduction of a third child, even though on the periphery, the game becomes a spirited competition, with Simone's chatter heightening the excitement:

RHONDA: Come on, we're almost done!
SIMONE: 4, we need a 4. That's what we need.
RHONDA: I got it!
SIMONE
AND RHONDA: A do ba do ba do ba [singing as they finish the numbers].
SIMONE: Look at Odette's. She has a *long* way to go. We need a 9,
             baby, and we're gonna win. Odette, we're gonna try to win.
             We're gonna *try* and we're gonna *win!*

The game is stacked in Simone's and Rhonda's favor since Odette is playing alone and Simone prevents her from getting help from a fourth child. Simone also cleverly tries to distract Odette from her own board, and when Odette has the temerity to question the number the two pals have reached, Simone shoos her away. Now the competition seems to be to complete the numbers before choosing time is over, but they keep an eye on Odette to make sure she is still lagging far behind. At this moment Ms. Allen announces the end of choosing time and will not allow the girls to finish their game.

SIMONE: Well at least *we won,* Odette. Let's say Happy Birthday America!

    While Simone's behavior toward Odette during this excerpt was competitive and manipulative, she can also be very helpful and thoughtful, especially to those she perceives as less adept than herself. In Ms. Allen's words: "If a child needs something, or someone is crying, Simone's very concerned. She'll go over and pat them and say 'don't cry.' She might kill the kid later on, but at that point, if the child is crying, she feels bad . . . She's very aware of what other children need. She's very kind . . . Now Kevin, she'll say to me, 'Can I help him?' Then she'll go by him and say 'Good work, Kevin.' I guess she imitates me a lot."
    We saw several instances of Simone's helpfulness in our observations. For example, Simone looks over at Jesse's paper and notices some errors. She takes an eraser out of her desk and erases his paper, saying, "Jesse, you made this backwards, see?" Simone writes the correct word for Jesse. She erases other parts of the paper while whispering, "I'll help you, okay?" Simone writes an answer and then passes the paper to Jesse. "Now all you have to do is color it in." Simone reports to the teacher, "Ms. Allen, I'm going to help Jesse." Ms. Allen replies, "That's fine, I'm not worried." A

long sequence follows in which Simone goes over Jesse's paper with him and tells him what to write. Jesse follows Simone's directions. Simone: "You need a 6 here." Jesse writes a 6. Simone: "Now a 7. Write a 7 right here." Jesse complies . . . Simone: "Now, Jesse, what do you think this is?" Jesse points to an answer. Simone: "No. Do you know how to do that? See, you have to write the things on the paper." Simone compliments Jesse on his ring. Jesse shows that he has two rings and gives one to Simone. Simone is pleased and in return offers Jesse a crayon, explaining, "It's part of the pencil. It's really a pencil but I use it for a crayon. You can have it. You can use my crayons but you can't put them back in your box." The two children continue to work on their separate papers, occasionally whispering back and forth.

While Simone assumes a superior directing role in this excerpt, she does so with a gentleness and sensitivity that are very reminiscent of Ms. Allen, whose behavior she seems to be consciously modeling.

The quantitative analysis of the observation data bears out this qualitative account in virtually every respect. Table 14 compares Simone's interactions with Ms. Allen with those of the average child in her class in the teacher-focused observations; table 15 makes the comparison for the child-focused observations. Because the target of the first method of observation was the teacher, only Ms. Allen's actual interactions with and reactions to Simone are included in these data. In contrast, the target of the second type of observation was the child. Here the observer recorded all of the child's behavior during selected periods of seatwork and play in the classroom, including Simone's interactions with other children and the teacher and her noninteractive behavior (for example, independent work, solitary play).

Although it now comes as no surprise, one of the outstanding features of table 14 is the amount of extra attention Simone receives from Ms. Allen compared to the average child. Nine percent of this teacher's interactions with individual children involves Simone, a figure nearly double that which one child in a class of twenty theoretically should receive (5 percent). Simone elicits attention from Ms. Allen in several ways. First, she more frequently exhibits "appropriate" behavior (for example, "Did I do this right?" "I love to read!"). This type of behavior usually evokes favorable reactions from Ms. Allen and consequently Simone receives more than an average share of special privileges. Simone is also not at all reluctant to express her opinions and engage her teacher in casual conversation. She does this twice as often as her average classmate and, in turn, Ms. Allen is much more apt to ask thought-provoking "process" questions and to engage in chitchat, humorous banter, and exchanges of affection with Simone than with the average student. These two strategies are clearly very successful in eliciting and sustaining positive attention from Ms. Allen and creating the

Table 14. Simone versus average child: teacher-focused observations.

Variable	Simone	Average child[1]
Interaction topic		
Academic	71.0%	69.8%
Nonacademic	4.8	3.8
Procedural	12.4	18.3
Privilege	3.8	1.5
Appropriate C behavior	1.0	0.2
Inappropriate C behavior	5.7	5.4
Health, distress	1.0	1.0
Selected child and teacher behaviors		
Appropriate C behavior	4.3	2.4
Positive T reinforcement	12.9	13.0
Expressive C behavior	7.1	3.5
T humor, conversation	6.7	3.3
Dependent C behavior	7.1	3.7
T grants request	5.7	6.2
T rejects request	3.8	1.1
Inappropriate C behavior	4.3	2.9
Negative T reinforcement	9.0	7.3
T open/free question	15.2	17.5
T process question	7.1	3.1
% total teacher-child interactions[2]	8.8	5.0

1. Average of all children in Ms. Allen's class.
2. Percentage of all teacher-child interactions for which the child was present and was a potential recipient.

basis for their special relationship. But Simone does not stop there. She is also much more prone than her average classmate to seek attention by asking for help, direction, information, and permission, even though this maneuver is counterproductive in that Ms. Allen rejects many of these demands and accedes to her requests no more often than to the average child's. It is important to note, however, that Simone is *not* conspicuously different from other children in frequency of "inappropriate" behavior, in how often this misbehavior becomes an issue with her teacher, or in the amount of negative reinforcement she recieves from Ms. Allen.

Table 15. Simone versus average child: child-focused observations.

Variable	Simone	Average child[1]	Range
Child activities			
Work	69.0%	46.3%	25.1-69.0%
Play	7.0	8.6	1.0-19.6
Talk	8.2	18.6	8.2-27.0
Self-care	1.6	3.0	1.0-7.5
Idle	9.6	15.4	2.7-29.6
Wild/disorderly conduct	0.0	2.8	0.0-8.5
Interacts with others	33.9	45.9	32.4-65.2
Child behavior when interacting with others			
Exhibits appropriate behavior	4.9	2.9	0.4-6.4
Receives appropriate behavior	0.9	2.3	0.8-5.5
Exhibits inappropriate behavior	1.6	5.9	0.4-22.8
Receives inappropriate behavior	1.8	2.4	0.7-6.6

1. Average of children observed individually in the four classes.

Consider now the child-focused observations of Simone during seatwork and play (table 15). Simone is clearly very task-oriented. In fact, she spends more time concentrating on work (defined as any academic task or quiet, constructive activity) than any child we observed in the four classes. Conversely, she spends relatively little time simply chatting with other children or in unfocused "idling." When she interacts with other children Simone is much more likely to behave positively than negatively. In 5 percent of the observations she is teaching, helping, or showing concern for other children as compared to 2 percent of the observations in which she may be bossing, teasing, or refusing them help.

The pictures of Simone that emerge from both the teacher-focused and child-focused observations are highly consistent with each other and with Ms. Allen's perceptions expressed in her interviews. We see here an intelligent, determined, highly academically motivated child, a child who is the leader, teacher, and helper of other children but who, at the same time, craves attention from adults and is clever enough to think of endless ways of attracting it. Simone strikes an observer as an outstanding student in so many ways that it comes as a shock to hear Ms. Allen predict that the system may very well destroy her. "I am willing to sit here today and tell you that Simone is going to be put in for a CASE [psychological evaluation as a problem child] . . . on the basis of her personality. See, the thing is we don't meet the child's personality, we meet our own personality . . . teachers don't look at the child and let them develop their personality and try to get the positive instead of the negative. And I'm afraid Simone does pout and get into these moods sometimes . . . They'll say she's emotional. But I don't think she's emotional. I just think she can work around you.''

Ironically, Simone may very well collaborate with the system in being designated a difficult child, if only to gain notoriety. "If she thinks she can give you a tale of woe, she'll give you a tale of woe. If she has her name put in as a child who's hard to handle, she'll play right into the psychiatrist's hands. You know, 'this poor fatherless child . . . ' "

It would greatly grieve but not surprise Ms. Allen if in the next year or two Simone did in fact become a problem child both behaviorally and academically despite her excellent academic achievements in first grade. Given Simone's hunger for attention and special status, her histrionic talents, her precocious social intelligence, her skill at manipulating adults, she may very well decide to gain her objectives through acting up rather than applying herself to work. So far her best insurance against this self-defeating course has been her mother, who Ms. Allen believes truly understands her daughter and has worked to bring out the best in her. But lately there have been some ominous developments. Simone's mother seems to be "going downhill." She often leaves Simone alone in the evening and no longer provides the solid support that was the child's mainstay. Simone's parents are now violently at odds and the child is bearing the brunt of their conflict. "I think we're seeing the effect in Simone's behavior in class. She's hitting people . . . The other day someone just looked at her and she up and punched them . . . nothing I do seems to stop her.''

This turn of events deepens Ms. Allen's trepidations about Simone's future. Will another teacher have the patience, the stamina, the love this child requires? The system, Ms. Allen knows, does not easily accept difference, uniqueness, individuality. It is easiest to label a child like Simone as abnormal and exile her to the limbo of counselors and experts. Ms. Allen will do all she can to protect this special child by conferring with her future teacher, by advising her to enlist the cooperation of Simone's mother, by challenging the CASE evaluation, by making herself always accessible to Simone. But her twenty years of experience tell her that these efforts may well be futile. Even at age seven, she knows that Simone must mostly be her own pilot. The love, the strength, the little bit of wisdom Ms. Allen has given her may not be enough to steer her safely home.

Ms. Prima

Interpretation　　*Sara Lawrence Lightfoot*

Ms. PRIMA, the other teacher in the Inner School, still lives with the family into which she was born thirty years ago, and her family continues to be the dominant force in her life. She was born on the south side of Conroy, the first child of second generation Italians. During the fifties and sixties the south side was the predominantly Italian section of the city and Ms. Prima vividly recalls the close feelings of community and ethnicity that were part of her early life. Her most intense images bring back the wonderful tastes and smells of Italian pasta. Food was symbolic of love and good living. "I would gorge. I loved food. When I was nine, ten years old I was a blimp. I was wearing size 16 dresses. Food, food, food . . . yes I liked it there. We had a big back yard. You know the house wasn't fancy or anything, but it was clean. You know my mother always kept the house clean." In more serious tones, she recalls the "deterioration" of the community when the Puerto Ricans began to move in. In recent years the neighborhood has changed radically and the Italians have escaped to other sections of Conroy and to the suburbs. Ms. Prima's voice expresses the threat, frustration, and bitterness of one who has been dispossessed from her beloved land, of one whose childhood memories have been shattered. She tells stories of the way the Puerto Ricans abuse the welfare system, how they hoard their money, and how their taste and style are opulent and offensive. She describes the disintegration of the schools and the low standards of instruction that result from their lack of skills and preparation. These negative stereotypes that she vigorously relates are not her customary manner of describing differences in people. The rush of anger at the Puerto Rican intruders seems to reflect the deep sense of loss that she feels in the destruction of her ethnic enclave.

Ms. Prima still identifies the south side of Conroy as home, although she has not lived there since early adolescence. When Ms. Prima was born, her father was running a radio and television business in Harper, a nearby suburb, and her mother was the head bookkeeper at a furniture company in south Conroy. "We used to live right around the corner from the store and when I was born, the owner liked my mother and so he allowed her to bring me to work. I mean the bassinet was there and I grew up in that furniture store. Everybody that came in knew me and the baby carriage and the playpen and the high chair." When her sister was born six years later, her mother hired a Polish woman to stay with both children during the day while her mother continued working at the store. Business became more lucrative for both parents as her father's store expanded to include furniture and toys and her mother rose in the hierarchy of her company and eventually bought the business when the original owner died. As part of their upward mobility, Ms. Prima's parents purchased a house in Harper as well as some other pieces of real estate around Conroy. They waited several years to move, however, because her mother wanted to remain close to her business and because they felt some ambivalence in moving away from their close friends and familiar neighborhood to the distant and immaculate suburbs. Ms. Prima still feels like a stranger when she drives home to the manicured lawns, the perfect houses, and the streets "with no children on them," although she has lived there more than half her life.

The dominant and moving force in Ms. Prima's family has always been her mother. The houses and businesses that the family has amassed are all in her name. She controls the household accounts and transactions, and she initiates and determines all the major decisions.

> My mother was one of the first liberated women that I know of . . . she had a very good head for figures and she's an Aries and Aries people are very dynamic, they're powerful, they're ambitious . . . so having children didn't prevent her from working because she took us right in with her . . . And my father never objected to any of this because even though she had children and she worked from nine to three, she still maintained the home. She still kept us well dressed and well fed and we never felt neglected or wanted for anything. We never came home to an empty house . . . If it was snowing or anything she'd pick me up then she'd go pick my sister up, so we never felt alone. We were always with my mother, I mean as many hours as we were home, she was home. She taught us to cook early and bake and clean the house and sew, crochet and knit.

Not only was Ms. Prima's mother an early feminist, she was also perceived as a superwoman who had a thriving career outside the family and also excelled in performing the traditional mother-wife roles. She speaks of her mother as having boundless energy and a kind of omnipresence that was somewhat overwhelming to her as a child. "I never had my mother's ambition, unfortunately. My sister does. She's a Scorpio. But I never had that ambition, that drive."

Religion played a prominent role in the lives of Ms. Prima's family. They were devout Catholics who attended church every Sunday, took Communion, and went to Confession. Church was not only a place for individual spiritual communication, it was also a central cohesive force in the community—a gathering place where everyone went in their finest to see and be seen, to meet and greet. Although church was a dominant force in her early life, it did not feel all-encompassing because Ms. Prima and her sister did not attend parochial school as did most of their friends in the neighborhood. Their mother felt very strongly that parochial education did not give children an adequate preparation for coping with the more diversified society beyond their immediate community. "My mother did not feel and still does not feel today that a Catholic education is a well-rounded education. She feels that if you're not involved with other children from different ethnic backgrounds you will not be aware of their lives and their contributions." So despite Ms. Prima's rather limited experience in living in a homogeneous, close-knit community, despite her family's fear of the impending threat of the Puerto Rican influx, there was an explicit and verbalized value within the family that supported cultural diversity and pluralism. The expressed value seemed to be a very pragmatic one—a necessary preparation for coping with adult life in the wider society—as well as one that reflected the religious dogma of the Catholic Church.

Catholicism remains a powerful influence on Ms. Prima's adult life, but her attitudes toward institutionalized religion have shifted slightly. She still attends church weekly, but now believes that regular church attendance does not define good Catholicism, neither must one use the priest as an intermediary to speak to God.

> My mother is still very religious. I mean she'll be in the office and every afternoon she'll take out the rosary and she'll say the rosary when there's nobody around . . . She might go to church twice a month or something like that, but my mother is more of a Catholic than half the hypocrites I know that go to church every Sunday, and then come out into the world and destroy people verbally. I don't think that one has to go to church to prove that you're a Catholic or to prove that you're a good Christian. I think you show it by the way you behave and the acts that you do. My mother always prays and always says her rosary. My father does as well. I still pray every night and my sister does as well. We have never stopped that.

Even though Ms. Prima has grown less committed to the idea of conforming to the constraints of institutionalized religion, her interpretation of

Christian ideology and practice has grown more profound and encompassing. Now that she feels that she "can go direct to God" rather than attend Confession and she has "Christ in her own room" to pray to, religion has become increasingly personalized and woven into her everyday experience.

The intimate and deep experiences of family, community, and church, therefore, have had a powerful influence on Ms. Prima's values and beliefs. These institutions have worked together in harmony and continue to have great influence in shaping her adult life. When she speaks now of her community, she is referring to the south side of Conroy rather than to Harper where she has resided for the twenty years since she was ten. When she refers to her family, she is talking about her family of orientation, the family into which she was born and with whom she still lives. Childhood and adulthood are very much entertwined and connected.

Ms. Prima's school career was a difficult string of failures and recoveries. For the most part, she relates her educational experience as painful, discouraging, and unfulfilling, and she still marvels at the fact that she chose a career that is intimately tied to those negative times. From the very beginning she was turned off by school. "I was never a very good student. I never really cared to study . . . It just never meant that much to me. Oh and I remember English. I hated English. I hated reading composition. And the teacher called my mother and said 'Your daughter can't write' and I couldn't write. I hated it . . . My mother was always push, push, push, you've got to do better." By the time Ms. Prima reached junior high, she discovered she was good in math. She found that she enjoyed and excelled in algebra and calculus, although she still hated reading and writing. But math was not valued by her mother, whom she described as a "literature and language" person despite the fact that she made a living in bookkeeping. Ms. Prima feels that her interest in math reflected her strong identification with her father ("who was math oriented")—an identification that was never fully encouraged or sanctioned.

The downhill trend continued in high school, where Ms. Prima was a straight C student. "Great, I'd get some As in math, but there were too many Cs to offset it. So I figured I was going to Secretarial School and I just didn't know what I wanted to do. Since I was a C student, there was very little opportunity for me to get into any kind of college." The first bright moment in her school career came quite unexpectedly when she was admitted to a local junior college and found a math teacher whom she "absolutely adored." For the first time, she felt special and talented. The math teacher was stunned that she only desired to be a secretary and convinced her that she could be a "terrific teacher." When Ms. Prima is asked *why* this math teacher became such an important figure in her life, she appears somewhat confused by the question and responds, "I don't know, something about her personality. She was very easy going, very calm. She demanded a lot but yet you wanted to do it. She was really a wonderful person, I really enjoyed her." She is aware of her attraction to her teacher's personality, but she says little about the behavior and style of this woman who caused an almost magical transformation in her attitude toward learning and teaching. More important, she does not seem to view the process of reflecting on these matters of great interest or consequence. Not only is Ms. Prima not intrigued by why and how she was turned on by this special teacher, she also appears uninterested in understanding or reflecting on the process of her *own* teaching.

I think that part of her indifference lies in the fact that she prefers things to be straightforward and simple, and untangling the social and psychological dimensions of behavior is a complex process. But there is also a certain quality of fatalism that underlies Ms. Prima's stories about her life. In her description of life events, she talks very little about making conscious and deliberate choices and decisions. Things unfold as if by chance, and this sense of determinism leads to very little reflection about what is below the surface. When she describes her mother's driving temperament, she blames it on the stars. "She's an Aries and that's the way they are."

Armed with new-found confidence and inspired by her reawakening with math, Ms. Prima finished junior college successfully and transferred to a large city university. Immediately she perceived it as a threatening place. "I hated it. It was too big. I got lost in it. I can't survive in a place like that." Her advisor was distant and unresponsive. He loaded her down with four heavy math courses and she flunked out within a semester. The university experience was crushing but not debilitating because Ms. Prima continued to search for an educational environment where she could thrive. She found County College, where she enrolled in the education program and took calculus, algebra, and physics over—this time with great success. "There were much smaller classes. The professors there cared. I was having trouble in physics and I would go practically every afternoon to the professor and he would sit down and he would go over it and over it." Throughout her recollections of successful past experiences, Ms. Prima often mentions her need for the support and intimacy of close-knit communities. She feels lost and alone in large, impersonal environments and more comfortable in smaller spaces with more possibilities for direct and continuous contact. This attraction to the familiarity of more circumscribed communities seems related to her childhood experiences in a very tight social network of families and friends where relationships were deep and sustaining and where social norms were clearly defined and largely unquestioned. In a sense, Ms. Prima seeks to establish the clarity and familiarity of her early upbringing in her own classroom, where she puts great emphasis on providing clear structure and regular ritualized routines.

The final shift in Ms. Prima's educational career came when she recognized that the program for math teachers at County College would take her a year longer to complete than courses in elementary education. Although she had no desire to teach reading and writing and was interested only in math, the thought of less time in school was too appealing to pass up, so she switched her major to elementary education. Even though she perceives this last move as a step down—she views a junior high math teacher as having higher status than a primary teacher—she still feels quite impressed, and even surprised, by her own accomplishments. Perhaps school was a painful and disheartening experience, but she seems to feel ultimately rather successful and special. "My English teacher in high school, I met him at my church about a year ago . . . I loved him. He was terrific, but I couldn't do English composition. There was just no way. So when I met him coming out of church, he said, 'I can't believe it, you lost all that weight' and he couldn't believe that I was an elementary teacher, 'You're kidding, you, of all people!' A lot of people couldn't believe I got the job."

Classroom management is the most important key to Ms. Prima's success as a teacher. She views her organizational abilities as the central force in the smooth functioning and productive learning of the children in her classroom. She likes things to move forward smoothly and quickly without a hitch, and when she describes her pedagogical and interactional style, she is likely to speak with a kind of speed and conviction that reveals no ambiguities or questions. Ms. Prima describes herself as very energetic (always getting things done before all the other teachers—her Christmas decorations were up before Thanksgiving), very organized and innovative ("I'm a frustrated decorator and everyone always steals my ideas"), and a natural leader ("I am always heading committees and taking all the responsibility").

Ms. Prima's preoccupation with speed, order, and control reflects her temperament, but it is also related to her conscious belief that energy should be spent economically and productively, that one should be visibly productive in one's work, and that reflection and uncertainty are distracting to forward movement. She points to her mother, who combined abundant energy and sharp organizational skills in her roles as worker, mother, and wife. She was a superwoman who excelled and profited in her work as bookkeeper, who managed to schedule her time so that she was a dedicated caretaker when her children arrived home from school, and who kept her children immaculately dressed and well fed. Ms. Prima's mother taught her daughters not only how to do bookkeeping and secretarial work but also how to organize their time and combine multiple roles. "She would tell us how she would manage . . . She's a great believer in using your time well. She would do all the cooking and put everything in the freezer, so that when she came home she was ready. She made a sauce and made seven containers of sauce and put it in the freezer. That way Monday, you just take your macaroni and you have your meat and your sauce ready to go.'' Ms. Prima recalls having once put a funny ad in a local paper to obtain a summer job. ''College girl desires summer employment. Can type, can bookkeep, can do general office work, 'cause my mother taught me!''

Although Ms. Prima claims not to have inherited the ''driving ambition'' of her mother, she does identify her early socialization as being the major force that shaped her notions of competence and professionalism. A primary component of Ms. Prima's self-image as a professional is her ability to organize and structure classroom activities and materials and her skills in attending to every detail of the day so that nothing goes unanticipated or unexpected. ''My lesson plan book is more detailed than anybody's in the building because I put everything in it. So that if someone comes in and wants to see what one group is doing, you can see. You know, they're reading that book, they're introducing new vocabulary and this is what is to be taught.''

Ms. Prima also believes that professionalism demands efficiency, an immediate and conforming response to bureaucratic details. When Mr. Hamilton, the principal, calls for reports from his teachers, she is proud to be the first to respond. Her immediate compliance with school regulations seems to be a mixture of wanting to please her boss and fulfilling her idealized picture of professionalism. But mostly it seems to be internally inspired. She simply becomes anxious when she begins to feel overwhelmed by unfinished business. She fears a loss of control. ''I try to get my reports in to him [the principal] because I don't want them hanging over my head. We have this interview and assessment and we try to write a big paper on it, and we have to cover certain areas. And I said to Mr. Hamilton when would you like it and he says anytime between now and the end of the school year. Well, I worked on it all weekend and tonight I'm going to copy it over, because I don't want to have that hanging around . . . so there is a lot of clerical work I have to do and I'd just as soon get rid of whatever he's giving me now.''

Much of the drive for the perfect completion of tasks and the orderly structure of events seems to have a competitive thrust. Ms. Prima not only desires to do well and be a good teacher, she also wants to do better than her peers. She prides herself in being the *most* organized and *most* hard-working teacher, and views some of her peers' less conscientious behaviors as unprofessional. ''There are a lot of teachers who do not live up to the profession they obviously have chosen. They use their free time very carelessly. I cannot get over teachers reading the newspaper . . . I'll walk by their rooms and they're at the desks reading the newspaper . . . or teachers who like to talk in the hall while classes are waiting . . . There are teachers in this building who love to waste time and I don't have time to waste.''

Ms. Prima's attitudes toward her work make her feel somewhat isolated from some of her colleagues. It is an isolation that grows out of perceived differences in professional standards and competence between her and some other teachers. She does feel a sense of superiority in relation to her colleagues, not so much a superiority based on natural talents but one based on her commitment to hard work and diligence. Her criticisms are mostly directed at teachers in the upper grades at the school who have been there a long time and grown lax. In general, Ms. Prima likes and respects the other primary-grade teachers who are similar in age, experience, and attitudes. Still, her professional alliances are not primarily with other teachers, except for occasional friends who share her professional point of view. Rather, her primary alliance seems to have developed with Mr. Hamilton, the principal, who values her institutional commitment, her organized and productive classroom environment, and her attention to bureaucratic details. Ms. Prima feels rewarded by his expressed approval of her efforts and feels supported by his protection of her individual interests. "I can go to him [the principal] any time something's bothering me, and we will sit down together and we will talk about it. You know, what his feelings are, what my feelings are, what I should do . . . He backs me 100 percent. I do not have to worry about him backing me up . . . If a parent gets on me, he gets super defensive and he gets on them and he doesn't let any parent talk to me wrong or anything. I don't think, though, that that is the general case . . . Any time you have a special person who will give that much, he'll back you 100 percent."

Throughout Ms. Prima's educational and professional career she has initiated and sustained this kind of special attachment with people in positions of authority, who have had a great impact on her development as a teacher. She describes these important others as role models whose behavior and style she wanted to imitate and whose approval and praise she valued highly. For example, one of the great cornerstones of Ms. Prima's teaching is her creativity, mostly defined in terms of the visible and innovative way she decorates her classroom. She can trace back her creative focus to a special relationship she developed with her supervising professor during her student teaching. "My advisor was a great believer in creativity . . . so I did a lot with games and went crazy with decorations . . . and little by little I developed the ability to be more creative in my teaching and in my lesson plan . . . You know, having fun while learning a skill, playing a game at the same time. So you see, when my advisor came to evaluate me I would definitely be more creative, because that is what he liked. And so perhaps I was pushed even more so by the knowledge that that's what he liked. Because I wanted to please him, to get a good mark."

Some of the central concepts Ms. Prima describes as part of her philosophy of education seem to be related to special relationships she had with people who played a central role in her professional development. These concepts emerged as she began to identify with her more experienced mentor and to form an alliance that was focused on pleasing her. For example, when describing her priorities in teaching and the structure and atmosphere she seeks to create in her classroom, Ms. Prima remarks: "I believe the children have to have skills, that there should be a degree of freedom in which to attain those skills. I like working with a small group and having children of an equal ability. I like the way the children know that when they finish what they have to do, they have the freedom to move to do what they want to within certain limitations." This commitment to a "traditional-open" classroom is connected to her experiences as a second-year teacher in a school where she was greatly influenced by the educational philosophy of the principal. During that school year, she had thoroughly incorporated the educational perspectives of her mentor and formed a very special relationship with her. "She believed very much that children have to learn skills . . . There can be a fun time where you fool around and things like that but you've got to get your basic skills in. If she liked you and liked the work you did in the classroom, she would do anything for you. If she didn't like what you did in the room or if you gave her trouble in any way, it would be like the North Pole freeze. But with me she and I got along very well and my room was right next to her office."

The professional development of Ms. Prima is, therefore, enmeshed in her strong identifications with role models who held positions of relative power and influence over the course of her life. From her mother she inherited great energy, organizational skills, and the tendency to act decisively rather than reflectively. Her creative talents developed out of her desire to emulate and please her college advisor, who admired innovative students. And her general philosophy of education reflects a special rapport that Ms. Prima enjoyed with a woman principal early in her teaching career. She admired the principal's values and style, recognized that their temperaments were mutually compatible, and very much enjoyed the special rewards and attention that came with being the "chosen one."

Ms. Prima gives her *whole* self to teaching. Teaching is at the very center of her life and is the role that most clearly defines her self-image. Most of her waking hours are spent preparing curricular materials, designing and creating decorations for the room, serving on numerous professional committees, working toward her master's degree in evening school. She does not make a clear separation between her family and work spheres and feels that one flows easily into the other. Ms. Prima's definition of her professional role is all-encompassing. It includes a deep commitment to effective teaching of intellectual skills and high reading scores for her children, but it also includes a wide array of other institutional and personal commitments to the prettiest classroom, the most detailed lesson plan, and the most conscientious response to administrative directives.

The most important agenda in Ms. Prima's first-grade class is learning to read. It is the pedagogical task that receives most of her attention, it is the primary basis for a child's social position in the classroom, and it is one of the chief criteria by which she judges her success as a teacher. Since reading is Ms. Prima's major preoccupation, she spends a great deal of energy choosing, shaping, and structuring her reading groups and finding the most effective and efficient pedagogical strategies to use with them. In assigning children to reading groups, she uses an array of sources that include standardized test scores, evaluations from the kindergarten teacher, and responses to reading readiness materials. She is also very interested in gathering any information about the children's family background that may influence their intellectual and social development in school. "The folder might say that parents are divorced, child is living with father. It might have some other kind of background information like a medical history record that might give you some help as to any problems that might develop in the room, maybe some social behavior problems." Although Ms. Prima does give weight to the background information in school records, she does not necessarily allow these data to influence her judgments. Indeed, a negative or pejorative evaluation from a former teacher seems to create a special challenge for her. She is inspired to overcome the prior difficulties, to save the child from further deterioration, and to increase her positive reputation as a teacher.

The most important source of information used in assigning children to reading groups is Ms. Prima's own judgment. She depends most heavily on her perceptions of the children's skills in coping with the reading materials presented at the beginning of the year. The first few weeks of school are a time for observation and listening, a time to remain on the periphery and discover the developmental potential of each child. Although this is a time of observation and relative inaction on Ms. Prima's part, it is highly organized and not at all haphazard.

Ms. Prima does not passively watch the natural and spontaneous interactions of children, neither does she wait for them to initiate contact with materials of their own choice. Rather, she presents materials and directs their behavior, then observes their competence in relating to the intellectual content. "In the beginning the groups were tentative so we didn't name them. I would just call up certain people and would try them in the group, and then some kids were too good for the group. Like some children that I did put in Group II, they were really too good for Group II, so I pushed them into Group I. And a couple of kids who I originally thought should have been in Group I, it became obvious that they were just floundering, and I put them back in Group II. Usually the people I chose for my bottom group were pretty well set.''

Ms. Prima remembers making two miscalculations in assigning children to reading groups. In one case a child was repeating first grade so that she assumed that he would not be eligible for placement in the top group. As she began listening to him function in Group II, she recognized that he had a large and sophisticated vocabulary and that he read quite fluently, so she moved him up to Group I. In the second case, Ms. Prima's fond recollections of the girl's older sibling obscured her objectivity. "I had Linda's older sister and her sister was in my first group, and I know the whole family, they are lovely children. So I figured that she should be in that group. But she doesn't retain her vocabulary words as fast as most of the [Group I] kids do. Most of them, you present it, in ten minutes they know it . . . all you have to do is reinforce it maybe two or three times thereafter. So Linda went from Group I to Group II.''

Interestingly, the main basis for Ms. Prima's decisions about grouping children is their ability to handle the intellectual material. She claims to give no attention to the psychological or social dimensions of the child when making group assignments; neither does she consider the chemistry of interacting personalities or the existence of already established social networks among children. When Ms. Prima is questioned about the place of these nonacademic considerations in her grouping of children, her response is almost one of surprise. It is not that she strongly argues against their inclusion or is opposed to progressive notions of attending to the "whole child." She simply appears uninterested. She seems to consider the dimensions of motivation, psyche, and personality structure complicating factors that obscure the picture and lead to confusion and inaction on the part of the teacher. So Ms. Prima clings to the relatively objective criteria of academic skills, and reasons that attention to the details of a child's psyche or to the development of his social skills is an unnecessarily complex way of dealing with a straightforward task and does not contribute to the positive experience of the child. "If there has been a personality conflict of some nature, I try to separate them in the group, have them sit at opposite sides of the table. But I have them stay in the same group . . . because most of them all get along with each other anyway.''

Ms. Prima's general lack of interest in the social and psychological dimensions of children is also revealed in her perceptions of competition in the classroom. She strongly believes that the children recognize no differences among the reading groups and that no competitive status system has evolved in the classroom. According to her, part of the reason why the children do not recognize differences is that the reading groups were not labeled by the teacher as I, II, and III or top, middle, and bottom. After assigning children to the three groups, Ms. Prima offered them the opportunity to name themselves, and they chose the Vanillas (Group I), the Chocolates (Group II), and the Pistachios (Group III). "They don't question the differences between the groups, maybe because they are so young . . . But they don't see any reason to be upset that they are in the Chocolates or with the Vanillas. And the people who are in the Pistachios aren't anywhere *near* the Vanillas or the Chocolates. See, the Vanillas and Chocolates are in the same book. They just happen to be maybe two or three stories ahead of the others. But the Pistachios are in an entirely separate program. They are in a linguistic program and they don't even question it."

Ms. Prima has never heard children exclaim, "Oh, you're in the dumb group," or "You're in that low group," or "You only read baby words," so she assumes that the children do not recognize the differences of competence and status in the classroom. She makes this claim even though she has deliberately accentuated the differences among the groups by designating some of the more advanced children as "helpers" in the classroom. The Vanillas are defined as surrogate teachers, and when one of the Pistachios is having difficulty with a reading or writing assignment, he is supposed to approach one of the Vanillas for help and advice. Only if one of the Vanillas is unable to give a satisfactory answer is the child supposed to appeal to the teacher. Not only are the Vanillas given high status as mini-teachers and knowledgeable ones, but their superior presence keeps the Pistachios at a greater distance from the teacher because she is available only as a second line of appeal.

The Pistachios are not only judged to be the least skilled academically, but are also thought to be the ones with behavior problems. Ms. Prima theorizes that there is a dynamic relationship between their behavior and their reading difficulties, but she usually tries to confront the problem by insisting on more academic structure and control. In fact, one sometimes has the feeling that Ms. Prima does not disentangle behavioral and intellectual crises in the classroom, that from her perspective they are such parallel phenomena that they should not be differentiated. So her attitude toward the Pistachios is one of tight control and supervision—over both their behavior and their skill development.

> I always like to work with the lowest group first. I like to get them because this way I can give them their work and they are not fidgeting; because sometimes they can disturb other groups. So I like to get them first . . . Generally that is where my talkers are, in that lower group, so I like to give them their work because their papers do take them a long time, because they are slower doing them. What tends to happen with the Pistachios is that they see the Chocolates finishing, or they see the

Vanillas finishing . . . and they couldn't *possibly* have finished yet . . .
and all of a sudden I see all they've done is shove the papers in their
desks.

Even though Ms. Prima regards the Pistachios as less skilled academically
and as potentially disruptive to the classroom, she claims to enjoy working
with them the most. Her special feelings for the Pistachios seem to be related to her desire to develop the potential of *all* children and especially to
work wonders on those who have special difficulties adjusting to school life.
She enjoys witnessing the transformations in their behavior and attitudes
toward the school. These significant and visible changes in "problem" children are more interesting to her than watching the smooth and steady progress of the more highly skilled and adaptive children. Ms. Prima also gets
pleasure out of the enthusiasm with which the Pistachios tackle their work.

I enjoy them all, but it seems that the lowest group is more spontaneous
and expressive . . . We play a game with a vocabulary word, start one
word going that way and one word going this way, and then they have
to switch. And there are a couple of them that really get so excited, and
they start laughing and giggling. It was funny. I only did it with the
bottom group, then the giggling and laughing was turning *me* on . . .
then I started hearing from the Chocolates, "Oh, can we play that
game?" And then I started hearing from the Vanillas. They watched
the enjoyment that the bottom group had and they wanted to do the
same thing.

Ms. Prima shares a very special kind of rapport with the Pistachios, one
that delights the children in that group and is inspiring to her as a teacher.
The children in the other two groups seem to perceive the special quality of
interaction and seek to replicate that experience in their own group.

The pervasive theme that runs through Ms. Prima's description of grouping patterns in the classroom is one of clarity, organization, and efficiency.
Even when she describes a period of tentative decision making in reference
to group assignments, one senses that she tolerates only the minimum of uncertainty and reflection in making her initial judgments of children's capabilities. Her need for structure and symmetry is seen in how she organizes
the presentation of reading skills and also in the numerical exactitude of her
grouping patterns. It is extremely important to Ms. Prima that groups have
identical form and follow identical formats. "I don't like to have one group
heavily weighted over the other, like one group have ten, another have
three. It doesn't benefit anyone. The most you really should have, ideally, is
seven, but most of my groups are eight. First of all, each child must be able
to comfortably sit at the table. You are able to get to each child more times
with more words, with board work, with problems, with giving sentences,
with oral reading, and with silent reading."

It also seems to be important to classroom structure that the groups be clearly differentiated. Ms. Prima claims that the skills and competencies of the children in groups I and II are very similar and one would be hard pressed to discern the differences among them. But after assigning children to these groups, she proceeds to *treat* them differently and thus create a differentiation that was almost invisible before. These differences are reinforced over time as the groups receive different reading assignments and respond to slightly different pedagogical modes from Ms. Prima.

> I like to keep the Chocolates a few stories behind the Vanillas. I purposely didn't start the Chocolates at the same time, I waited. I did more reading readiness with them, maybe two or three days, while I got the Vanillas going. What I do is get one group going at a time . . . Once I get that first group going, then maybe two days later I'll start the second group and I'll spend two days with them, getting them going in the exact procedure . . . and then the following week I'll get the third group going . . . and so by a week and a half everybody's going at their own pace.

Her decision to accentuate the differences between the reading groups does not seem to reflect unconscious or conscious favoritism of one group over the other. It does appear to be related to Ms. Prima's wish for clarity and classification. If there are three groups, then they should be distinguishable as representing the top, the middle, and the bottom. This is true even when the distribution of children's talents do not easily conform to those configurations, when, left alone, the only group that might spontaneously emerge would be the lowest group of readers. The irony of the structured cleavages among groups is that once Ms. Prima has established the differentiations, the pedagogical structures and methods of presentation she uses are almost identical within each group. "The basic setup is always the same . . . I spend one day introducing the story, doing my vocabulary, doing one or two skills, and silent reading. I will help them if they forget how to spell a word. I'll say, well, put your sounds together and see if you can come up with it. And then on the second day I review the vocabulary; they put it in a sentence, their own sentence. We might review the previous day's skills or perhaps introduce two more skills and then we do oral reading."

Grouping children for instruction corresponds to Ms. Prima's pedagogical style and educational values. She strongly believes that organizing children into groups based on intellectual skills is the most effective and efficient mode of structuring learning. In fact, she is so wedded to the grouping tradition that she finds it difficult to imagine other classroom forms that would be realistic and workable. Ms. Prima views grouping as the optimal strategy for individualizing instruction. She thinks of the group as supportive of individual expression, rather than limiting or inhibiting it, and she imagines that true individualization (that is, teaching children on a one-to-one basis) would be impossibly chaotic and energy consuming. Most important, Ms. Prima recognizes that teaching small groups of children is adaptive to her temperament and personality. She prefers the orderly, structured environment and ritualized patterns of behavior that grouping permits. Also, grouping seems to allow her a comfortable relationship with the children—one that is close enough to know students' capabilities and needs and therefore teach effectively, but one that is not so intimate that it might obscure her objectivity and status as a teacher.

Ms. Prima's perspective on groups of children in her class is far more insightful and comprehensive than her perceptions of individual children. In other words, she conceives of the class in terms of a structure of small groups rather than an array of individuals. She always knows exactly where a reading group is in a certain book, what skills they have just mastered, and what they will need to review the next day. She not only carries these curricular agendas around in her head, she also has the details of each group carefully written into her lesson-plan book.

The process of evaluation is also highly systematized and group-related. Each day Ms. Prima publicly evaluates the behavior and accomplishment of the three reading groups rather than making judgments of individual academic development. The children, therefore, tend to become more concerned about the group score and very intolerant of those individuals whose failures and mistakes might diminish the collective effort.

> The way they behave at the reading table, the way they listen to their lesson, the way they read their books, the way they answer questions, the way they do their vocabulary words, and also their seat work is evaluated after all three groups have had their reading. So they get a mark not only for everything they do up here at the reading table, but they get a mark for everything they do at their desks. The whole group does . . . whether they work up here together or whether they work at their desks singly . . . The whole thing is encompassed. So at the end of the morning they'll ask me how the group did. And I rate them . . . They came in first, they came in second, they came in third. Well, there have been many many days when the Pistachios came in first and the Vanillas came in second or third . . . and the Vanillas are the top group . . . so that kind of diminishes the fact that the Vanillas will always be on top.

Perhaps because the group is her major focus, her primary unit of description, Ms. Prima does not give the same perceptive attention to the individual development of children within each group. Part of her tendency to respond to groupings of children is, I am sure, related to her wish to give structure and order to the classroom environment. It is certainly much easier to keep a few group agendas in one's mind than to be in touch with the individual social and intellectual patterns of each child. Trying to be responsive to the unique qualities and special needs of each child would be a complex and confusing process for Ms. Prima, who seeks to diminish the differences and reduce the complexities of classroom life. "If an open classroom is run correctly, it is much more demanding than my job. I have seen very well run open classrooms and I would *never* run one. Because I could not have everything so precise, knowing all these things going on at the same time. This boy has got his card and it tells where he is, on what page in reading and math . . . you have got to track every single child. You know, I couldn't do it."

One also has a sense that Ms. Prima does not really believe that a preoccupation with individual needs is a good pedagogical strategy nor does she feel it is necessarily beneficial for the child. One of her favorite ways of getting children involved in their reading groups, for instance, is to play a fast-moving game that demands the same thing of each child around the circle. Children get involved in the momentum, the spirit of the moment, and quickly learn the skill that is being taught. She does not permit stopping for the recalcitrant one nor indulging the individual wish of a single child, because that would be giving in to their weakness and that would destroy the cohesion and direction of the group. Nonrecognition (or at least nonindulgence) of the individual needs of children, therefore, is viewed as a deliberate pedagogical method.

Although Ms. Prima resists making differentiations among children within the classroom, she is cognizant of differences in their lives outside of school. She is very knowledgeable and expressive about the family backgrounds of each child and often draws parallels between home conditions and intellectual competence in school. In some ways Ms. Prima relates to individual children by reference to their parentage: "You look at the mother and you see the child." Children are primarily seen as miniature versions of their parents, and the sociological dimensions of race, social class, religion, ethnicity, and family structure become the primary factors for discriminating among them. Some of the differentiating themes that Ms. Prima identifies as having a perceptible impact on the child's patterns of behavior and achievement in school follow:

(1) Children who live in a home with a mother and a father have a better chance for school success than children of single-parent families. "Mark comes from a very solid family. They expect certain behavior . . . They live in a two-family house, two parents, a good home, well dressed, well-kept. He has loads of uncles and aunts who love him and take him on trips. He's going to go into school solid and he's going to come out solid."

(2) Children who live in homes where the parent takes a caring, attentive

attitude toward learning and responds to the teacher's requests for tutoring at home will be higher achievers than children whose parents are uncooperative and irresponsible toward their children's education. "Some of the children have parents who just don't care. They give that job and responsibility to the teacher. You take care of it. They don't realize that if it's not reinforced at home, that some of these kids just won't progress."

(3) Children whose parents are highly educated and attend the university are more likely to be intellectually gifted and academically achieving than children whose parents live in the public (low-income) projects. "Generally if you get a class that has a lot of university children in it, you generally have a good class . . . Parents are very concerned about their education. The children come in brighter because they have the opportunity. They have the environment, they have their parents. They have books, they have parents who sit down and read with them."

(4) Children whose families are on welfare and public assistance are less likely to be good students than those children whose parents work hard for a living. "The family has all kinds of problems. The mother especially. She's alone, she's on welfare, she's completely disheveled . . . Jason will come to school with pants not fitting, undershirt inside out, shirt not properly buttoned, hair not combed, sometimes a dirty face."

(5) Children who come from families with only one child are likely to have more difficulty in school than children who have siblings at home. The single child experiences more pressure to succeed and has a relationship with her parents that is too overwhelming and intense. She probably knows less well how to get along with peers. "Sibyl had a very difficult time in the beginning of the year . . . couldn't remember words day to day, couldn't remember sounds. So she started taking some of the lessons home and her mother started working on them . . . Her mother works at the university library. Sibyl is an only child. So I would give homework and they would fight every night, and I mean fight. They would have battles before she would do two papers. And I said forget it, and she started doing the papers on her own. Then, her reading improved."

Ms. Prima frequently characterizes children in these terms and speaks with certainty about the power and influence of home background on school performance. For instance, Jason and Dennis are described as coming from infamous, disorderly housing-project families. Jason's mother has three boys, each with a different father. He comes to school slovenly, is easily distracted, does not attend to school tasks, and has little self control. He has a very high IQ, but his social and psychological problems seem to get in the way of his academic progress. When Ms. Prima tried to enlist the help and cooperation of his mother, she showed the same irresponsibility as her son and responded in a hostile way when she was prodded by the teacher.

Dennis is the son of a mother whom Ms. Prima describes as "out of it," perhaps retarded and very slow. She rarely cooperates with the teacher's requests for conferences and is generally unresponsive and lazy. Dennis's mother and Jason's mother have been known to enter into physical battles over their sons, often arguing over fights their sons have had in school. Ms. Prima finds parallels between the social deviance and disorderly conduct of the mothers and the similar behavior of their sons in school.

But Ms. Prima is quick to point to exceptions, examples of children and families living in the horrible, oppressive environment of the same housing project, whose lives are well ordered and secure and whose relationship to the school is productive and positive. Linda, a black Puerto Rican girl, lives in the same environment as Jason and Dennis where "you find kids who are fourteen or fifteen and have been arrested five times and kids who are sky-high on dope; they black out and have to be rushed to the hospital," but she comes from an "intact" family who dress her beautifully, who spend hours combing her hair and making it neat for school, who have structure and discipline in their household, and who have a great appreciation for the work of the teacher.

Ms. Prima is also aware of those university children who experience a great deal of economic and intellectual abundance but are neglected emotionally by their parents. She feels that many of these parents become overly preoccupied with their own lives and give minimal attention to their children. Also, she disagrees with their overly progressive and indulgent attitudes toward child rearing and their unstructured home environments.

Ms. Prima seems most perceptive when she distances herself from stereotypic categories long enough to recognize the exceptions, surprises, and paradoxes of reality. Her special attachment to Linda, for instance, seems to be related to the fact that Linda defies the rule; she dramatically contradicts the stereotypic image of a young black Puerto Rican living in conditions of extreme poverty. Ms. Prima greatly admires this child's fortitude and character and recognizes the incredible strength of her family. This admiration is expressed in a classic teacher-pet relationship. "I go up to her and I hug her all the time . . . she's one of my favorites. I told her one day that I was going to take her home and her mother said I could . . . I could take her for a whole weekend . . . Everybody likes Linda and I give her a lot of responsibility. If I have an errand to go on, she'll go up to the third floor. She knows exactly what to do."

Although Ms. Prima uses the sociological variables of social class and family structure to differentiate the academic potential of children in her classroom (but readily pointing to exceptions and paradoxes), she is very skeptical of the psychological labels that are often attached to children's behaviors in school. Her skepticism reflects her general tendency to avoid and negate the psychological roots of behavior and personality when she is teaching children; but it also reflects a very profound concern that negative psychological labels can do irreversible damage to the child and his parents.

The story of Nicky reveals Ms. Prima's attitudes toward psychoemotional explanations of behavior problems. Nicky, a white boy from a single-parent, middle-income family, has had a great deal of trouble adjusting to the demands of school life. Ms. Prima describes him as extremely bright and articulate, with the vocabulary of an adult, but very immature psychologically and socially. Before coming to first grade, Nicky had great interpersonal struggles in kindergarten and gained a school-wide reputation as angry, wild, and belligerent. His anxious and helpless mother began to seek help for Nicky from teachers and counselors within the school and from a mental health center in the community.

By the end of kindergarten the counselors at the mental health center suggested that Nicky repeat the year in order to give him more of a chance to mature socially and adapt more positively to the constraints of the school environment. Ms. Prima argued strongly and persuasively for his promotion to the first grade and committed a lot of her energy to reversing the disruptive patterns in Nicky's behavior. Her commitment to Nicky's improvement became a serious challenge that seemed to touch a stubborn nerve—one that defied defeat. She kept saying, "I'll see this through to the end. I'll keep him in my class and he'll finish first grade even if I have a heart attack in the process." Her persistence and dedication seemed partly related to a genuine interest in tapping Nicky's unusual intellectual potential, but Ms. Prima also saw this as a challenge to her professionalism as a teacher. In her mind, a good teacher succeeds not only with easy and good students but also with those who present difficulties and problems. As a *very* good teacher she should be able to overcome the problems that the previous teacher has not adequately solved. Ms. Prima rises to the challenge of responding to classroom "problems" and gets great pleasure out of winning over a child whom everyone else views as a disaster. She also believes that judgments about grade placement should not be made on the basis of social-psychological dimensions.

How can you put Nicky back into kindergarten when he is so bright and intelligent, regardless of whether he is working up to his ability. That will come. I'm not worried about that. My idea of keeping a child back is to keep him back because he's not performing adequately in most of his subjects. Social behavior comes into it but I don't think social behavior should count as much as academic behavior . . . perhaps three quarters academic and a quarter social. I don't think you say, well this child gets kept back because he was socially unacceptable for first grade . . . How do you as a teacher, a psychologist, or an educator justify that kind of premise?

In Ms. Prima's view, therefore, academic talent and potential should be the primary focus of all who are concerned with the child's school life. Psychological explanations of classroom problems are unjustifiable in terms of the explicit purpose of school in this society. More important, psychological labels obscure the intellectual problems and potentially damage the child's motivation or will to change. During the year, a psychologist from the mental health center determined that Nicky was "minimally brain damaged" after administering a series of perceptual tests to him. This diagnosis was told to Nicky's mother, who was depressed and overwhelmed by the news, and to Ms. Prima, who mistrusted and challenged the psychologist's perceptions. "This Dr. Anderson [at the mental health center] really psyched this mother out! I don't think a doctor has the right to do that . . . she came in here practically destroyed. She'd never heard of minimal brain damage. She's a supersensitive person and she started crying . . . 'What have I done to Nicky? What was it in my genes that made me do this to Nicky?' All kinds of guilt complexes . . . I don't think the psychologist had any finesse, he just went *bang!*"

Ms. Prima was greatly angered by the lack of sensitivity on the part of the psychologist in translating clinical information to a layperson, and she was also critical of the diagnosis. Although she recognizes that in the eyes of society a psychologist is the presumed authority on mental disorders and is generally given more deference than a classroom teacher, she feels that psychologists are often less knowledgeable about the child's response to real-life conditions than teachers and are oriented toward identifying pathology rather than health. Despite their lofty status, the psychologists' limited vision often leads to misdiagnosis and mislabeling. Once a "problem" child is labeled and categorized by a psychologist, school personnel feel justified in their lack of success with him. Ms. Prima speaks critically of this process of rationalization for failure. It releases the teachers from feeling any responsibility for showing improvements in the child, and it increases the amount of subsidiary funds given to the school to support problem children.

> Every kid that's got something wrong with him either has minimal brain damage, learning difficulties, or he's hyperactive. I've got a funny feeling we're labeling too many kids so that we can get the money from the federal programs to support those things. When you see twelve out of twenty-two in a class who are classified LD [learning disabled] . . . when you see those kinds of statistics, I become suspicious of them and I certainly don't trust them . . . And I'm getting a little tired of teachers who say, "I've got to get him into the LD program." I think too many teachers are rushing into classifying him. Get him out of the room so he can go somewhere else and they don't have to worry about him.

THERE ARE consistent themes that move through Ms. Prima's childhood, schooling, and teaching—themes that reveal an energetic, focused, and straightforward person who engages the world by structuring and ordering the environment and events over which she has control; who is not much interested in reflecting on her own behaviors or attending to the motivations of others; who leads an adult life that is very much influenced by her childhood experiences.

A certain fatalism seems to underly Ms. Prima's temperamental bias toward nonreflection. One thinks of her in motion, moving with great speed and rarely pausing to consider the consequences of her actions or stopping to anticipate and ponder future directions. Her tendencies toward action rather than reflection, her wish not to confront the complexities of life, her history of stumbling into circumstances rather than making deliberate choices seem related to a view of life as being already determined. She feels comfortable describing personality types by referring to the astrological sign under which a person was born, rather than searching out the psychodynamic origins of personality.

Ms. Prima feels that in a smoothly functioning and well-structured classroom, individual differences will be almost invisible. Observation and diagnosis of the individual needs of children will diminish as the routines and rules of the classroom are thoroughly internalized by children and as *groups* become the primary focus of the teacher. Ms. Prima, having socialized her children to the prescribed patterns of classroom life, spends her energies attending to the progress of groups of children. When she is asked to give holistic descriptions of individual children in her classroom, she is somewhat at a loss. She finds it difficult to fully describe a child without reference to family background variables. In fact, she sees a correlation between social background variables (home environment, family structure, education, and social class) and the child's chances for success in school. Ironically, Ms. Prima does not view these sociological differentiations as potentially discriminatory, but she does believe that the psychological labels used by school personnel are prejudicial, unjustified, and potentially damaging to children and parents.

Ms. Prima's mediocre history in school seems to have given her a perspective on good teaching and a special identification with those children who have difficulty in school. Because she experienced the pain of academic failure and the boredom of being on the periphery of school life, she sees her professional task as one of including *everyone* in the classroom and permitting no one to fall by the wayside in failure. Her favorite group of students are those who have the most severe academic and behavioral difficulties, because in them she can see the most visible and promising changes, and perhaps because in them she sees herself. Also, they provide the active challenge, the test of whether she is a "good" teacher. Finally, the "problem" children give her the opportunity to outdo her colleagues, who are most often viewed as competitors rather than allies. Competitiveness is one of the traits that pervades Ms. Prima's teaching and inspires her to encourage and support the success of children who were once labeled impossible failures.

Ms. Prima sees herself as very fair and just in her treatment of children. Fair, to her, is defined by the structured inclusion of everyone in classroom life. The structure defies inequality. Everyone must follow the rules, which are made visible and understandable to all. Her strategies for teaching reading are the same for all groups, and everyone in the reading circle gets a chance to participate. Fairness and equality are assured by providing an unbiased, highly anticipatable environment and set of classroom procedures.

Dividing children into hierarchical and differentiated reading groups is not perceived by Ms. Prima as unfair or discriminatory because the groups receive equal amounts of time and are presented with work that conforms to their abilities and makes them feel equally successful. Grouping is also viewed as a method for responding to initial differences in academic abilities and moving children toward greater homogeneity. The educational goal is to have a class full of readers. There will obviously be some who are very advanced and reading at third-grade level, but Ms. Prima stresses her goals for the class in terms of realistic and attainable minimums—everyone should have completed the first grade reader by the end of the year.

Ms. Prima's ability to teach everyone has gained her a reputation as one of the school's best teachers. Based on her excellent record in raising reading scores, parents often make special requests that their children be placed in her classroom, and the principal speaks proudly of her talents as a creative and demanding teacher. Her professional success is very much related to her realistic assessment of her own strengths, weaknesses, and preferences. Her choice of teaching strategies and curricular goals stresses those aspects of the educational process that emphasize her best qualities and make her feel most comfortable. She is aware that she is fast-moving, impatient, and nonreflective, that she thrives on organization and structure; thus, she creates a classroom environment that supports those aspects of her character. Ms. Prima purposely does not venture into the more complex and "messy" world of open classrooms because she knows that would match neither her skills nor her temperament. Likewise, she focuses on intellectual content and ignores the psychosocial issues of classroom life because she devalues those dimensions of interaction and feels uneasy searching out the motivations and personalities of children.

Beyond the personal comfort of an ordered classroom environment, Ms. Prima also believes that structure encourages the intellectual agenda of school. In her view, school should be a place for learning to read and write. She works to counterbalance the "modern" rhetoric of the educational literature that talks about the development of the "whole" child, and she reacts negatively to the highly-educated, liberal parents or the "unrealistic" school psychologists who expect her to appreciate and respond to the unique and complex nature of the individual child. Ms. Prima thrives in the autonomous context of the classroom, isolated from the intrusions of parents and community and from the petty, nonprofessional behavior of her colleagues. There she is free to create an environment that is full of hard work, structure, achievement, and beauty.

Synthesis   *Jean V. Carew*

The major themes that emerged from our many conversations with Ms. Prima are well reflected in the quantitative analysis of our direct observation in her classroom. The two sets of data are generally consistent, although not on every point. One particularly tantalizing contradiction concerns Ms. Prima's relationship to black children. We shall address this issue after we have considered the many points of correspondence between the interview and observation data.

Like Ms. Allen, Ms. Prima placed considerably more emphasis on academic instruction and classroom management than did the two teachers' counterparts in the Outer School. Nearly 90 percent of interactions between Ms. Prima and her pupils occurred in structured academic contexts, 77 percent in reading-activity contexts, and 61 percent in small reading groups. These percentages are similar to her co-teacher's at the Inner School and considerably larger than the corresponding figures for the two teachers in the Outer School. In both classrooms at the Inner School reading was clearly the primary item on the day's agenda. Ms. Prima's three clearly ranked reading groups, the Vanillas, Chocolates, and Pistachios, were called up in set order, low to high rank, on every one of our observations.

The quantitative analysis also provides a picture of Ms. Prima as a highly efficient manager of her classroom. Generally, the less efficient the teacher, the more time is absorbed by procedural matters. Of the four teachers, Ms. Prima spent least time in management activities (7 percent) and least time interacting with children on procedural issues (15 percent). Her brisk, well-structured approach is also well indicated by the fact that 49 percent of her interactions with children were easily coded in the Structured Interaction Observation protocol.

These data are entirely in accord with the previous description of Ms. Prima as a teacher highly skilled in structuring and controlling her classroom environment, one who plans carefully, moves with speed and decisiveness, and applies the same set of clearly visible rules and expectations to all her pupils. But there is another side to this picture of super-efficiency: academic focus, clarity of goals, and brisk management are not always associated with superior skill at interpersonal relationships. Ms. Prima is a case in point. On variables denoting "child-centeredness" such as the use of open and free questions and positive evaluations of children's responses, she ranked third or fourth among the four teachers, considerably lower than Ms. Allen, her equally academically-oriented and efficient co-teacher at the Inner School. Conversely, Ms. Prima was the teacher who most often took issue with children for their inappropriate behaviors, scolded and criticized them, and rejected their requests. Concomitantly, children in her classroom engaged in relatively less appropriate and expressive behaviors and in more dependent and inappropriate behaviors than in her co-teacher's classroom. In Ms. Prima's case, therefore, it seems that academic goals and efficiency were achieved at considerable cost. The children in Ms. Prima's classroom certainly spent large amounts of time enjoyably engaged in learning basic academic skills, and this concentration paid off impressively: at the end of first grade all fifteen children who were tested were reading at or above second-grade level, and five were reading at or above third-grade level. Where they may have come up short is in precisely those aspects of socioemotional development that Ms. Prima seemed to dismiss in our interviews as unimportant to her concept of teaching.

It will be recalled from the previous section that Ms. Prima's approach to children exhibiting emotional or behavioral problems was to focus even more heavily on rules and academic tasks. In the interviews she seemed uninterested in temperamental or other socioemotional differences in the behavior of individual children unless these blatantly interfered with their academic performance or adherence to rules. This lack of interest in children as individuals along with her emphasis on control and order affected her relationships with her pupils in a curious way. The observation data show that she was *more* likely to discriminate among individuals, treating certain children very differently from others. Thus, five of the twenty children in her class received either very high or very low amounts of attention as compared to Ms. Allen's, her co-teacher's, class in which only one child received such exceptional treatment. Not surprising, excessive attention from Ms. Prima mostly came in the form of negative reinforcement for inappropriate behavior, which the children in question also exhibited disproportionately.

We turn finally to an issue on which the interview and observation data are, at first blush, less in accord. In the behavior observation data Ms. Prima was the only one of the four teachers who consistently seemed to discriminate between black and white children. In her classroom, blacks were the favored group. On academic matters Ms. Prima treated black and white children similarly, but she was more likely to positively reinforce black children, grant their requests, engage in humor and in nonacademic playful exchanges, and to ask open questions of them. Thus, one might characterize Ms. Prima's behavior toward blacks, especially black girls, as being relatively more child-centered, accepting, indulgent, playful, and relaxed, a description that also fits Mses. Allen's and Edwards' interactions with all their pupils, both black and white. The enigma in this case is that Ms. Prima gave little hint of special consideration for black children in our conversations with her, although one might have expected her to do so explicitly when speaking to a black interviewer.

But the puzzle is not as difficult as it first appears. Ms. Prima often referred to variables such as social class, family structure, and parental attitudes as directly influencing the child's progress and behavior in school, the perceived connections being the conventional ones that give children from stable, two-parent, educationally-oriented families a decisive advantage. At the same time, there were two groups of parents with whom Ms. Prima felt particularly uncomfortable: the snobbish, overeducated, permissive, and demanding university students and the aggressive, undereducated, disorganized, and irresponsible parents who failed to show respect for her authority as a teacher. In contrast, the parents she felt closest to and the children with whom she identified most strongly were those from the stable, diligent working class who believed in education and appreciated and supported the teacher's role in the classroom. It so happens that in Ms. Prima's classroom this year several of the black children, particularly the girls, belonged to this special group of quietly "supportive" families. Given Ms. Prima's own lack of success as a child in school and her need to prove her present superiority as a teacher, it is not surprising that she chose as favorites children whose family virtues make them very likely to succeed in Ms. Prima's class but whose success, as lower-class blacks, will make the rest of the school community take notice.

Ms. Prima's relationship with different types of parents is best conveyed by comparing two children in her class: Linda, a black girl from a poor, stable, two-parent family, and Nicky, a white boy from a poor, single-parent family. Linda lives in a neighborhood housing project. Her mother, however, is far from being the *quietly* supportive black parent that we have alluded to earlier. She is a strong-willed, progressive, and powerful woman who makes her views felt in the classroom, the principal's office, and the PTA. Ms. Prima, in fact, was initially apprehensive about having Linda in her class because Linda's oldest sister's teacher had felt the brunt of her mother's disapproval. But it so happened that Ms. Prima had taught another sister with great success, and Linda's mother requested, indeed demanded, that Linda be assigned to Ms. Prima's class. Timorous at first, Ms. Prima went along with the request at the principal's urging. Looking

back, it turned out to be a fortunate concession. Linda was a beautifully behaved, highly intelligent, extremely responsible student, and her mother,
having made the choice of Ms. Prima, swung her powerful support behind
her. As Ms. Prima put it, "She is the not the sort of woman you'd want to
cross." But then, in Linda's case, there never was any need.

Nicky's mother exemplifies a different kind of parent—one less strong-
willed, less sure of herself, more vulnerable to pressure and criticism. Nicky
and his family are white. His parents are divorced and Nicky lives with his
mother in an apartment in a neighborhood similar to Linda's. In kindergarten Nicky had earned a reputation for behavior problems. A CASE evaluation was carried out at the end of the year and the psychologist diagnosed
minimal brain damage with borderline hyperactivity symptoms. The psychologist and Nicky's mother concurred that Nicky, only five-and-a-half
years old in September, should repeat the year in kindergarten. Ms. Prima
argued forcefully that the child was intellectually very advanced and would
languish for lack of stimulation. What he needed was more structure, control, and focus on academic work and his behavior problems would take
care of themselves.

The initial parent-teacher conference of Nicky's first-grade year saw the
first confrontation between the two women. According to Nicky's mother,
Ms. Prima "blasted her in front of all the other parents," describing Nicky
as "a terror" and implicitly placing the blame on his mother; Ms. Prima
sees her as having exacerbated Nicky's lack of self-control and poor work
habits by babying him and giving him too much freedom and attention. Ms.
Prima's prescription was more insistence on discipline, rules, and work at
home, but when Nicky's mother tried to discuss his academic problems with
his teacher, Ms. Prima brusquely dismissed her questions, regarding them
as personal criticisms. On more than one occasion, worried or genuinely
curious about Nicky's progress in math or reading, she had queried Ms.
Prima, only to be brushed off with blunt retorts: "Yes, of course he knows
his numbers! Yes, of course he can read!" although his mother's observations of Nicky at home told her otherwise. On other occasions she had tried
to intercede for her son when she felt that Nicky could not finish all his
homework or that the problems assigned were too difficult. But again Ms.
Prima merely saw her as indulging Nicky: "He *knows* how to do it! Leave
him alone!"

And so a not-quite-so-polite tug of war went on, one in which Ms. Prima
saw Nicky's mother as irresponsible, weak, and undermining of her efforts
in the classroom, and Nicky's mother perceived Ms. Prima as too strict,
controlling, overbearing, insensitive, uninterested in her child's problems,
and hostile to her. This mother judges that Nicky's year with Ms. Prima has
done him some good; he has learned to read, he is calmer, he has more self-

control. But she wonders whether a softer approach, one that was more forgiving of Nicky and welcoming of his mother's insights, might not have been more successful. Indeed, she notes that over the course of the year, through the intercessions of Nicky's psychological counselor, Ms. Prima did modulate her style, and this gentler approach may have accounted for the modicum of success that was eventually achieved.

Hearing Nicky's mother talk, one is struck not so much by the differences between the teacher's and parent's understanding of the child but more by their contrasting views of the causes of his present problems and of appropriate strategies for helping him. Nicky's mother acknowledges that he has behavior problems: he is too playful, too easily distracted, too intent on getting attention, too talkative, too given to challenging statements from adults and asking questions. She relates an incident when Nicky came across two laborers digging up the street in front of their apartment. Nicky asked, "You laying in pipes?" One man said yes, the other said no. "Hey," said Nicky. "What's this? What's really happening? How can he say yes, and you say no?" The men thought Nicky obstreperous and angrily chased him away, not appreciating that the boy simply wanted to know what was going on. Nicky is a very bright child with a large adult-like vocabulary and an inquiring mind. In his mother's view this is one cause of his problems in school. The other causes, Nicky's mother acknowledges, are the fact that he is an only child, used to a great deal of adult attention and unused to sharing this attention with other children, and that he has no masculine role model at home.

Ms. Prima's perceptions of Nicky are similar to his mother's, although she is much less inclined to accept the psychologist's labels and their ominous implications. She sees no evidence of minimal brain damage or hyperactivity in Nicky. As she tells it, "Brain damage means you can't operate as a human being, right? Hyperactivity means you can't sit still for two minutes, right? A child who's brain damaged couldn't exist in a class like this. There are too many things going on. I couldn't even wear my rings around them, that's how distractible those kids are."

Ms. Prima refuses to hang such labels on Nicky with their frightening connotations, preferring instead to use the familiar, understandable terms—inattentive, easily distracted, attention-seeking, too playful—that she and the mother can accept as describing the boy. Where Ms. Prima and Nicky's mother part company is not in the diagnosis of Nicky's difficulties but in their prescription. Ms. Prima sees the mother's way of relating to Nicky (along with the circumstances of her divorce, single parenthood, and the fact of her having an only child) as a major cause of his problems and insists on a change toward her own style: more structure, more control, more focus on academic tasks. Nicky's mother acknowledges the need for some change along these lines but sees Ms. Prima's approach as too stern, harsh, and uncompromising, not loving and caring enough of children, and especially of her own complex, sensitive, individual child.

The general picture of Ms. Prima depicted in the analysis of the teacher-focused observation data lends some support to Nicky's mother's point of view. But this analysis, of course, does not describe Ms. Prima's interactions with Nicky as an individual, only her interactions with the class as a whole and with the mythical average child. Does Ms. Prima in fact treat Nicky appropriately, given her perceptions of his needs? We can address this question by examining in table 16 the profile of interactions between Ms. Prima and Nicky in the classroom and comparing it to similar profiles for the average child and for a model child such as Linda.

Let us consider first Nicky's own behavior during the teacher-focused observations. Compared to the average child, Nicky diverges markedly in only one respect. He is twice as likely to behave *appropriately* when interacting with Ms. Prima (7.7 percent versus 3.9 percent). Specifically, he is more likely to show enthusiasm for work in her presence and to request evaluation of his performance—in other words, to show the proper interest in appropriate tasks. On other counts Nicky's behavior is about average. He is no more or less expressive, dependent, or misbehaved than the average child in his class—a surprising finding in view of how much we heard about his talkativeness, attention seeking, and distractibility. However, it must be borne in mind that these figures come from our teacher-focused observations and hence refer only to behaviors on Nicky's part that are responded to by his teacher or are responses to her behavior.

Given that Nicky showed more than average appropriate behavior during the teacher-focused observations, one might expect that Ms. Prima would more often make this a topic of her interaction with him, commenting favorably on his initiatives and praising him. But she does not do so. Nicky's appropriate behavior is no more often noted by his teacher than the average child's, and he is no more often recognized by his teacher than his typical classmate. Conversely, since Nicky's inappropriate, dependent, and expressive behaviors are like the typical child's in his class, we might expect the corresponding behaviors on Ms. Prima's part to be about average. But again this is not the case. Ms. Prima more often scolds and criticizes Nicky than the average child, she is more likely to reject his requests for help, less likely to engage him in social conversation and other playful, relaxed interchanges, and she is much less likely to ask him open and free questions or to award him special privileges. To put it succinctly, Ms. Prima seems less appreciative, admiring, and trusting and more disapproving and critical of Nicky than he seems to deserve.

The contrast sharpens when we consider Ms. Prima's responses to Linda.

Table 16. Linda and Nicky versus average child: teacher-focused observations.

Variable	Linda	Nicky	Average child[1]
Interaction topic			
Academic	72.7%	57.1%	66.9%
Nonacademic	4.4	5.8	4.4
Procedural	9.8	18.6	15.0
Privilege	3.8	0.6	1.5
Appropriate C behavior	1.1	0.6	0.4
Inappropriate C behavior	6.0	14.7	11.2
Health, distress	1.1	2.6	0.5
Selected child and teacher behaviors			
Appropriate C behavior	7.7	7.7	3.9
Positive T reinforcement	7.1	7.7	7.0
Expressive C behavior	7.1	3.8	4.0
T humor, conversation	9.3	2.6	3.6
Dependent C behavior	7.1	9.0	8.8
T grants request	6.0	6.4	4.6
T rejects request	1.1	3.8	2.2
Inappropriate C behavior	5.5	9.0	6.9
Negative T reinforcement	8.2	26.3	17.6
T open/free question	5.5	0.6	5.6
T process question	10.4	9.0	10.2
% total teacher-child interactions[2]	6.9	6.4	5.4

1. Average of all children in Ms. Prima's class.
2. Percentage of all teacher-child interactions for which the child was present and was a potential recipient.

Like Nicky, Linda behaves appropriately about twice as often as the average child (7.7 percent versus 3.9 percent). But unlike Nicky, her appropriate behavior is recognized by Ms. Prima considerably more often than the average child's. Again like Nicky, Linda shows about an average amount of dependent and inappropriate behavior. But in contrast to Nicky, Linda's requests are less often rejected by Ms. Prima than the average child's, her behavior less often becomes an issue with her teacher, and she is scolded or criticized much less often than is typical. Equally important though more subtle are the clues indicating that Linda and her teacher have a rather special relationship. Linda clearly feels more at ease in expressing her opinions and initiating chitchat with Ms. Prima than the average child, and her teacher in turn is much more likely to engage her in conversation, to show her affection, and to single her out for special privileges.

One problem about data based exclusively on teacher observations is that one does not know what the child is doing when he is not interacting with the teacher. The teacher may choose to respond to only certain of these activities that she has observed (for example, when she reprimands a child for idling at his desk or disrupting the other children), but she may ignore or simply not perceive others. In a classroom of twenty children the teacher sees only a subset of the behaviors going on around her and responds to an even smaller subset of those she perceives. Everyday experience also suggests that children may behave quite differently when directly interacting with the teacher or when they are aware of her scrutiny than when they believe their activities are going unnoticed. Indeed, the more dominant and controlling the teacher, the more likely children may be to modify their behavior strategically. One wonders therefore what Nicky and Linda are like in situations where they are more removed from Ms. Prima's immediate presence. To answer this question, we turn to the child-focused observations (table 17).

Linda was observed on six separate occasions, for a total of one hour and ten minutes over a four-month period. Five of these observations took place in the morning when seatwork or other quiet activity was appropriate, and one took place in the first half hour of the day before reading turns and serious work were started. So much of the day in Ms. Prima's classroom was allotted to specific activities designated by the teacher that there were no truly unstructured contexts within the classroom in which a child could be observed for a reasonable length of time. The picture of Linda that one draws from these child-focused observations is indeed very like the one based on the teacher-focused observations. Linda is rather highly task-oriented. As a designated "helper" in the class, she is often called upon to assist other children with problems and she usually responds positively and promptly. Indeed, she takes her responsibility so seriously that from time to time she takes it upon herself to check up on others and report her findings to Ms. Prima. For example, on one occasion Linda overheard Ms. Prima telling Charles that he couldn't possibly have finished his work. Linda immediately volunteered to check. An observation of her behavior follows.

Linda goes to Charles's desk, calmly sits and takes out his papers, checking whether they are completed. Charles: "Stop! I did them!" Linda: "No, you didn't." Linda continues checking the papers and takes a set of them to the teacher as proof. Linda goes back to Charles's desk and continues carefully checking his work. Charles protests: "We have only half a day. I can't

Table 17. Linda and Nicky versus average child: child-focused observations.

Variable	Linda	Nicky	Average child[1]	Range
Child activities				
Work	54.1%	45.4%	46.3%	25.1-69.0%
Play	6.4	1.0	8.6	1.0-19.6
Talk	15.7	21.2	18.6	8.2-27.0
Self-care	7.5	5.9	3.0	1.0-7.5
Idle	14.6	16.7	15.4	2.7-29.6
Wild/disorderly conduct	0.0	4.3	2.8	0.0-8.5
Interacts with others	32.4	45.8	45.9	32.4-65.2
Child behavior when interacting with others				
Exhibits appropriate behavior	3.6	2.3	2.9	0.4-6.4
Receives appropriate behavior	2.9	1.6	2.3	0.8-5.5
Exhibits inappropriate behavior	2.5	4.3	5.9	0.4-22.8
Receives inappropriate behavior	0.7	3.6	2.4	0.7-6.6

1. Average of children observed individually in the four classes.

finish them.'' Linda: ''Yes, you can do them right now!'' Charles: ''I can't!'' Linda sighs . . . arranges the papers for Charles to start. Linda: ''Start on this one. Tell me when you're finished, then I'll give you another one.'' She sits by, in the posture of a supervisor, watching as Charles reluctantly begins his work.

Linda's officiousness is sanctioned by Ms. Prima. In fact, in the child-focused observations, we saw very little behavior on her part that Ms. Prima would deem inappropriate—no fighting, verbal or physical, only occasional refusals to share, and more often the kind of tattling to the teacher that in Linda's role as ''helper'' comes very close to being correct behavior. Linda clearly earns her position as her teacher's ''number one honey.''

Like Linda, Nicky was observed on six separate occasions, for a total of one hour and fifteen minutes, spaced over a four-month period. All of these observations took place in the morning when paperwork at one's desk or some other quiet activity was appropriate. Reading through these observations and tabulating the codes, one is struck by how little evidence there is of the problematic behaviors that teacher and mother are so agitated about. Nicky's profile in table 17 shows that he spent about 45 percent of his time on work, 21 percent chatting with his friends, and 17 percent of his time ''off task.'' He helped and received help from others equally often; he was aggressive toward others and was the victim of aggression equally often. In many respects, Nicky seems quite similar to Linda, and his overall profile of behavior when apart from Ms. Prima is probably not much different than that of the average child in his class. Yet in some ways he is most unusual, and, curiously, our best evidence of this came from our interview with him.

All the children whom we observed individually in class were interviewed in a separate room toward the end of the year. The material we obtained from these interviews was generally disappointing. Although most children seemed at ease and liked having themselves tape-recorded, their answers to our questions were often vague and stereotypic. Our interview with Linda excerpted below is typical.

INTERVIEWER: Do you like to come to school?
LINDA: Yes.
INTERVIEWER: What about the kids in your class? Who do you like?
LINDA: I like Valerie, Cathy, Patrick, and Debra.
INTERVIEWER: Why do you like Debra?
LINDA: 'Cause we always used to play together.
INTERVIEWER: Why do you like Patrick?
LINDA: 'Cause he plays with me.
INTERVIEWER: Are there any kids you don't like in school?
LINDA: No.
INTERVIEWER: Do you like Ms. Prima?
LINDA: Yes.
INTERVIEWER: Why do you like her?
LINDA: She's nice.
INTERVIEWER: Is there anything you don't like about her?
LINDA: No.
INTERVIEWER: Who do you think Ms. Prima likes of all the kids in your class?
LINDA: She likes me . . . and Cathy, Valerie, and Debra.
INTERVIEWER: Why does she like you?
LINDA: 'Cause we're nice.

Now, contrast a similar interview with Nicky.

INTERVIEWER: Do you like to come to school?
NICKY: Ya . . . I do . . . But you know what? Everytime in my class when the clock goes to twelve o'clock and the bell rings . . . my class goes Yeah! Yeah! [cheering].
INTERVIEWER: Is there anything you don't like about school?
NICKY: Let's see. One thing I get so bored of . . . When you have to make words, big words and things like that.

INTERVIEWER: What about the other kids in your class—who do you like?

NICKY: Oh, Mark. I just learned him a new joke. What's Fonzie's favorite holiday? Give up? Easter, 'cause that's when all the *chicks* come out!

INTERVIEWER: Are there any other kids that you like?

NICKY: Reggie. But I don't like him for one reason. He goes to bed real late, like 9 o'clock!

INTERVIEWER: What about somebody like Christopher?

NICKY: No. Not at all! He lies! He lies to my teacher!

INTERVIEWER: So you don't like him. What about Linda? Do you like her?

NICKY: Yeah. But it's amazing because Linda doesn't like me.

INTERVIEWER: Why doesn't Linda like you?

NICKY: 'Cause today she told Gary: Don't help Nicky.

INTERVIEWER: What about Jason? Do you like Jason?

NICKY: Yeah, a lot. But he used to be an old slob and dumb and creepy and a sneak. BUT . . . he turned into a great, nice man like me!

INTERVIEWER: What about Ms. Prima? Do you like her?

NICKY: Yeah. Because she plans nice lessons.

INTERVIEWER: Is there anything you don't like about Ms. Prima?

NICKY: Ya. When she yells at me. I say to myself, I'm not coming to school tomorrow.

INTERVIEWER: Why does she yell at you, Nicky?

NICKY: Well . . . some kids know how to turn it off fast, but I don't. I just get real mad and I'm still fighting . . . and then I look around and I say, oh, no! . . . there's Ms. Prima . . . and then she's on me!

INTERVIEWER: Who do you think Ms. Prima likes of all the kids in your class?

NICKY: Sometimes me . . . but I'd say Valerie, Debra.

INTERVIEWER: Anybody else?

NICKY: No. They're all girls. That's exactly it!

This six-year-old boy's insights into what was going on in his class and the subtlety of his perceptions of the people around him are impressive. His mother hinted that it might be this precocity that put off some adults like his teacher, but we think this is unfair. Ms. Prima seemed genuinely to admire Nicky's imagination and intellectual talents, although she was unduly irritated by other aspects of his personality. Perhaps what we mostly have here is a mother's unrealistic desire that her own child be the loved one, the one who captures the teacher's special feelings. This wish may have complicated roots in her own history—the late age at which she bore Nicky, her divorce, her role as a single parent of an only child. But it is a recurring phenomenon in our observations of first-grade classrooms. The pity of it is that the two women—both enormously significant people to Nicky—were so much at odds. Paradoxically, Ms. Prima reported that she and Nicky's mother had an excellent, trusting relationship. In her words: "She'll do whatever I . . . the school . . . thinks is good for Nicky. She doesn't know anything much about the educational process. She'll go along with what we say." In fact, Nicky's mother thought quite otherwise and had strong feelings about how his teacher might change *her* behavior to help her son.

As an outsider, one wonders whether in Nicky's case his alleged problems have not in part been created by the therapeutic institutions supposedly designed to mitigate them. The conflicting messages about himself bombarding Nicky from his mother, his teacher, and his counselor must be thoroughly perplexing to such an insightful child. It can hardly be clear to this six-year-old just what his difficulties are, only that he has many, since powerful people in his life repeatedly tell him so. Yet to a dispassionate observer and interviewer, Nicky seemed a pretty normal child, unusual only in his exceptionally articulate, reflective, and insightful perceptions about himself and other people. We recall Simone in Ms. Allen's class and worry, as her teacher did, whether Nicky may not soon learn to define himself as a problem child and to act so as to fulfill the expectations that others have for him. His verbal precocity, his fertile imagination, his emotional responsiveness, his budding tendency to introspect and "psychologize" make him a therapist's ideal patient. But would Nicky not be better off if the opinionated, anxious, concerned adults in his life simply let him *be*? It is a fine line that separates intrusion from guidance, dependence from support, freedom to become from pressure to conform.

These remarks may seem presumptuous, coming from one who watched Nicky only briefly and in one circumscribed setting. But observing this six-year-old in his classroom going about his seatwork or having fun with his friends, one could hardly help asking, "What's the fuss about?" It was at least plausible to imagine that the behavior problems that Nicky's teacher, mother, and counselor were so agitated about had little to do with the child himself and more to do with a clash of adult personalities, styles, and values. An initial, perhaps faulty, diagnosis of Nicky at the end of kindergarten had provoked a process of confrontation, mistrust, and disrespect among these adults that continued all through first grade. As time went on Nicky's behavior problems seemed to take on a reality of their own in the minds of these protagonists, a reality that was divorced from the boy himself and apparently unrelated to developmental changes in him. To us, the one hopeful note is Nicky's ability, glimpsed in the interview, to distance himself from this adult conflict and to come to his own conclusions about the contenders. Counterbalancing this, though, is Nicky's desire—the desire of any child in similar circumstances—to continue to attract the exceptional attention he receives. Ultimately the choice to define himself or to let others define him will be his to make. But one wonders how a child of six can come to understand so subtle a distinction and who will help him grasp it.

8

Ms. Edwards

Interpretation   *Sara Lawrence Lightfoot*

WHEN WE FIRST met Ms. Edwards she seemed friendly and interested in our research. Her questions were insightful and she sought information that would help her make an informed decision about whether to participate in our research. Before responding affirmatively to our request, she pondered her decision for several days. Her initial response of interest and enthusiasm mixed with caution was to be her approach to our work throughout the year.

Ms. Edwards saw our research as a potential intrusion into her private life with her husband and son as well as a source of confusion and chaos within the classroom. Her skepticism was also intensified by her general wariness of academicians and researchers who come into schools to scrutinize, evaluate, and learn but never seem to give. She had been aware of too many esoteric volumes by professors about child self-concept, teacher pedagogy, or the organizational character of the school—volumes that were written in highly technical language and just gathered dust in the libraries of scholars. Ms. Edwards was not prepared, therefore, to become the object of a nonreciprocal relationship. Throughout the research she maintained her skeptical spirit even as she grew closer to us, comforting herself with the knowledge that at any point she could withdraw from the process. "The feeling that I could stop it at any time was always there. So I thought that if it became a nuisance, then I'd just tell you that I'd rather not be bothered with it. And I was really concerned with the fact that you said that you could come into the room and really not be seen. If that couldn't happen, then I was going to say forget it. If it would create a problem, I would say it would have to be over."

One reason, therefore, that Ms. Edwards was able to respond affirmatively to the research was that she felt a sense of control over her classroom environment and saw us as the bidding supplicants. Beyond the psychological feelings of choice and control, Ms. Edwards also anticipated that she might learn something by joining our study—that participation in our research might enrich her teaching experience or help her improve pedagogical methods and teaching strategies. "Even though we're evaluated, it's just not a fair way of evaluating. And sometimes I like to sit back and have someone sort of point out the kinds of things that are going on and then sort of put it together in my head as to whether it is worth it or whether it is crazy and bizarre."

She did not perceive our research as a critical evaluation but as a descriptive (though perhaps somewhat threatening) process that expressed one point of view that might be useful to her. Ms. Edwards did not see it as *the* authoritative perspective, but one that might or might not be valid and functional for her teaching. There was always an abiding confidence that her insights, confused though they may be, were legitimate and that no outsider, no matter how expert, could diminish her central role as teacher of her classroom. This underlying confidence and skepticism of academic strangers made her the most questioning and discerning of all the teachers we worked with. She did not automatically agree to each of our research requests but always asked why the information was important to us. For instance, although she consented to our initial request to the taping of interviews, she demanded to know why it was necessary and how the tapes would be used. At the beginning of each interview she wanted to know the general topic of inquiry and the relevance of the interview questions to the basic framework of our research. Sometimes our responses to her inquiries did not seem totally satisfying to her, and the initial phases of the interview often reflected her wariness of our purposes. Most often there seemed to be a need for a warm-up period, a space of time when Ms. Edwards would slowly relax to the interview process, begin to bear the intrusion, and finally trust our purposes. But there always remained a measure of healthy skepticism.

Ms. Edwards' pursuit of our intentions, her continuous questioning, and her tendency to never trust us completely raised some instructive and tough questions about the nature of our research and underscored some of the critical dilemmas that evolve between practitioners and researchers. Her prodding encouraged us to ask questions that we believe should be part of the self-critical agenda of responsible researchers, questions that demand that investigators constantly engage in self-conscious reflection on the nature of their own participation in the research and on the potential impact of their presence in the setting. Ms. Edwards' skeptical reactions pointed to the following questions: Did her distant and critical response to our research reflect a more general attitude of teachers who have become increasingly politicized and unwilling to submit to being "subjects" of research inquiry? Was her response more related to an individual style of inquiry, her wish to know more, her tendency to feel more relaxed when she had gathered abundant and comprehensive information? Was her skepticism part of a more universal response of blacks in this culture who seek to protect themselves from the abuses of those in power (related perhaps to the healthy paranoia that Grier and Cobbs refer to in *Black Rage,* a kind of protective defensiveness that is socialized early in black children—a functional and necessary response to an oppressive and racist society)? Could her questioning have been part of a genuine interest in understanding research, an intellectual curiosity about the connection between research theory and the process of data collection? Did her reaction to our research reflect a more general difference in perspective between researchers and practitioners, who tend to have different orientations toward time and toward the form and substance of data? Practitioners seek immediate feedback and want practical and functional information that will relate to the daily lives of teachers and children in schools, whereas researchers are generally more concerned with engaging in a reflective and analytic process and accumulating a knowledge base that might affect the lives of some future generation.

The issues raised by Ms. Edwards' skepticism, therefore, seem to combine the universal concerns and barriers faced by all researchers whose work is beyond the controlled environment of the laboratory as well as the range of issues particular to this teacher. Whether the barriers and inhibitions to research arise out of universalistic or particularistic concerns on the part of practitioners, they should be a constant source of interest and analysis for the researcher. We believe that only when naturalistic research becomes a self-critical and reflective process can many of the traditional divisions between researchers and subjects be minimized and more comprehensive and perceptive data emerge.

Ms. Edwards came to the Outer School four years before our research began, after one year at another Conroy school and a maternity leave. She was pleased to find an opening at the Outer School because it is close by, enabling her to make short trips home to check on her new baby, and because of the ethnic and racial diversity of the school. On her first day of teaching, she experienced the wonderful surprise of walking into a class that was "beautifully proportioned . . . I had children from India, children from the Islands, children from the Orient . . . It was the League of Nations." She also enjoyed the initial pleasure of being in a new and clean modern building with excellent facilities. But very soon the impressive newness began to fade and the building began to feel cold and unlived in. The architectural design did not make good use of space, nor take into account the needs of young children, nor encourage easy social interaction among the people inside. "It looks more like a prison than a school . . . it's just too cold looking. I'd love to see them paint some beautiful murals on the walls."

The scale of the school is also a critical factor in defining people's approach to the environment and to each other. Ms. Edwards described the fear of first graders as they entered this impersonal, massive structure for the first time and the reticence of some parents, who felt the unwelcomeness and impenetrability of the facade. The large scale also decreases the opportunities for teachers to feel themselves a part of a community that works together. "Because the school is so big, we don't see other people . . . only people on our wing . . . We only see the others at meetings and we have very few meetings. There are some teachers upstairs that I see but I don't know their names." The physical space, therefore, seems to have a profound impact on the young children's introduction to the school, on the parents' perceptions of school and community relations, and on the quality of teacher interaction.

The social network of which Ms. Edwards is a part is located in one wing of the school and includes teachers of the primary grades. She describes their interactions as generally supportive and useful. Their relationships seem to permit a comfortable degree of autonomy as well as a reference group for discussing common institutional concerns and curricular issues. Ms. Edwards compares her life in the Outer School with her year at the first school in which she taught. She had been surrounded by older, more experienced and conservative colleagues who scrutinized her work and who were threatened by any talk of innovation and change. But her most immediate colleagues at the Outer School are generally of the same age and experience and seem to share a sense of protective and supportive togetherness. "Most of the teachers here are young . . . I think we floundered together. We made some mistakes together. We had some difficulties initially just relating to each other and that got worked out and I think the relationships are good. We'd get together and sit down and talk about problems within our classroom, problems at the grade level, and sometimes we were able to work things out. Sometimes we act together, and sometimes it's just a place to dump our grief."

Initially, the difficulties among the first-grade teachers, according to Ms. Edwards, were primarily caused by personality clashes that were modified and modulated over time. It was a new setting for all of them; they were all new teachers with an intense desire to do an excellent job. Their uncertainty and ambition was initially expressed in competitiveness, but these competitive struggles diminished as they recognized that sharing of resources was essential and more productive and as they began spending formal and informal time together around lunch and in curricular meetings. "It's just sort of a natural happening because we do see each other pretty much every day and also because if something's happening that you're not satisfied with, you run to somebody and if the person is pretty much in accord with what you're thinking, then it's even more of a place where you can relieve your frustration.''

Coming together is often in response to a problem that the teachers are experiencing. Their meetings, therefore, tend to revolve around a perceived crisis, are responsive rather than initiating processes, and are called for the purpose of working out a collective strategy. The enemy in these meetings tends not to be children or parents but the administration, which is blamed more for its inaction, indecision, and lack of commitment than for purposeful malice or ill will. For example, when Ms. Edwards needs to talk with someone about a problem she is having in the classroom, she tends to consult her trusted fellow teachers or the resource teacher for the primary grades. She is less likely to search out the principal because she does not view him as a capable or wise supervisor of teachers and because he is unwilling to offer a substantive opinion or take decisive action. ''I think that we should have somebody that we can talk to . . . that could make some sort of stand, commitment. Now I feel that I would be left totally alone to plead the cause, whatever it is.''

Not only does Ms. Edwards feel a lack of support for her own decision making from the principal, but she also claims that he views his role as lofty and superior to teachers' and lowly and inferior to the bureaucrats' of the central administration. She sees him as preoccupied with defending his place in the bureaucracy and reluctant to do anything or push any issue that might compromise his position. ''The teachers I've talked with feel that he will do anything to avoid a bureaucratic hassle . . . If he can dole out anything else that may not meet your need, he will try to avoid going up there and creating any pressure or problem for the higher ups . . . Maybe he feels because he is way up there and we are down here . . . that it is not important.''

The principal's commitment to and fear of the hierarchical order has a very real and direct impact on arrangements the teachers are trying to make for special programs, workshops, and trips. Because the principal refuses to act as advocate and conduit of his teachers' requests, the central office tends to neglect the Outer School. In desperation, at one point the teachers went over the head of Mr. Barry, the principal, to make a request for a workshop on discipline from the director of primary education. When word came back to Mr. Barry, he was angered and annoyed that they had defied the order of command and that his role had been compromised. Ms. Edwards, therefore, would prefer a principal who more strongly identified with the process of teaching, who was a decisive and forceful leader, who both initiated action and was a responsive listener. Mr. O'Connor, the assistant principal, comes closer to being her ideal. "Mr. O'Connor is a more forceful person. He comes on a lot stronger than Mr. Barry . . . Mr. O'Connor is the kind of person who will listen to you, sympathize with you, and then he may give you the bad news that there is nothing he can do about it . . . If there is no solution, or he can work toward a solution, he'll get back to you."

Ms. Edwards' first-grade classroom gives the visual appearance of being relatively unstructured and open. There is not the traditional pattern of desks and chairs. The physical space is casually organized into interest areas, and children are likely to be found sitting around tables working in small groups, lying on the rug reading alone, wandering about the room aimlessly, or approaching Ms. Edwards for attention and help. The curricular and social action is not centered around the teacher but is dispersed throughout the room. In fact, the teacher often appears peripheral to the experience of children and spends much of her time observing the whole scene from the sidelines.

The rapid movement of children and the fluid use of classroom space sometimes creates a chaotic impression, and one is surprised to count only sixteen children in the room. The class is well-integrated, with equal proportions of black and white children, middle-class and poor children, and a smattering of children from foreign countries. Ms. Edwards greatly enjoys the small size of the class because she feels it gives her the opportunity to work with individuals and know each child more deeply; she also values the range of ethnic, racial, and social-class backgrounds because she believes that public schools should be culturally pluralistic environments.

The individual nature of each child is a constant source of interest, dismay, and struggle for Ms. Edwards. She approaches the task of discovering the temperament, style, and skills of each child as the primary agenda of her teaching. Her descriptions and diagnoses of children reveal details about how they function socially and intellectually in the classroom and often refer to the psychological dimensions of motivation, self-concept, anger, and anxiety. Learning and development are considered very complex processes by Ms. Edwards, who describes the subtle interactions of the socioemotional and intellectual spheres in a child. She often talks about how poor development in one sphere may inhibit or distort functioning in the other. She is aware of basic limitations in the development of even the most highly skilled children in her class. Bridget, for instance, reads at a third-grade level and is quick to learn, but she is also a very threatened and insecure little girl who has difficulty working with other children. She insists on being at center stage when she initiates something but shyly withdraws when Ms. Edwards calls on her without warning. Not only does Ms. Edwards recognize the various dimensions of personality structure in the children in her classroom, but she also continuously searches for ways of interacting more successfully with them, by observing and monitoring their behavior and redefining her pedagogical strategies. Often she admits to being "baffled" and "confused" about which direction to take with a particular child. She talks openly about how she has miscalculated a child's potential and expected too much of him.

Her descriptions of children are full of insight, but one often has the feeling that the abundance of information that she absorbs about children inhibits her ability to move quickly and take action. Ms. Edwards clearly enjoys the process of reflection provided by our interviews, but she often appears overwhelmed with the complexity of human behavior and mesmerized by its subtle and obscure dimensions. This fascination with individuality seems to limit her effective and purposeful action in the classroom. Her approach appears tentative and hesitant. Her timing, her spontaneous reactions, seem to be held in check by her tendency to struggle with the motivational and developmental roots underlying the child's behavior.

Part of Ms. Edwards' understanding of a child's individuality recognizes the power of the environment on the child's expression of self. In her descriptions of children she often distinguishes between that part of the child which finds expression in school and that part of the child which is revealed with family members and peers. Ms. Edwards is very aware of the constraints and demands of the social context, and she recognizes that her vision of the child is but a partial one that is situationally defined. Her broad perspective gives a very generous thrust to her statements about children. Even if a child is not functioning well in school, he may be thriving in other environments. No child should be thought of as a total loser, nor should his self-image be defined entirely in terms of school criteria. When Ms. Edwards speaks of Jackie, for instance, she describes her shy, withdrawn character in the classroom and her aggressive, assertive behavior with her older siblings. "That is not the Jackie we see in class."

Ms. Edwards' interest in the family backgrounds of the children in her class seems to be related to her concern with understanding the other powerful influences on their lives and the potential impact of these forces on their development in school. Her interviews are rich with details about the families from which her children come, information that she believes will give her a more realistic perspective on their behavior and attitudes in school. For Ms. Edwards, family background material does not merely seem to be a way of rationalizing stereotypes and labels. Rather, she uses this information to draw a more complete and comprehensive picture of individual children and to elaborate and expand her repertoire of behaviors toward them. For instance, Ms. Edwards has abundant information on the disruptive and sad home life of Robert that helps her understand and value his highly complex imagination and his expressions of dreams and fantasies in his sophisticated drawings. She also feels that her knowledge of his background gives her more patience in coping with his negative behavior. "Knowing this about Bobby, I can deal with him. I can grin and bear it a little longer. I can look at it and see the other side of Bobby, not the repulsive side."

Family background, environmental variables, and personality structure all contribute to Ms. Edwards' perception of the child's individuality. She also recognizes that her perceptions might be at variance with those of the children in her class. She is aware of the emergence of different status systems in the classroom that often conflict with her values and priorities. Behaviors and attitudes that the children might value are not necessarily the ones she is trying to teach. Ms. Edwards describes Daniel as "the class everything . . . the class clown . . . the class leader. He can terrify during the class. You know, he says, 'I'm gonna knock you down; I'm gonna kick your butt.' But everyone in the class likes him. It seems as though he's everyone's idol." This description of Daniel as seen by other children is quite at variance with Ms. Edwards', who recognizes his magnetic and powerful personality but is also aware of his academic and intellectual inadequacies and the softness behind his tough exterior. "As strong as he is in spirit, as dynamic as he is . . . you know this powerful little image, he's nothing inside. He's really just as soft as one of the most frightened little kids in the class. But he's got an exterior."

Part of Ms. Edwards' diagnosis of individuality, therefore, searches behind the facade in an attempt to explore the discrepancies between her judgments and those of others. Her perspectives on individuality seem to focus on the basic contradictions and distortions that emerge in the classroom—the differences between the child as family member and the child as pupil, between the images projected to peers and those projected to the teacher, between external behaviors and internal motivations. For Ms. Edwards, an important part of teaching is to understand the basic contradictions of personality, behavior, style, and image making that are expressed in and out of the classroom.

In responding to different individuals, Ms. Edwards consciously offers different kinds of attention and guidance and makes different kinds of intellectual and social demands. Her definition of fairness does not seem to be limited to giving equal favors to every child but requires giving attention and offering resources that are consonant with what she perceives to be the child's needs. Sometimes her notion of justice in the classroom leads to conspicuous differences in her interactions with children. Daniel, for instance, is the recipient of many specialized favors. Ms. Edwards justifies and rationalizes her unique efforts by describing his relatively deprived condition—his chaotic home background, his difficulties in learning basic skills, his superior but distorted status among his peers, his obsession with being the first at everything. Often Daniel comes to school late, looking unbrushed and unkempt, and is embarrassed to enter the classroom. Ms. Edwards and he have a private arrangement. "Daniel has come to school as late as quarter to nine. Other teachers have come in and said that he is out in the hallway. And often his hair is not combed and his face is not washed. It's really a job for him to come to class . . . But he doesn't feel good about coming through the door looking the way he looks. He's very conscious of what he looks like and what he should look like . . . So we have a comb for him and he can go into the next room and get his face washed and it does wonders for him . . . This is his little thing, his little private thing with me."

In her special treatment of individuals, Ms. Edwards shows the ability to empathize and identify with children's feelings of anger, defeat, and embarrassment. She takes their feelings very seriously and seeks to find ways of helping children avoid or handle emotional distress. But at the same time Ms. Edwards has some very strong feelings about the optimal development of a child. She voices distinct preferences for children who are independent and autonomous and who show the ability to focus and sustain interest in a task. She also admires leadership and assertiveness—not the kind of aggressiveness that is competitive, hostile, and defensive but the kind that reflects a child's sense of confidence and security. Ms. Edwards describes Heather as having these characteristics and therefore "being good for the classroom." She counts on Heather to be a surrogate teacher and to help her with classroom structure and control. Interestingly, Ms. Edwards does not view Heather's surrogate role as simply a passive imitation of the teacher or as a yearning to appeal to the authority figure but rather describes it as reflecting the child's independence, competence, and maturity. "Leave it to Heather to come out with a directive. In doing this she can get a following . . . she is a leader."

For Ms. Edwards, leadership and power are compelling and valued qualities in children. Abdul, a strong and magnetic little boy from Africa, symbolizes the positive qualities of self-confidence and individual style. She speaks as if knowing him has been a transforming, almost spiritual experience for her. "He talks very slowly, very distinctly, and you *must* stand there and listen . . . it is almost like you're really just held there by this little child . . . he's a very powerful little boy." Ms. Edwards also values the distant experiences that Abdul has brought to the classroom through his vivid descriptions of his land and religion. She admires his strength and his charisma, but she seems to especially like his good feelings about himself, his proud feelings about his blackness, his culture, his history, his full expression of uniqueness and individuality. "The school needs a boy like Abdul, such a proud little black child . . . we don't see that very often."

Although Ms. Edwards focuses a great deal of her energy on discerning and supporting individuality among children, she is also concerned with developing their sense of commitment and responsibility to group life in the classroom. One of the cornerstones of her teaching has to do with developing the social self in children. Although she considers the adequate learning of basic cognitive skills to be critical to the child's success in school, Ms. Edwards is even more concerned about the development of social skills. Children must learn less egocentric behavior and find effective strategies for coping with the realities and constraints of group life. "I'm almost at the point of thinking that kindergarten should definitely be a socialization kind of program. And I'm beginning to wonder whether maybe first grade should be more socialization than academics. Looking at the way some of the kids are coming each year, it's almost amazing that the immaturity level just seems to continue to get lower and lower . . . and I'm beginning to wonder about the whole process. Maybe we shouldn't expect them to do the kinds of things that we expect them to do . . . They have so much trouble relating to each other, getting along with one another, just solving problems amongst themselves."

Ms. Edwards is generally frustrated by and critical of parents who send their children to first grade without fundamental social skills, and is appalled that parents expect her to teach academic skills when they have not taught their children basic manners and decorum. "These mothers expect us to do things in one year that they haven't been able to accomplish in the first five years of the child's life." Because children arrive at first grade lacking some of the fundamental skills of social interaction, Ms. Edwards feels that primary socialization is not only an important and legitimate agenda but also that it must become part of the didactic ritual of classroom life. The teaching of social skills demands the same kind of systematic and serious attention as cognitive interactions, although the ways of coping with interpersonal struggle may appear somewhat less directive. When children become aggressively competitive, for instance, Ms. Edwards is not likely to discourage their behavior directly and explicitly. She will, however, urge children to recognize the differences among themselves and feel positive about what they each can do. "I'd like them to sort of find where they are and what they can do best . . . we don't all have to be the same thing; we don't all have to be the best in everything." She sees the expression of and respect for individual differences as a critical ingredient of healthy and productive group behavior.

When real conflict and violence erupt, activity is stopped and Ms. Edwards often tries to draw from the particular interpersonal struggle more general and universal principles. The issues raised in the following excerpt reflect the basic values she maintains about social interaction and social responsibility. "We can sit down and talk about what causes a fight, what makes you angry and how you can deal with it other than striking out. Because if you strike out at someone they're going to strike back at you. So how can we handle it differently? It takes so much repetition . . . discussion and role playing before it seems as though most of them have gotten to the place where they'll say, 'We need to get together and *talk* about it.' "

Ms. Edwards' concern for social development in children reflects a fundamental pedagogical notion that underlies all her teaching—the belief that the essence of teaching and learning is problem solving. When she speaks of problem solving, she is referring to the learning of both social and cognitive skills. Ms. Edwards wants children to be able to ask appropriate questions and search for answers in a systematic and structured way. "The entire picture is solving problems, whether it is math, reading, or social problems."

Very much related to problem solving is the issue of autonomy within a structured environment. One of Ms. Edwards' educational goals is to create a classroom environment that enhances the possibilities for children to make individual decisions and act without the constant supervision and intervention of the teacher. In a sense she seeks to become increasingly redundant to children and to give them the social and intellectual tools to solve their own problems. This process of socialization for self-reliance is a slow and arduous task. It includes a variety of strategies that focus on helping children learn rules that will provide them with a structure and order that is rational, dependable, and anticipatable and one that demonstrates the connections between the various steps so that children can get a sense of the whole process, whether the process is academically or socially focused. Both of these stages require a long preparatory period filled with ritual, routine, and reinforcement, but eventually these ritualized behaviors begin to provide an internal structure for the child that supports autonomous action.

In reinforcing autonomy in the social sphere, Ms. Edwards often purposely remains on the periphery of struggles among children. She reasons that her interventions will substantially transform the moment and, in fact, that children might work out a better resolution of their problems themselves. "If I inject anything in there at all, you know, it may go the way that they think I want it to go. Whereas they may be able to resolve it quite well alone." Further, Ms. Edwards believes that her nonintervention allows her to learn something about the children through observation. She thinks their behavior is more authentic and their responses more believable to one another when they are left alone to work things out. Brian finally began to believe that his classmates cared about him when one of them said spontaneously after a struggle, "I'm your friend, Brian. I like you. I don't like what you do all the time. You cry too much, but I like you." His peer's words were so much more convincing than the proclamations of his teacher, who had given him continuous assurances that he was liked by his classmates.

Although her policy of helping children toward independence is a fairly generalized pattern in her teaching, Ms. Edwards recognizes great differences in the learning styles and personality structures of children that cause her to restructure some of her basic pedagogical approaches. She modifies her strategy of nonintervention with Daniel, who needs constant individual attention and abundant positive reinforcement in order to successfully make it through his day. "The trouble with Daniel, I think, was that he was so impatient, so anxious to do something, that before he looked into what he was doing, he would come up with an answer. And the minute he was wrong, that took him down five pegs and it seemed as though he would discontinue and be defeated and stop; and as a result, it always seemed as if we were spoonfeeding him everything."

In her interactions with children, Ms. Edwards is well aware of the potential dangers of individualized and specialized attention for a child. She fears that the strategy of interaction that she adopts might begin to define and reinforce negative patterns in the child. She also recognizes that developmental shifts or behavior fluctuations in the child may disrupt the patterns that the teacher has grown to expect. She is constantly asking herself whether her interactions are reinforcing weakness or strength and how she can remain responsive to the inconsistencies and changes in the child. "Sometimes I don't know whether I am making enough demands on Daniel. Maybe he can do a lot more than he is allowing us to see." Ms. Edwards constantly searches for the balance between a structured, consistent pattern of interaction with an individual child and the danger of stereotyping the child so that his behavior remains prescribed and unchanged. In order to be a good teacher, she feels, one must work toward consistency and continuity in one's interactions with children, but one must also anticipate, welcome, and "tune in" to changes and fluctuations in their behavior.

The theme of problem solving is also evident in Ms. Edwards' attitudes toward the structuring of reading groups in the classroom. She conceives of the organization and monitoring of reading groups and of her interaction with them as an exercise in putting together a difficult and complex puzzle. The process of choosing reading groups begins with careful and deliberate observation—observing children functioning in the classroom, observing their response to reading-readiness exercises, observing their interactions within a group, observing their ability to focus on a task: "The whole thing is observation." The children are tested before entering first grade, and Ms. Edwards is aware of their scores when she forms groups, but she is also convinced that test scores are often very discrepant with actual ability to function in the classroom. "Test scores don't often seem to coincide with what children are doing . . . I don't take them too seriously, but consider other

things first . . . I had a child last year who was reading well above the second-grade level and she tested in the lower half of the class . . . and that is
not only last year, but that's right along.''

Ms. Edwards assigns her children to reading groups on the basis of a fluid
and complex mixture of several ingredients; she gives minimal attention to
test scores, and maximal attention to reading-readiness skills, general patterns of functioning and accommodation in the classroom, and the optimal
size of the group and the social-psychological match of children within it.
For those children who seem to be having difficulties, Ms. Edwards probes
into their family background and seeks out the previous teachers' perceptions of them, but she recognizes some of the limitations and biases of this
information. Family-background information contained in school files can
obviously be used to justify a child's school failure. Further, in recent years
this written information has become vacuous and imprecise because teachers fear legal repercussions from placing negative assessments in official records. They still pass on their judgments informally, by word of mouth;
hence the potential for distortion, rationalization, and prejudice is even
stronger—an alarming turn of events that makes Ms. Edwards increasingly
wary of using the opinions of other people to guide her behavior toward
students.

Once the groups are initially formed, Ms. Edwards focuses her attention
on the chemistry of interacting personalities and learning styles. One of the
differentiating factors that she often refers to is the ability to focus on the
task and absorb oneself in work, the ability to pursue the task without supervision or intervention from an adult. She thinks of restructuring one of
the groups because the children have comparable intellectual skills but different abilities to concentrate; and yet she worries that separating out the
focused, on-task children may remove the potential sources of inspiration
and modeling from those who are more distracted.

There are three reading groups in Ms. Edwards' classroom: the Whales
(Group I), the Seals (Group II), and the Dolphins (Group III), and they require varying degrees of direction and intervention from her. The Dolphins
demand the greatest amount of guidance. "It's almost like you are spoonfeeding the material for many reasons—not only because of their capabilities but because of distractibility. It's almost like holding their hands." The
more advanced groups may require many of the same skills in learning vocabulary and listening to directions but less of the constant prodding and intervening by the teacher. The most advanced, independent children require
minimal skill training or behavioral direction but need clarification of concepts presented in the reading.

Ms. Edwards claims to get the most enjoyment out of working with the
Whales because of their energy, focus, and drive. They are the "natural

leaders" of the class and have an attitude of "I can do that!" "It's exciting to watch and see how far they push themselves." Because she enjoys their style of attacking the material, Ms. Edwards seems to identify most closely with the relatively advanced and successful children, but she is critical of their competitiveness and seeks to protect other children from invidious comparisons. For example, Raymond and Samantha were initially placed in the Whales because of their outstanding performances on the reading readiness material. Very soon it became evident to Ms. Edwards that they were unable to move at the same pace as other members of the group, so she decided to reassign them to the Seals. The transition was made very naturally and smoothly. It was introduced casually by Ms. Edwards (after discussion and agreement with their parents); she invited them to work with the Seals on a day when the group was involved with active and attractive tasks in which Raymond and Samantha immediately experienced success and reward. They did not raise any resistance to working in their new group and in fact seemed to enjoy the relative comfort and ease of functioning in a less competitive and pressured setting. Samantha, who had been shy and withdrawn among the Whales, began to flourish and actively respond among the Seals.

Ms. Edwards' work with the Dolphins causes her the greatest stress and demands the most patience and endurance. She describes the Dolphins as being children who seem to have learning blocks or emotional difficulties. Several go for special tutoring and psychological counseling outside the classroom. Her interactions with them inside the classroom are laborious and frustrating to her. Her pedagogical style is slow, systematic, and repetitive. "When I feel that they have gotten an understanding of whatever the concept is that I'm trying to get across to them and I'm ready to sort of introduce something that may ask a little more of them, I'll start reviewing what they have already learned and they bomb right out."

The practice of grouping children for reading strikes Ms. Edwards as an effective and productive way of structuring the class for basic skills learning. She cannot consider the possibility of whole-group instruction (because the range of abilities is so vast that one could not find a single style or curriculum that would work for the majority of children), nor can she imagine totally individualized instruction (because she could never cope with the chaos of responding to the individual agendas of every child). For Ms. Edwards, grouping seems to be a realistic and comfortable compromise that provides for some individualized attention as well as some sense of being a part of group life. However, reading groups can be limiting and oppressive settings for children if the teacher does not see them as fluid and flexible structures. She seeks to gain the advantages of small-group work by preceding the assignment of children into groups with several weeks of observation and diagnosis of their skills, behavior, and attitudes toward learning; by structuring groups that take into account the chemistry of interacting personalities and social skills as well as intellectual abilities; by rearranging groups when children do not seem to be functioning optimally; by making movements of children from one group to another as casual and comfortable as possible in order to minimize the child's sense of failure; and by quietly discouraging the competitive urges among children, especially the very advanced children who like to assert their superiority. The task of monitoring the children's progress in reading groups remains important and continuous throughout the year. The constant reevaluation of each child's abilities and needs is her basis for deciding whether the reading groups are productive, comfortable environments or stagnant, competitive ones.

Ms. Edwards was the youngest of several children in a West Indian family who had migrated to the United States when her parents were young adults. In the West Indies her father had been a teacher and her mother a dressmaker. After coming to Conroy, her father took a job as a carpenter and eventually was called to service in the ministry. Education and religion were central and dominant forces in the life of her family. Even though her father was no longer a practicing teacher, he greatly valued the educational process and continued to enjoy reading books for his own development. Ms. Edwards' mother and father took an active interest in the schooling of their children, all of whom attended the public schools of Conroy. Although they stressed the critical importance of education, they recognized and reinforced differences in the interests, skills, and abilities of their children. Everyone was expected to work to the utmost of his abilities, but everyone was not expected to succeed equally well or to pursue identical interests. "I did very well in school and I had some members of my family who did as well as they could do but it wasn't at the same level as the others. We were expected to do what we could do. I have a brother who was very good in school. I didn't have to do what he did but I had to do my *own* best. I have a sister who became a seamstress, she didn't go to high school, but to trade school. She did her best at what she was doing."

This tradition of working for one's own individual reward, as an expression of one's unique combination of strengths and abilities, seems to be reflected in Ms. Edwards' interactions with children in her classroom and in her consciously articulated educational philosophy. Throughout her discussions about children there is a preoccupation with finding the essence of their individuality, with learning as much as possible about their intellectual and social potentials, and then with finding appropriate strategies for directing their potentials in productive directions.

Ms. Edwards' parents appreciated diversity and variation among their offspring, but they had a single behavioral and social standard which all the children were expected to meet. Good behavior was considered critical for young black children who would be entering an unjust world and who would have to learn to meet indignities with a controlled and civilized presence. "Behavior was more important than grades in school because we were always told that when you go out into the world . . . there were certain things that were expected of you . . . because you were black, things would come down harder on you . . . that you had to do a lot better than what other people did."

This behavioral and moral standard was monitored and reinforced by the close-knit West Indian community in which Ms. Edwards grew up. Neighbors and friends served as surrogate parents and extended family in making sure that her brothers and sisters were appropriately behaved. The fact that her father was the minister who served this community added an additional burden of rectitude and decorum. "My father had a small congregation not far from where we lived. My parents had been in Conroy for several years and they knew all their friends that came from the Islands and had settled in Conroy, so that it was like a community. If we weren't home and something happened, my parents always knew about it before we got home. I think it was also maintaining a standard—a moral standard."

The themes of good behavior and spiritual morality were, therefore, closely mingled in Ms. Edwards' early life. She experienced a sense of consistency and harmony of values between home, church, and community that acted in powerful unity to shape her. These dominant values were expected to be transferred to the school environment. She recalls that her parents were in continuous communication with her teachers and that they viewed the authority of the teacher as ultimate and irreversible. If one of the children misbehaved in school, her parents would assume an alliance with the teacher unless the evidence was clearly to the contrary. The strong alliances between parents and teachers in her early life gave Ms. Edwards a view of the education process that emphasized the clarity and asymmetry of child and adult roles. Children did not dare cross the moral boundary. "Our classes went a lot smoother than today. The kids were petrified of the teachers, so that a lot of things that happen in class now just wouldn't happen . . . kids held the teachers up as gods, so that whatever the teacher said was God's law."

Ms. Edwards reflects on these times with nostalgia because in some ways the order and control of the old days seem so much more comfortable and appealing to her than the relatively chaotic and questioning contemporary world. Life yesterday always seems simpler than today. A real contrast seems to exist between the behavioral and moral expectations of her youth and the present realities of her professional life. She talks about the persistent clash of these two perspectives in her daily teaching. "Some of my [family] tradition really did carry over . . . I find it very difficult to hear a six- or seven-year-old child telling a teacher to go to hell . . . I just can't deal with that.''

Ms. Edwards' history of spiritual and moral training seems to bear some relation to her attitudes toward social development in the classroom. Although they have taken on a modern expression, great similarities exist between her parents' concerns about good behavior and moral attitudes and Ms. Edwards' primary focus on helping children learn the standards and protocol of correct social interaction. Individuality is seen as important, but productive functioning of the social group and participation in the social networks of the classroom are seen as the primary agenda of her first grade. The recognition of individual differences and individual needs becomes part of a diagnostic process—strategies used by the teacher to identify the appropriate pedagogical methods and interactional styles to be used with that child. But the ultimate goal seems to be to help children "fit in," to establish an authentic and productive relationship between the individual and the social group.

In Ms. Edwards' reminiscences of her early years, one discerns a deep longing to return to the days when life was less complex and more orderly. We hear this wish in her remembrances of her school life and also in her description of the meaningfulness of religion for young people today. She recognized the importance of spirituality in her own life only recently. "I appreciate it more now than I did as a child. I think it gives another dimension to life and what it is all about . . . It seems to give me a feeling that there's got to be a better way, and there's hope somewhere." Although her adult life has taken on a powerful spiritual dimension, she remembers the church during her childhood as an important environment for providing young people with good, honest fun, with trips, conventions, formals. She regrets that the church no longer serves this social and socializing function. Instead of providing disciplined fun, it has attempted to become "liberated and it seems that something is missing."

Much of the chaos and lack of discipline that Ms. Edwards perceives as prevalent in today's world are the repercussions of plenty and abundance. She values her heritage of poverty and restraint—a heritage that molded her into a resourceful and hard-working person, a heritage that appreciated the value of earthy, manual work as well as the value of the intellect. "I think that's part of the West Indian culture and I think it is probably part of the black culture as a whole. The fact that in the Islands—and probably most of the minority cultures—you don't have abundance, you have to learn to survive. In the Islands they had gardens. You planted and whatever you ate was from your own land . . . and everyone had something that they could do with their land." From poverty came struggle, pain, and strength that abided for the rest of one's life. People were more resourceful, more "whole" because they had to confront the simple and harsh realities of survival.

Ms. Edwards held a very special place in her family. The last of several children, she experienced all the advantages and disadvantages of being the baby. Mostly she recalls the good parts—the many siblings who protected and cared for her, the tendency of her parents to overlook her misbehavior. "I was allowed to do a lot more things, like just going out, and going different places after school . . . There was always a time that I had to be in. When I went over my time limit, I could always depend on someone to come and get me before my father came looking for me. And the story was always put together, so that by the time I got home everything was normal . . . I think my parents probably caught on to it. I don't know why they didn't dole out the punishment, but they never seemed to."

So she had a very special, protected place in her family—one that was part of a more general atmosphere of admiration and closeness. Along with the demands for excellent decorum at home, in the school, and in the community, the children also received large doses of approval and love. They were encouraged to feel they were beautiful and special and worthy of recognition from the outside world. "My mother especially felt that her children were magnificent . . . She was blind with love . . . She used to say that her sons were handsome and her daughters were beautiful. And we were taught that very early."

The recollections of Ms. Edwards' early years were told with eloquence and emotion. After a brief period of awkwardness and reticence about revealing this kind of personal information as well as a healthy suspicion about the relation of this material to the purpose of our research, she seemed pleased to tell her story. Throughout the interview she would often recognize parallels between early training in her family and the primary values and attitudes that are expressed in her teaching. There was an impressive correspondence between her notions of the social responsibility and contribution of children to life in the classroom and the emphasis in her early upbringing on moral and behavioral training. Also, it seemed that her balanced combination of making clear and firm demands on children and at the same time offering abundant positive reinforcement was learned early at her mother's knee where she heard that she was special and beautiful but also knew that she must be a responsible member of a family seeking to survive in an unjust society.

The path to becoming a teacher was not smooth for Ms. Edwards. She took a long and winding route, even though she remembers always wanting to be a teacher. After high school she briefly enrolled in a large city university; but fearing that it would be too expensive for her family to support, she withdrew and attended a much smaller, relatively inexpensive school nearby. Still trammeled by the economic burden of college upon her family and yearning to use the secretarial skills in which she had excelled in high school, Ms. Edwards went to work as a stenographer for the telephone company during the summer after her first year in college. She found the salary and structured life-style very appealing and decided not to return to college but to remain employed at the telephone company. It was a good job because it offered experience on a variety of business machines and she gained important office skills. After a few years, she began to grow weary of the standardization and lack of choice. She looked at some of her older colleagues and began to fear that she would become deadened and hardened by the process. "The phone company was good to me—a good experience and a bad experience that sort of compelled me forward."

The structure and regimentation of her job began to seem burdensome and personally unrewarding, and she decided to begin work toward the career that she really wanted. "I always felt that I wanted to be a teacher. When I was young I used to make up stories and tell them to the rest of the family. And they were delighted naturally. And then when I was a teenager, I was a Sunday School teacher. And it worked out pretty well. Then I worked in a community center with children . . . I was interested in teaching retarded children. I had a friend who had retarded children and I used to tutor them and I enjoyed that."

Receiving a partial scholarship, Ms. Edwards returned to a local college, where she completed her training. During her years at the telephone company and throughout college, she continued to live at home with her parents, an arrangement she recalls as warm and supportive rather than burdensome and limiting. Throughout her college years, she consistently held part-time jobs, usually working with children in community agencies. Her life was hectic and fast-moving and she enjoyed coming home to mother's cooking and care. "It was just unbelievable because I'd leave home in the morning at eight and get home about eleven at night, dinner was there. I don't know how mother put up with it because she never knew when I was going to be home but there was always some food there. And there was always money there." During this long and arduous journey through college, home remained a place of solace and comfort. Ms. Edwards' parents were of steady, working-class means, but education was their clear priority and they did everything in their power to support and encourage their children's schooling.

Not only did Ms. Edwards early recognize her calling as a teacher—a "calling" because the choice to become a teacher seemed more like a spiritual, other-worldly response similar to her father's call to the ministry than an explicit and conscious decision—but she claims to have always wanted to be a teacher and always to have known that she would eventually reach her goal. Her lack of clear, rational reasons for her career choice and her seeming unconcern about the various distractions that impeded her progress forward make it seem as if she was counting on some external guiding support, perhaps some divine intervention. She was also very much inspired by teachers she had in the seventh and eighth grades, whom she admired because "they both demanded an awful lot of order and you knew the rules and definitely had to obey them. They were in charge, very much in command." Ms. Edwards identified strongly with her seventh grade teacher, her first black teacher, but her absolute favorite was a high-powered German woman who was totally committed to teaching and who exuded a positive and encouraging spirit through a somewhat frightening, demanding facade. "She seemed like a very strong and dynamic person. She used to walk to school every day and she was straight and healthy. She taught for years and years and years and everyone in the community knew her. She was never sick a day in her life. Her job, her role in that classroom was the most important thing to her. You had to learn in her classroom or something was really wrong with you."

Interestingly, although Ms. Edwards speaks of these two teachers with awe and admiration, she does not view her own style as anything like theirs. She recalls their sense of order and control, but she often describes herself as confused, open, and relatively unstructured. She remembers them as being totally absorbed by and committed to their role as teacher, but she proudly speaks of being able to separate the worlds of home and school and reveals a great dedication and joy in mothering. So perhaps these two women stood as inspirations but were unreal models of professional behavior. Perhaps Ms. Edwards also has a lingering sense that her definition of professionalism is slightly compromised by her nonorderly temperament and her deep commitment to family life.

Ms. Edwards was married to her husband, a small-businessman, several days before graduation from college. The early years of their marriage were economically lean. She still had school loans to repay, her husband started his own firm and was struggling to become established, and she immediately became pregnant. To add to all of these burdens, Ms. Edwards began her first year as a teacher—a year she recalls as difficult and trying, in which she found it almost impossible to separate her schoolwork from her home life. With each year of teaching she has become more successful at differentiating the two environments and not permitting the negative feelings from a bad day at school to affect her interactions with her husband and child. Even though she has completely stopped bringing schoolwork home, she cannot stop bringing her concerns about children home in her head. Sometimes she even entertains fantasies about bringing one of her pupils home and giving him "the treatment," washing him from head to toe, combing his hair, and making him attractive and presentable. Her husband responds adamantly, "My God, they'll probably take you to court for it," and she soon recognizes the lack of wisdom revealed in her fantasy.

Only after one has made Ms. Edwards feel comfortable and trusting does she reveal the pain and isolation of being one of two black teachers in a large school whose student population is over fifty percent black. Her words and her images take on an emotional dimension that one rarely hears in her discussions about teaching. But once given space to focus on the experience of tokenism, the continuous and subtle assault of racism, she recalls her feelings and responses vividly.

Her experiences of exclusion, difference, and subtle oppression take hold in a variety of forms. At the most distant level she recognizes her black status when bureaucratic counts are being taken. Once a year a population census is made and an administrator circulates around the classrooms making sure the racial balance directives are being adhered to. Although Ms. Edwards feels very strongly that classes should be heterogeneously composed, she thinks that counting black and white heads is a simplistic and superficial measure of heterogeneity. If the school is to include an authentic mixture, then administrators must consider a variety of other dimensions—social class, ethnicity, religion, individual personality.

Also Ms. Edwards feels just as concerned about the racial balance of the teacher population, a topic which is scrupulously avoided by the school system. How can one be serious about providing an environment of positive white *and* black experience if there are negligible numbers of black teachers? What is a black child to think of his chances for success and excellence in a school where he has so few opportunities to see successful and productive black role models? And what sort of distorted experience are white children receiving when they view white teachers as virtually the only source of learning, culture, and knowledge?

Beyond the distortions that tokenism produces for the child's perspectives on learning and life, the productive efforts of the token black are diminished by the heavy burdens of isolation and high visibility. Ms. Edwards talks about the response of her white colleagues during Black History Week. They suddenly panic at their ignorance and incompetence in this area, and they look to her to represent and reflect the essence of "The Black Experience" in the United States. Ms. Edwards has ceased responding to these once-a-year requests for pictures of Martin Luther King and quick biographies of Harriet Tubman and Frederick Douglass because she feels that these events and heroes of black history should be considered important enough to be thoroughly integrated into the curriculum during the year. She becomes annoyed at these empty rituals and at the ignorance of her colleagues about the lives and experiences of blacks. "Every year when

Black History Week comes along, there's a bunch of people who come in wanting to know about black history, which I find very annoying . . . I'm supposed to learn about everyone else and you'd think people could learn about us . . . but I think this is representative of the actual feelings . . . the concern is over the number of black children [not their experience] . . . We have to meet a kind of numbers game.''

Ms. Edwards is also angered by what she believes is a general pattern of discrimination against black children in the school. The discriminatory policy regarding black students is not explicit nor immediately visible and harsh. In fact, it almost has a benign expression—black children are simply not taken seriously as students. Ms. Edwards perceives an expectation among her colleagues that blacks have minimal potential, that they will never develop academic competence, and that for them school serves a custodial function. ''It can be frustrating to me because sometimes I feel that most of the kids that are being pushed along are minority children . . . There are no demands being placed on these children or their parents because they are black and the feeling is that 'Well, they don't care.' ''

There is a great discrepancy, in her view, between the masses of black children who are passed through the system and graduate from the eighth grade as functional illiterates and the very special children of university parents who receive all the advantages of excellent attention and resources and for whose superior success in school the teacher is held ultimately accountable. In contrast, the black child's failure is either obscured and falsified by passing him on to the next grade regardless of his achievement and competence, or his failure is ultimately blamed on his poor and chaotic home background. The final blame rests with him, not with the teacher. The more privileged white child is taken seriously as a potential contributor to society, and his failure is more often perceived as a reflection of the teacher's incompetence.

When Ms. Edwards witnesses these extreme inequities, she feels angry and isolated from the mainstream perspective. Her isolation is increased by the additional burden of her perceived special competence as a black. ''As far as being a black teacher, you are in a sense expected to solve all the problems of black children.'' Her blackness makes her an immediate authority on disciplining and teaching black children; her blackness makes her better able to control and dominate their threatening actions; her blackness gives her a mysterious ability to communicate with and manipulate black children. All of these misperceptions by her white colleagues about the dark and mysterious side of blackness add to Ms. Edwards' more intense concern for the fate of black children in public schools and society in general and dominate and shape her relationships with her colleagues and her feelings about her professional role.

Interestingly, although people seem to think of her as relatively more competent and experienced in relating to black parents and children, they do not seem to take her professional ideas about learning and curriculum seriously. When talking about general issues related to the substance and process of schooling, her competence seems to suddenly diminish. "Sometimes in group discussions, when you're discussing something, about a problem or a particular child, and you offer a suggestion . . . (it is) sort of looked upon lightly . . . and when the suggestions are written up as a result of the meeting, there have been instances when none of those suggestions that you offered have been included . . . and sometimes you don't know whether it is paranoia or will it ever end."

So Ms. Edwards experiences extreme fluctuations of high visibility and invisibility in her status as a black teacher in this school. She is highly visible and much sought-after in her role as expert on blackness and in her function as problem solver for black troublemakers. But she is relatively invisible and neglected as a competent and functioning member of the school staff. Ms. Edwards is angered by both of these distortions and disfigurations of who she is and what she can do. She is asking to be taken seriously as a professional with a unique array of talents and skills as well as her share of weaknesses and prejudices. She is not asking her colleagues to pretend she is not black or to ignore the central part blackness plays in her personal identity, but she is asking them to look beyond her blackness to discover the richness of her individuality. And in the same breath, she is asking them to give the black children in their classrooms the same careful, thorough, and nonstereotyped attention.

EVER SINCE she can remember, Ms. Edwards wanted to be a teacher, but her career path was not direct, and she continues to reflect critically on her commitments to the profession and her skills and competence in relating to children. She seems to approach all aspects of her life with reflection, struggle, and self-criticism. Her initial approach to our research revealed those qualities, as do her interactions with children in the classroom.

For Ms. Edwards, teaching is a complex process of observation, analysis, and action. A great deal of energy is spent searching for the social, psychological, and intellectual nature of each child and trying to design effective pedagogical and interactional strategies to support his individual growth. Her efforts to know the dimensions of each child's personality and competence often diminish her ability to act quickly. Her focus on the complexities and subtleties of a child's world and her concern for the motivating forces underlying behavior frequently seem to overwhelm her and can stifle her spontaneous, intuitive interventions with children. She often claims to be "baffled" by the abundant information she has stored up on a single child and "confused" about how to proceed with him. Her movements in the classroom, therefore, sometimes appear vague even though her descriptions of events and experiences are precise and insightful.

Although the child's individuality is a constant source of interest and struggle to Ms. Edwards, she strongly believes that children must learn to function collectively. In fact, individual expression is viewed as critical to healthy group behavior. Most important, she believes that first grade should be a time for teaching children the basic social skills needed for responsible and caring participation in groups. Most six-year-olds arrive at school very used to the all-encompassing, nurturant attention of their parents. Their social and psychological needs tend to be self-centered and their visions of life egocentric. Teachers must take on the socioemotional task of restructuring the child's basic ways of relating to others. Ms. Edwards feels that socialization to the group environment is the primary agenda of first grade, but that it cannot be easily disentangled from the academic curriculum. When she structures reading groups, for instance, she is concerned with matching not only the intellectual competence of children but also the developing "chemistry" of personalities. And when she reviews the class for promotion to second grade, she stresses the social and emotional maturity of the child as well as his cognitive achievement.

Ms. Edwards does not believe that socialization of young children is a spontaneous process that emerges naturally when children come together in a group. It is not something that should be left to chance. Acculturation of children to the social demands of school requires the deliberate and systematic attention of the teacher. In training children to develop social responsibility, Ms. Edwards uses a didactic method of explicit value clarification and ritualized learning. When struggles develop among children she is likely to use the occasion to talk more generally about how and why conflicts arise, how people feel about them, and effective ways of resolving them. Her goal is to get children to the point where they will not feel the need to call on her to negotiate or intervene in the struggle but will be able to resolve it themselves. She seeks to slowly remove herself from center stage in the classroom and support her children in becoming more autonomous and more accountable for their own actions.

Many of the basic values that emerge in Ms. Edwards' teaching seem to reflect the traditions and history of her family of origin. She remembers a house filled with love and caring, the voices of many siblings, the wonderful smell of West Indian cooking, and the magic of making a little into a lot. She learned early to share, to feel responsible for her brothers and sisters, and to use her resources wisely. Each of the children in her family had different intellectual talents and were encouraged to develop their skills to the fullest. Her parents were firm disciplinarians and demanded correct behavior from their children. Good behavior, manners, and decorum were considered critical to a black child's success and assimilation in school and more important than academic excellence. One can trace in Ms. Edwards' teaching her parents' conceptions of social responsibility and individualization—the need for a dynamic interaction of individual expression and group accountability.

Ms. Edwards' history is mirrored not only in her interactions with children but also in her feelings of isolation and tokenism within the school setting. Her experience of being one of two black teachers in the entire school is alien to her upbringing in a very close and encompassing West Indian community. Her parents were not her only caretakers; the community served as an extended family, offering advice, support, love, and even punishment. The circle of love and intimacy was black and spread far beyond the boundaries of the nuclear family. Her professional environment is in stark contrast—a place where she lives a token black experience, a place where she feels the daily micro-aggressions of racism. The institutional and interpersonal racism that she perceives distracts her from her teaching, gives her a pervasive sense of aloneness, and affects her interactions with children.

Because she recognizes the subtle discriminatory treatment many of the black children in school receive from teachers who assume that black children are academically weak and who do not push them to achieve or else, out of guilt, award inflated grades for poor work, Ms. Edwards finds herself, almost unconsciously and alone, trying to reverse the pervasive institutional patterns. She works to counteract the negative, distorted views of black children and struggles to negate the categorizations made by colleagues who want her to play the multiple roles of consultant on black studies, counselor for black students, and spokesperson for the black world.

In her classroom, Ms. Edwards seems to respond to the subtle forms of discrimination she receives by reserving her special energies for the promising black children who have energy and style, whom she wants to save from the destructive forces of school and society. Her great admiration for Abdul, the "powerful" black boy from Africa, and her deep feelings of identification and empathy with Daniel, whose great potential is being slowly eroded by poverty and neglect, are part of her wish to support and celebrate children who might go unnoticed or unrecognized as special people.

Synthesis   *Jean V. Carew*

The two observers who visited Ms. Edwards' class both agreed that hers was the most difficult of the four to observe. The open structure of her class, the

fluid and sometimes disorganized nature of activities within it, the unpre-
dictability of the class schedule, Ms. Edwards' ambivalence about appropriate academic goals for her first graders, and her reluctance to act quickly, decisively, and according to set rules made observations in her classroom
both confusing and challenging. Whereas for the other three classes two or
three visits were sufficient to form a stable, subjective impression that one
could feel confident would be borne out by exact quantitative analysis, this
was not the case here. In a real sense Ms. Edwards' behavior seemed too reactive and too individualized to be captured by a coding system that worked
best when the teacher took the lead and there was a clear structuring of activity within a framework of explicit rules.

It was therefore surprising to us that the quantitative analyses of our observations did in the end provide a highly differentiated, sensitive, and apparently authentic picture of this teacher. The deeper and more intangible
aspects of her motivations and goals are most evident in the interview material, but the degree of congruence between this material and observation
data is remarkable. An outstanding characteristic of Ms. Edwards is her
highly reflective and self-critical approach to teaching. These are perhaps
the qualities that make her perceptions of herself so consonant with our objective observations of her behavior.

A salient feature of Ms. Edwards' class was the relative lack of emphasis
on teaching reading and other academic skills. Although nominally there
were three hierarchically structured reading groups in her class (the Whales,
Seals, and Dolphins), it was difficult to discern from observations who were
the stable members of each group, since Ms. Edwards called her reading
groups much less often and regularly than the other teachers. During our
eleven visits to her class, the Whales were never observed, and the Seals and
Dolphins were each called only five times.

Our observations of Ms. Edwards' interactions with her pupils also clearly showed that she and Ms. Ryan, the other teacher in the Outer School, devoted less time to teaching reading and academic skills in general than the
two teachers in the Inner School (reading: Mses. Edwards and Ryan, 29 and
48 percent, versus Mses. Allen and Prima, 75 and 77 percent; academic
skills: Mses. Edwards and Ryan, 74 and 69 percent, versus Mses. Allen and
Prima, 85 and 90 percent). These differences may be traceable to dissimilar-
ities between the two schools in policy standards, methods, staff, student
body, and so on. However, in her interviews Ms. Edwards described how
she deliberately and independently sought to keep her reading groups open
and flexible and to emphasize social development rather than academic
skills as the primary goal for her pupils. She saw the school administration
and other teachers as giving her little support or respect for pursuing these
principles. Thus, whether or not one agrees with Ms. Edwards' convictions,

it is clear that this was a conscious and deliberate strategy born of conviction to a different view of what was important to the education of children in first grade.

A related theme touched upon several times in the previous section was Ms. Edwards' characteristic tentativeness in planning and decision making, her preference for teaching on a one-to-one rather than a group basis, and her reluctance to impose undue structure and direction on the learning activities of children. In the terms of our observational system, this pedagogical approach shows a lack of organizational ability as indicated by an excessive amount of time spent in class management and in explaining and implementing classroom procedures. It is not surprising, then, that our analysis of their interactions in the classroom showed that the two teachers in the Outer School devoted almost twice as much time to procedural matters as the two teachers in the Inner School (Mses. Edwards and Ryan, 31 and 32 percent, versus Mses. Allen and Prima, 18 and 15 percent). But again, the finding seems to have a different significance for Mses. Edwards and Ryan. In Ms. Ryan's case excessive time spent on management and procedure was also associated with a relatively high amount of time spent on disciplining children for inappropriate classroom behavior. In contrast, the observation data show that Ms. Edwards spent relatively little time on behavioral control and discipline and that her interactions with children were considerably more positive than Ms. Ryan's (control of inappropriate child behavior: Edwards, 7 percent, versus Ryan, 11 percent). This finding is of course consonant with Ms. Edwards' interest in understanding and responding appropriately to the individual personalities of the children in her class and with her emphasis on their socioemotional development.

The observation system focused specifically on four types of teacher behavior toward children that are pertinent to this discussion: the use of an open versus a directive style of asking questions or requesting work; the asking of questions allowing free responses; positive evaluation of children's performance; and positive versus negative reinforcement of children's behavior. On all of these variables Ms. Edwards ranked first or second among the four teachers, her behavior being similar to Ms. Allen's and often conspicuously different from Ms. Ryan's, her co-teacher at the Outer School. Thus, in Ms. Edwards' classroom the percentage of open questions was 17 percent (compared to 8 percent for Ms. Ryan); the percentage of free questions was 6 percent versus 4 percent; the percentage of positive evaluation of children's responses was 19 percent versus 5 percent; and the percentage of positive and negative reinforcement of children's behavior was 5 and 18 percent (versus 4 and 23 percent). These statistics are the objective evidence for the central theme that emerged in interviews with Ms. Edwards—the care she takes to make children feel worthy and competent, her responsiveness to their needs, and her reluctance to impose on them her direction and authority.

Further evidence of Ms. Edwards' skill in socializing children comes from our observations of the actual behavior of pupils as she interacted with them. Four types of child behavior occurred frequently enough in our teacher-focused observations to be quantitatively analyzed: appropriate behavior (including achievement-oriented behavior and prosocial behavior such as helping and sharing); expressive behavior (expressing opinions, commenting); dependent behavior (asking for help, materials); and inappropriate behavior (including disrupting and annoying others and not attending to one's work). The children in Ms. Edwards' class ranked first or second on appropriate and expressive behavior and third or fourth on dependent and inappropriate behavior. As was the case for teacher behavior toward children, the behavior of Ms. Edwards' pupils closely resembled that of Ms. Allen's and contrasted strongly with the profiles of child behavior characterizing the other two classes.

It is important to note the consistency between these observations of actual child behavior in her classroom and Ms. Edwards' social developmental goals for her pupils. Ms. Edwards wanted her first graders to learn to treat each other considerately; she wanted them to be able to express their opinions and feelings without fear of contradiction or ridicule; she wanted them to be independent and resourceful and able to work and get along with each other without her constant supervision and control; and she wanted them to learn to find socially acceptable ways of expressing negative feelings. This litany of virtues is one that many a first-grade teacher might compile. The impressive thing about Ms. Edwards is the objective evidence of her success in meeting goals that are more easily idealized than realized. One must be chary of inferring cause and effect from correlational data: it is possible that the behavior of children in Ms. Edwards' class was not attributable to anything she did but rather that they were like that to start with. Although the many points of correspondence between Ms. Edwards' goals and the actual behavior of children make this alternative explanation implausible, the precise attribution of cause and effect is an issue that this study cannot resolve.

An important purpose of this research was to examine whether teachers treated black and white children in their classes differently, and if so, why. As the one black teacher in our sample, Ms. Edwards was a particularly valuable case. During our recruitment efforts, she was the only teacher who asked whether we were particularly interested in the experiences of minority children. She was also the only one who talked in the interviews about a special feeling of connectedness and empathy with black students and expressed a deep concern that they be taken seriously, with the same social and academic standards being applied to them as to whites. Ms. Edwards gave so sensitive and vivid an account of what it meant for her to be the token black teacher in her school and to be seen as being uniquely competent to guide and teach black children that we looked forward with particular curiosity to analyzing her actual behavior toward these two racial groups.

Our first task was to find out whether there were any significant differences in Ms. Edwards' treatment of black and white children and how she compared with the other three teachers in this respect. The results of this analysis showed that Ms. Edwards, like Ms. Allen, was remarkably fair. In fact, on *none* of the twenty variables included in this analysis was there a significant difference in Ms. Edwards' behavior toward black and white children or their behavior toward her. This finding is the more remarkable when one considers the open nature of Ms. Edwards' classroom, her emphasis on psychosocial development rather than the teaching of academic skills, and her tendency to interact with children on a one-to-one basis rather than in the context of a group, where rituals such as reading turns often serve to curtail the teacher's discretion and to equalize opportunities for children.

Another way in which teachers may discriminate among children is by assigning them to hierarchically distinct reading groups or seat locations which afford different opportunities for interactions with the teacher and with other children. On the basis of our observations it seems that the racial composition of reading groups and of seating patterns in Ms. Edwards' class was also impressively fair; her reading groups were each 50 percent black, precisely paralleling the racial composition of the class as a whole.

As to seating patterns, Ms. Edwards favored an arrangement of several clusters of adjoining desks, casually distributed around the room, with two or three desks to a cluster. This arrangement permitted each child to have one or two neighbors sitting at desks adjoining his, but neighbors were occasionally changed so that the typical child had about six different neighbors over the course of the year. Fifty percent of the children in Ms. Edwards' class were black and 49 percent of all neighbors were black. Thus, if seating patterns were color-blind in this class, one might expect that about half of the average black child's neighbors would be black and half white. Instead we find some evidence of overcompensation: 63 percent of the neighbors of black children were white and 58 percent of the neighbors of white children were black. Ms. Edwards seems to have gone out of her way to bring children of different races together as neighbors, a strategy that of course was very much in keeping with her interest in helping her first graders learn to tolerate and appreciate diverse cultures and personalities.

Another aspect of seating patterns that is often revealing of a teacher's values and relationships with children has to do with the isolation of certain pupils in the classroom. A familiar device for controlling troublemakers or distractible pupils is to place them close to the teacher's desk or to relegate them to seats with no neighbors. Ms. Edwards used this tactic more frequently than the other three teachers. She nearly always placed three boys close to her desk and set five other children apart from the class for short periods of time. Our observations show that overall, precisely 50 percent of children given this exceptional treatment were white and 50 percent were black. Ms. Edwards' reasons for doing so are instructive and best illustrated by our individual observations of Daniel, a black boy whom Ms. Edwards always placed close to her desk.

Ms. Edwards had a special relationship with this six-year-old black boy "from the project." Daniel has four brothers and sisters. His mother supports the family by working at two jobs, as a waitress and cab driver, while struggling to get her high school equivalency diploma. At twenty-nine, and without a husband to help, she works far into the night and sleeps late into the morning. Daniel has to get his own breakfast, dress himself, and catch the bus out of the project to school. He is often late, inadequately dressed, dirty, disheveled, and hungry when he gets there. But Daniel is very conscious of his physical appearance. He is a handsome, flirtatious boy, much admired by girls. To come to school with matted hair and a grimy face is unbearable. Ms. Edwards senses Daniel's feelings and has worked out a private arrangement which permits him to use a bathroom at the school to wash and brush up before coming to class. Now, everyone looks up when Daniel makes his entrance. Girls rush up to hug him, boys to shake his hand. With his radiant smile, sparkling eyes, and sculptured Afro, Daniel is a prince among the first graders. Only Ms. Edwards knows how he looked before.

Ms. Edwards understands a lot about Daniel that his classmates may perceive only dimly. Daniel has many sides to his personality. One is that of a natural leader—an active, dynamic, charismatic, powerful boy who can fire up the class and direct their energies and enthusiasm to any purpose. Authoritative, affectionate, playful, and easygoing, this is the Daniel that draws his classmates toward him and makes him sought after, even idolized. There is, however, another side of Daniel that repels and frightens his many admirers. Suddenly, and with no apparent provocation, he may strike out, shoving, kicking, teasing, and bullying his victims relentlessly. The third side of Daniel, which perhaps only Ms. Edwards perceives, is his deep insecurity: his feeling of being unloved, unprotected, incompetent, his constant need for approval, reassurance, and encouragement.

The other children in Daniel's class may not know that about a year ago his fourteen-year-old brother was killed in an accident as he tried to escape pursuit by the police in a stolen car. Daniel at the time was in kindergarten and a second brother, George, was in the first grade at the Outer School. The older brother's death "tore George to pieces. He would run out of the classroom, up to the third floor, and jump from the third-floor landing to the basement. He'd take scissors and just throw them at other children." Now, at long last, George is pulling through. In Ms. Edwards' words: "I guess that if I never again see a child make progress, George will be enough to last the rest of my life." But what is in store for Daniel? After his kindergarten year in which he seemed fairly oblivious to the catastrophe, Daniel is beginning to act out his repressed feelings by persecuting the now subdued George and by victimizing his classmates. Part of the reason seems to be his mother's constant comparison of Daniel to his "criminal" older brother, whose fate she is sure Daniel will inevitably meet and deserve. Yet Daniel adores his mother. Seeing in him the makings of her older son, she spurns him. At Christmas he gets no present, at Halloween no costume, on his birthday no remembrance. Promises to visit his class are always broken, and an inadvertent remark from Ms. Edwards that Daniel is causing trouble at school provokes his mother's wrath in the form of a terrible beating.

Why then does Ms. Edwards place Daniel close to her desk and give him much more attention than she pays the average child? One reason certainly is Ms. Edwards' responsibility to protect other children from Daniel's unpredictable aggressive outbursts. Another is his need for constant supervison in his schoolwork, for he has fallen behind and is easily distracted, frustrated, and defeated. But an equally important reason in Ms. Edwards' mind is Daniel's need for physical and psychological closeness to an adult. Lacking this closeness with his mother, Daniel seeks to find it with the only other significant adult in his life, his teacher. As a black female, Ms. Edwards is conscious of her unique ability to meet this boy's needs for a black mother figure. She is also well aware of the dangers inherent in playing this surrogate role. But Daniel's present needs are so pressing, the consequences of ignoring them so ominous, that she sees no real ethical alternative.

Thus, it is hardly surprising that the quantitative analysis of the observation data (table 18) shows that Daniel engages in more interactions with Ms. Edwards than any child in his class and considerably more than the average child (12 percent versus 7 percent). Clearly Daniel is the student who captures most of Ms. Edwards' attention, but are her interactions with him qualitatively distinctive? In most respects Ms. Edwards seems to treat Daniel as she does the typical child in her class. She spends 53 percent of her interactions with him on academic activities, 5 percent on nonacademic activities, and 28 percent on procedural topics. She provides him with positive evaluation of his behavior and responds positively to his requests 11 percent and 8 percent of the time. These figures are virtually the same as the corre-

Table 18. Daniel versus average child: teacher-focused observations.

Variable	Daniel	Average child[1]
Interaction topic		
Academic	53.3%	53.7%
Nonacademic	4.6	3.8
Procedural	28.2	32.2
Privilege	3.1	3.2
Appropriate C behavior	0.0	0.2
Inappropriate C behavior	10.3	6.2
Health, distress	0.5	0.6
Selected child and teacher behaviors		
Appropriate C behavior	8.7	7.4
Positive T reinforcement	10.8	11.3
Expressive C behavior	12.3	7.1
T humor, conversation	6.7	4.1
Dependent C behavior	6.7	7.3
T grants request	7.7	7.9
T rejects request	1.0	2.0
Inappropriate C behavior	6.7	5.1
Negative T reinforcement	18.5	12.8
T open/free question	3.1	8.3
T process question	0.5	4.5
% total teacher-child interactions[2]	11.7	7.3

1. Average of all children in Ms. Edwards' class.
2. Percentage of all teacher-child interactions for which the child was present and was a potential recipient.

sponding figures for the average child in his class. The two respects in which Ms. Edwards seems to treat Daniel somewhat differently are that his inappropriate behavior is more likely to become an issue between them (10 percent, versus 6 percent for the average child), and she gives him more than an average share of negative reinforcement (19 versus 13 percent).

Is this difference in treatment warranted in the sense that Daniel really is more likely than his classmates to behave in inappropriate ways? To answer this question we turn from teacher-focused observations to child-focused observations in which individual children were watched during free play and seatwork (table 19). These activities seemed to us to provide appropriate contexts for observing the normal behavior of the child vis-à-vis schoolwork and classmates when the teacher's influence was less dominant. Daniel's behavior stands out in the following respects: he is very social (62 percent of the time he is interacting with someone), he is often inattentive to his work (14 percent), and the ratio of the negative to positive interactions he initiates with others is two to one. The extent to which this profile of Daniel's behavior accords with Ms. Edwards' overall perceptions of him is worth noting. Ms. Edwards described Daniel as a natural leader whose classmates both loved and feared him. She saw him as charming and sociable but also aggressive and distractible. Nothing in our quantitative analysis of Daniel's behavior contradicts this characterization. Once more, Ms. Edwards' insights seem to be precisely on the mark.

We end this account of Daniel by juxtaposing some of Ms. Edwards' comments in the interviews with excerpts from our actual observations of Daniel in school. First his ability to assume authority and act as a leader:

Ms. Edwards: "Suppose everybody is screaming at one another, Daniel can bring them right down. He'll say, 'Hold it, how many people are supposed to be talking at one time?' But he's not a tyrant. He's a good guy to have in class." Ms. Edwards' remarks are illustrated by the following observation, during which Daniel takes it upon himself to organize the after-

Table 19. Daniel versus average child: child-focused observations.

Variable	Daniel	Average child[1]	Range
Child activities			
Work	25.1%	46.3%	25.1-69.0%
Play	19.6	8.6	1.0-19.6
Talk	26.2	18.6	8.2-27.0
Self-care	1.7	3.0	1.0-7.5
Idle	14.1	15.4	2.7-29.6
Wild/disorderly conduct	7.5	2.8	0.0-8.5
Interacts with others	61.7	45.9	32.4-65.2
Child behavior when interacting with others			
Exhibits appropriate behavior	4.0	2.9	0.4-6.4
Receives appropriate behavior	1.7	2.3	0.8-5.5
Exhibits inappropriate behavior	10.1	5.9	0.4-22.8
Receives inappropriate behavior	1.7	2.4	0.7-6.6

1. Average of children observed individually in the four classes.

noon Show and Tell. Daniel: "Go ahead, Scott!" Daniel sits and watches, smiling. Daniel: "Now, come on, Judy!" Judy declines; she has to work. Daniel: "Hey Brian! Bring your Show and Tell up." Raymond is ready to start. Daniel: "Raymond, wait! Brian's not here yet." Ms. Edwards reprimands them briefly for the noise. Daniel looks around. Daniel: "Yes sir, Raymond, you're going next! I can see your [Show and Tell] thing. Shhh!" (to children who are making noise). Daniel watches Scott put on a record for his Show and Tell. Daniel: "Hey, he's got a record!" Daniel sings and moves rhythmically to the music. "Ooh! ooh! ooh!" Jackie asks Susan if she's going to turn off the lights during her Show and Tell. Daniel: "Eeee! I hope you do" (pretending to be scared). "Shhh! Be quiet, one at a time, Tyrone! Brian, come on. Let Brian play. Let him show." Daniel watches Brian prepare his Show and Tell. Daniel to Bridget (who is getting in Brian's way): "Get out! Let him show." Daniel helps Brian take the toys out of the bag for his Show and Tell.

So far as academic work is concerned, Daniel is "at the low level of the totem pole." Ms. Edwards: "There seem to be so many things that play into this—anxiety chiefly. You can give him a letter, give him the sound, and ask him to give you some words or even pictures. He's so anxious to do it that the minute he makes a mistake, if you don't handle it carefully, he's defeated completely. There's no gradual thing, he's down to the bottom. And there's a constant need for that little extra attention, patience, and understanding to get him up. He can be a hard worker. He enjoys math and he can really get it finished, go into other areas and not distract anyone. It's amazing how he can work at times, then at other times he's just *raw* with distraction . . . especially if he's had a bad time at home."

Consider the following observation, during which Daniel is supposed to be working on his math.

Daniel: "5 take away 1." Daniel counts on his fingers, then looks at the teacher. He writes an answer on the paper, stretches, yawns, sits, and stares at the other children. Daniel picks up his pencil and waves it. He stretches, gets up, walks around. He gets a piece of paper, sits, scratches on it, and squishes the paper up. Daniel goes back to get a new paper. Teacher: "Do this one." Daniel: "I did." Teacher: "All the ones without answers are wrong." Daniel looks at his paper, frowns, and erases. Daniel: "2 take away 1." He erases the answer and mumbles to himself. He taps the pencil on the table, then pounds his fist on the table. He erases, looks at the teacher, erases, brushes erasures off, erases, and brushes. Daniel looks at the problems. Daniel: "2 take away 1." He counts on his fingers, writes an answer. "5 take away 5." He counts on his fingers. He rubs his eyes, mumbles to himself, covers his eyes with his hands, leans back and stretches. He rubs his eye. He sits and stares at the others. He rubs his other eye, rubs both eyes, scratches his head, rubs his eyes, sits and kicks his desk. He rubs his eyes, yawns, picks his nose, wipes his hand on his pants, looks at his arm, and rubs his nose . . .

Of the three minutes of coded behavior in the above observation, Daniel was on task only about half the time. Ms. Edwards' phrase "raw with distraction" could hardly be more apt. Now contrast this with the following observation made toward the end of the school year. Daniel is working on a reading-writing exercise at his desk.

Daniel reads aloud to himself: "The dog ran." He erases his paper. Daniel reads: "The dog is yellow." He colors the dog yellow. Daniel reads: "The cat is purple." He writes on a slip of paper, *p u r p.* He looks at the book, writes *l e,* then closes the book. Daniel opens to the page with colors on it and looks at the colors. Daniel tries to sound out words and match the spellings on his paper. He turns the paper over and reads the words. He writes *p i g* under the picture. Daniel sniffles, taps his pencil on the desk top, looks at the pictures, and writes *p o p* under the picture of a popsicle. Daniel puts his pencil to his head. Daniel: "Tyrone, what's that?" Tyrone: "That is a pad." Daniel: "Which word is that? This one?" Daniel writes *p a d* under the picture. He writes *p i n* under the picture of a pin, and turns the paper over to look at the next picture. He tries to guess its name. Daniel writes *p o d* under a pea pod. Daniel checks his words. He writes *p a n* on the page. Daniel: "I'm all done, Ms. Edwards! The work I have to do is all here!"

In this observation we see marked improvement in Daniel's ability to focus on his work, although he is clearly well behind grade level in the material and skills he has mastered.

Regarding evidence of improvement in Daniel's ability to control and express aggression in socially acceptable ways, Ms. Edwards says: "He can really terrify you in the class. You know, 'I'm gonna knock you out, I'm gonna kick your butt!' . . . it is very, very difficult for him not to strike out and just tear somebody up. But now I see him coming in and saying that he wants to *talk* to somebody . . . somebody did something to him and he wants to *talk* it out rather than retaliate."

In our very first observation of Daniel we witnessed the following.

Daniel is walking toward the playground. Suddenly he runs over and pulls Susan's hand. She tries to get away. He holds her and pulls her up the stairs with two other boys, then lets go, laughs, and smiles. She holds him. Susan: "Get the heck off me!" Daniel: "Shove off!" Daniel takes the ball from Judy, bounces it, kicks it high. Daniel and Eric chase another girl and grab her. Daniel pulls off her coat, walks with it, drops it, then runs and grabs the girl. He then chases the child with the ball, takes it, and bounces it. Other children take the ball from him. He pursues them, yelling at Eric for taking it. He and Eric watch the older kids play basketball. Daniel chases a girl and tries to pull off her coat. He watches another child, goes over and kicks her, then chases Eric and knocks him down. Daniel gets the ball and runs around bouncing it. He suddenly goes after a girl, grabs hold of her coat, and pushes her away. Daniel now chases the child with the ball. The child throws the ball, Daniel gets it, bounces it, then walks over, pulls Eric away from George, and kicks him. Daniel watches Eric chase George, tugs at Eric, and throws the ball at him. Daniel wrestles with a girl, pulls her to the stairs, and she screams. He pulls her over and laughs; three boys gang up on her. She pushes Daniel and gets away. He sits on the stairs for a minute, then runs after Tyrone, who has the ball, and knocks him down.

In this five-minute observation the observer coded thirteen instances of physical aggression by Daniel against other children, mostly girls. In the following observation Daniel's aggressiveness is still clearly evident but is more modulated and obliquely expressed.

Daniel and Tyrone are playing with clay. Tyrone: "I'm making Raymond." Daniel: "Me too! That should be fun!" Daniel rolls clay in his hands, makes a ball "head," then squishes a flat piece to the ball. Daniel: "This is Raymond, right? And here comes Ms. Edwards. Bam! Then here comes Ms. Edwards and his head fell off, and he gets it! Bam!" Daniel laughs as Tyrone plays. Daniel: "Make Bridget for me. Hey, make Bridget for me!" Daniel watches Tyrone do so and laughs. Daniel gets the cover of a can to squash the clay, then cuts the arm off "Bridget," Tyrone's clay doll. Tyrone: "Look at Raymond! He's every which way except good!" Daniel: "You should make a long shape. I'm making a long one. Lookit, a cigar." Daniel puts the clay cigar in his mouth. Daniel: "Bridget's nasty like that."

Finally, two months later we see Daniel and his pals playing cards.

Daniel: "Bert, want to play cards?" Daniel goes to get the cards, smiling. Daniel, Eric, Scott, and Bert sit around the table. Daniel: "Scott, you can sit over here." Daniel arranges the cards. Bert: "No, this way." Daniel smiles and watches as Bert shows him how. Daniel picks up the cards as they are passed out. He's the first to open. Daniel: "Oh! Deuces are wild!" They play the first round and Bert wins. Daniel: "Ooh! Over! You must say, 'I declare war!' Say, 'I declare war!' " Daniel smiles as Eric says it. Daniel picks up some cards. Eric: "Danny, gimme my cards." Daniel complies. Daniel: "I'm still gonna win!" Daniel puts down a card. Daniel: "That's yours, Scott. Go ahead, Eric. Oh! I want to knock him out!" (of the game). Bert: "Hey Danny! Don't put your cards on the top of the deck. That's [not fair]. That's how you win." Daniel complies and the game stops as Ms. Edwards announces it's time to go out.

In these observations we see a child who seems to be slowly learning to control his violent impulses and to observe the rules of give and take. Daniel may be no one's ideal student but with a less perceptive teacher he might have fared far worse. In our private interview with him, this six-year-old came straight to the point. Queried why he liked his teacher, the typical child often gave the stereotypic reply, " 'Cause she's our teacher. 'Cause she's nice." Asked this question, Daniel replied without hesitation: "Oh, I really *love* her. She's my *buddy,* don't you know. She's my friend!"

9

Ms. Ryan

Interpretation   *Jean V. Carew*

"I FEEL like I come into school sometimes and all I am is a disciplinarian. I'm not here to teach at all which is what I should be here for . . . But my problem is . . . I've got such a limited experience and limited background, what else am I qualified to do? I only know how to teach." I felt great sympathy for Ms. Ryan as she said these words. I saw her as conscientious and hard-working and I wondered why she has had such difficulties, for there is much in her background that might have equipped her to face her urban classroom. Ms. Ryan comes from a very large, close-knit, loving, well-run family in which the children were expected to take care of one another, to do their share of household chores without too much complaint, to be well-mannered and obedient, to live in reasonable harmony. As a girl Ms. Ryan accepted her responsibilities cheerfully, delighted in being a surrogate mother and teacher to the younger ones, and found herself rather effective in the role. It seemed only natural that as a teenager she should quickly settle on teaching as a future career. It was a job she was likely to be successful at, one she would enjoy, and most important, since she would have to pay for her college education, it was financially feasible. "A lot of my background and reason for going into teaching goes back to enjoying working with the younger kids in my family. I had a lot of experience babysitting, helping with homework, doing chores around the house . . . I went into teaching because I guess I felt successful in what I had done and again maybe being familiar with kids, it wasn't like going into something completely strange. That's been my security blanket . . . I don't ever remember having frightening, overwhelmingly scary thoughts about going in and facing twenty kids. I felt pretty confident about teaching."

Immediately after high school, therefore, Ms. Ryan attended a local college and in due course earned her degree and teacher certification. Her first and only regular full-time job was at the Outer School, where she has been for the last five years.

Ms. Ryan did not say a great deal more about how her parents, siblings, teachers, husband, or other people in her life influenced her as a person or prepared her to be a teacher. But she remembers her father's insistence on effort and good behavior in school and sees the connection with her present mode of teaching. "We had the whole range of academic achievement in our family, and it always stuck in my mind that Dad was pleased with our accomplishments, but it was much more important to him how we were behaving and how hard we were trying . . . we really got laid into if our behavior and effort were not up to par . . . that's why in my own teaching I'm concerned not with what you're producing, but how you're producing it, the effort involved."

Ms. Ryan thinks also of the parochial schools that she attended all her growing-up years in Ashton, a town adjacent to Conroy. She describes with mock horror classes of forty to fifty children sitting submissively in rows, totally dominated by the nuns, but she recalls also the explicit rules and standards, the order and good conduct that prevailed; these memories of children happy, productive, and well-behaved in a sternly disciplined setting have remained with her to this day.

Ms. Ryan's training in college was also along traditional lines, her exposure to "open-education" concepts coming mostly from workshops and other voluntary courses she took subsequently. In her first two years at the Outer School Ms. Ryan taught "the way she thought she should," mostly following the traditional mode, but the following year she experimented with a more open framework which worked well with the particular class she then had. She has since come full circle, moving back toward a more traditional, structured approach, a reversal based on her gradually evolving perceptions of "what the kids are able to do and what type of organization they need to function." Nevertheless, like the other three teachers in this study, she rejects the labels "traditional," "structured." She sees her classroom as an eclectic blend of open and traditional modes tailored to suit the children she has to work with and herself. "I don't like to think I'm putting kids into a mold. At the same time there has to be a certain code by which we operate and I'm trying to set up standards for what I know are *my* limits and what I hope is appropriate for these children."

In explaining her approach to teaching Ms. Ryan shifts back and forth from a description emphasizing the values of openness and of personal and social development in children to one stressing order, discipline, and academic achievement as priorities. Asked to put herself in the place of an observer and describe her classroom, Ms. Ryan replies: "I think the first thing I would like to see happening is interaction with children, showing how they can get along socially and academically in a helping type of way, rather than constantly using physical language . . . I'd like to have them feeling good about themselves, feeling successful and feeling they are accomplishing something . . . learning how to get along with other people . . . not so much learning to learn but learning to *live*. I'd like to get a more frequent sense of this happening. I think that a lot of the time it is happening, but I get blinded by the fact that I'm so hung up on academic progress that I can't look beyond that.''

Ms. Ryan's concern for academic progress was in accordance with demands of the school administration and parents. But she also impressed me as having somewhat idealized expectations for how children so young should behave—expectations that seemed to cloud her appreciation of her first graders' personal and social achievements. Very likely these expectations trace back to memories of well-behaved, responsible classmates in parochial school, even though this good conduct came at some cost to self-expression. Whatever their roots, it seemed to me that Ms. Ryan's high standards, her narrow definition of good behavior, and her intolerance of immaturity were factors detracting from her effectiveness as a teacher. In one interview carried out three months after school had started Ms. Ryan was asked to give a thumbnail sketch of each child in her class in whatever terms she saw fit. She was the only one of the four teachers who described a majority of her first graders in predominantly negative terms. Of the twenty children in her class, Ms. Ryan depicted only four or five as not having notable academic or social problems. Of the rest she portrayed eight as excessively "babied, spoiled, overly dependent." Others were "immature," "lazy," "distractible," "disorganized," "disruptive," "uncontrollable," "wild." Later, when asked to review their progress over the year, Ms. Ryan still perceived most children as having some academic or social deficiency. Her warmest praise went to those who were polite, well-behaved, and hardworking and her sharpest criticism was of those who were either "little babies" in class or uncontrollable "difficult children." Consider these three vignettes:

Gregory, "a good kid." "He definitely has some kind of learning disability. Even at this point he can't identify his letters. He puts out a lot of effort but it just isn't coming to him. But he's a good kid. A real nice little boy. He'll be the first one to volunteer to help clean up or something, or pick up something that's knocked over. A lot of behavior like that comes from his background. His mother considers these things are important—being nice to people, saying thank you, and helping. He's got four or five brothers and sisters and he's expected to do a lot of things at home to help out."

Madeline, "a baby." "She's a bright little girl but knows how to be a royal pain. She has a minor hearing problem but I feel that a lot of the time that she doesn't hear it's because she doesn't want to . . . it's her way of getting attention, her way of complaining about something . . . Academically she has no problem but she's really sloppy in what she does. Look at her name tag on her desk. When everybody else's is laying flat, hers has to be rolled up . . . Socially she's a disaster. There's not one single child she's really friendly with . . . The other day I had the kids write down the name of the first and second person they liked to play with most. Then the name of the person they liked to play with least. Madeline did not get a single number one vote and ten of the sixteen children said they liked to play with her least! I think the problem is that she's been the baby in the family . . . she's treated like she's the queen of the house, catered to, and has everything done the way she wants it. So she really doesn't have to consider other people's needs or wants or considerations."

Kenneth, "a difficult child." "He's my 'child of the year' type of kid. Every year I have one who I am not going to let get the best of me. He's a very demanding child, demanding of attention and time . . . He's definitely a child whose behavior interferes with his academics . . . he just can't sit still . . . he can't do without adult supervision or help. He's a real disruption to the class . . . He's no dummy. He's a bright little kid. And he knows exactly what he's doing to me. He just seems to crave doing it."

Ms. Ryan sees parents and the home as the main source of her students' personal and social deficiencies. She seems to place children into two main categories. First, a large group of "babies" whose immature behavior is variously manifested in their continually seeking help with their work and requiring directions to be repeated; in their lack of impulse control, constant interruption when others are speaking, and frequent attention seeking; in their inattentiveness, playfulness, inability to concentrate on a task for long without supervision; in disorganization, dreaminess, and lack of common sense; in their lack of skill in relating to other children in play or in abiding by the ground rules in group activities. Ms. Ryan's explanation in nearly all of these cases is that the child in question is "spoiled" and catered to too much at home. The classroom "baby" is often an only child, the last child in the family, or the child of a single parent, and typically is surrounded only by attentive, indulging adults and has little contact with other children. His mother does everything for him when and how he wants it, and he or she is not required to wait, take turns, share, help. Used to being a little queen or king at home, a child like this finds it very difficult to adapt to the group setting of a classroom, where the teacher cannot play the role of an indulgent mother and where other children make similar selfish demands. It is easy to understand why Ms. Ryan might leap to negative judgments of parents who "spoil" their only children: the experience is so far from her own upbringing, which stressed shared responsibility and mutual support among several siblings.

Although Ms. Ryan has no opportunity to observe the babying relationship directly in the home, she sometimes sees it firsthand when parents bring their children to class in the morning. A case in point is Nina. "We'd go through this ten- or fifteen-minute procedure in the morning when her mother was leaving the classroom. She'd come into the room and help Nina put her coat away. Then Nina would have to go out in the hall and throw kisses to her, and her mother would say, 'I caught it, Nina.' . . . This ritual would go on every single morning!"

Mostly, however, Ms. Ryan infers the parent's overindulgence of the child by observing the latter's behavior in the classroom, as in the sketch of Madeline given above. By a similar process of reasoning Ms. Ryan attributes the disruptive, defiant, aggressive behaviors of boys like Kenneth and Russell to their rough, chaotic, unstable homes and parents who provide little approval, affection, or security. Ms. Ryan has never had the opportunity to visit these boys' homes, but her brief, guarded contacts with their mothers, her direct experiences with their children in school, their mothers' reputation with other teachers as inadequate parents, and the notoriety of the housing project in which they live suggest to her that the home is at the root of their problems.

This is not to say that Ms. Ryan's actual relationships with parents are unconstructive or unfeeling. She recounts the details of conferences with several mothers in which she displayed sensitivity, discretion, and concern for a child in trouble. For example, Donna's mother was at her wits' end about her daughter's temper tantrums at home. Ms. Ryan reassured her that she saw nothing so extreme in Donna's behavior in class but encouraged her to consult a guidance counselor for a third opinion. Ms. Ryan also met with the mother of Anko, a Korean boy, about his constant requests to have her repeat directions. Ms. Ryan had had Anko's hearing checked, and having ascertained he had no hearing problem, she and the mother discussed other possibilities: bilingual interference, culturally-derived perfectionist standards, absent-mindedness, too little contact with other children. Ms. Ryan also conferred with Vanessa's mother about whether her daughter would be promoted to second grade. An airline stewardess, Vanessa's mother was away from home much of the time, so for most of the year Vanessa lived with a grandmother in Conroy. When the grandmother became ill and unable to care for her, Vanessa went to live with a grandfather in another town a considerable distance away. Already far behind in her schoolwork, Vanessa began to miss weeks of school and her promotion was in grave jeopardy. Ms. Ryan worked out a system of homework assignments with Vanessa's mother plus tutoring from a neighborhood teacher which saved the day for Vanessa. Even in the case of Kenneth's mother, Ms. Ryan initially took a sympathetic, constructive approach. Knowing the mother already had her hands full with problems concerning her other children, Ms. Ryan went out of her way to find something to praise in Kenneth. "Just the fact that I was able to comment how clean Ken is and that he's always so well taken care of, that his clothes are so clean and he's always dressed for the weather. Little things like that made her feel good." Later, however, as her frustration and difficulties with Kenneth intensified, Ms. Ryan adopted a very different stance.

Curiously, Ms. Ryan often admits she is at a loss to understand why some of her first graders behave the way they do or why they fail to respond to her attempts at changing them. She does not "really know" why Donna has her temper tantrums, why Vanessa is so immature, why Cheryl is so disorganized, why Madeline is so self-centered, why Kenneth is so obstinate, defiant, and aggressive. Unsure in her diagnosis, Ms. Ryan seems ambivalent and inconsistent in her attempts at treatment. For example, in Vanessa's case she reasons that a more playful approach with liberal amounts of praise for effort may do the trick and she tries this strategy for awhile.

> Vanessa . . . academically, I'm very concerned about her because I think that her attitude is really interfering with her work. She lives with her grandmother in a very adult world and isn't given the opportunity to get involved in kid-type activities. So when she comes to school, there's so much going on she gets bombarded and flits from one thing to another. Everything is taken with a very playful attitude. And she gets into sulking moods, too, which doesn't help. If anything is in the least bit challenging to her, she may not even make an attempt. In a reading group or even if we're just reading a story, she gets very restless and fidgety and starts fooling around with the person next to her. . . . So, I've been trying to boost her ego and make her feel good about what she's doing and make a lot of situations more playful, more of a game than a work-type situation. But it's the type of thing that at the moment it's effective, but it doesn't have a long-lasting effect. It doesn't carry over to the next thing. She needs immediate approval, praise for almost everything. And I can't give it to her with so many other demanding children in the class.

Ms. Ryan's lack of confidence in herself, her frustration, are more vividly illustrated in her account of her steadily deteriorating relationship with Madeline. Madeline is the "baby" who uses her minor hearing problem to get her own way and whom the other children selected as the child they least want to play with.

> In the last couple of months she's really rubbed me the wrong way. Anything I say she has to say the opposite. If I say sit, she says stand . . . I have to build up my tolerance, my willpower not to say anything, to avoid getting really angry at her. Because she won't back down. So in order to not get myself upset I have to back down. I don't know

whether it really has gotten worse or . . . maybe because it's getting late in the year, my patience is wearing thin. But I've had enough of her pulling this act on me all year long. I can only take so much. So I've got to the point where I don't even answer her because I end up getting mad myself. Like the other day when I told her to finish clearing her desk and she said "No!" and began to argue. I just ended it. "Finish clearing your desk and I don't want to hear another word from you!" I said. And now, when we're playing a game and she won't play by the rules I just up and walk away. I don't give her the chance to walk away from me first.

But it is Kenneth more than any of the other children in her class who has made Ms. Ryan doubt her effectiveness as a teacher. Three months after school started she described him as her "child of the year," the one whom she would not let "get the best of her." But by year's end Kenneth had so undermined Ms. Ryan's self-esteem and had attained so powerful an influence over other children that according to Ms. Ryan his sheer presence or absence ensured two completely different classrooms: one in which she, the teacher, was more or less in control versus one in which she might as well be "talking to the walls."

There are two topics that really rouse Ms. Ryan's ire: Kenneth and the school administration. The two topics are interwoven because Ms. Ryan often has to turn to the office for help in controlling Kenneth, so she has strong opinions about the principal and his staff. What upsets her most about the principal, Mr. Barry, is his indecisiveness, his timidity, his lack of leadership. She sees him as a nice person and acknowledges his past reputation as an excellent teacher, but finds him not well-suited to his present role as the head of a large, ethnically and socially heterogeneous urban school. For example, despite many recommendations from teachers, there is still no book of rules and operating procedures in the school for handling discipline, tardiness, absences from class, and so on so that teachers, students, and parents know what is expected and what the consequences are for failure to conform. Lacking explicit rules, there is little consistency in practice from administrator to administrator, or teacher to teacher, with the result that some teachers do as they please, often taking the line of least resistance. Ms. Ryan describes a recent meeting of the school staff on this issue and her feelings of anger and helplessness as it became clear what some other teachers were getting away with, how certain parents were sloughing off their responsibilities, and how unlikely it was that the principal would take steps to bring them into line.

A recent incident involving Kenneth brought these issues to a head. Kenneth simply left school one day, maneuvered his way across heavily trafficked streets, and went home with the news that his younger brother,

Thomas, was missing from class. Ms. Ryan had seen Ken leave her class-room and warned the office, but no action was taken. His mother called the school when Ken showed up, and the principal checked and assured her that Thomas was safely in class. It did not occur to Mr. Barry that the real issue was not Thomas's alleged absence but Kenneth's walking out of school, a very serious and dangerous infraction for a seven-year-old and one he had committed before. It was Ms. Ryan who had to point this out to Mr. Barry and insist that he call Kenneth's mother and tell her that if Kenneth broke the rule again he would not be allowed to come back until his behavior im-proved. Ms. Ryan compared Mr. Barry's handling of this situation with the tough stance of another principal, who kept a boy sitting in his office for days until his mother showed up to discuss the child's offense. The boy "has been a peach since then" and so would Kenneth, if only the adminis-tration was clear, consistent, and tough about the rules of the school. "He probably considers it a privilege to come to school, so if this privilege is taken away from him and he has to stay at home and listen to his mother complaining and yelling at him all day, maybe he'll start shaping up. Be-cause he certainly has been given too many privileges right now. I know he needs a lot. I try to appreciate this fact and keep it in the back of my mind, but he's just gotten away with too much; he's pushed me too far."

Ms. Ryan is a conscientious and committed person who puts a great deal of effort into teaching and spends many long hours after school preparing lesson plans, completing paperwork, and doing the many extra tasks re-quired of a responsible teacher. She also frequently attends workshops and conferences designed to improve teaching styles and curriculum content. She is therefore dismayed that in this school "there is no incentive for being good," for abiding by the rules. This slackness carries over to the classroom and the home, for teachers, children, and parents soon realize that they can act as they please with impunity.

In describing the Outer School as a system, Ms. Ryan is most concerned about issues of governance and control. She seems less concerned about the more insidious practices that so disturbed Ms. Allen and Ms. Prima: the overuse of remedial tutors and adjustment counselors, the labeling of chil-dren on the basis of psychological evaluations, the IQ tests. Six of the twen-ty children in her room go to a remedial tutor regularly, and this is clearly a relief to her, especially in the case of Kenneth, whose absence guarantees a relatively controllable class. Ms. Ryan does not seriously question whether this practice is deleterious to the children involved because in her view the particular remedial tutor to whom her first graders go is excellent and has helped them considerably. In general, for Ms. Ryan it is not the system that is at fault but individual administrators who, lacking qualities of leadership and forcefulness, fail to impose clarity, consistency, and discipline and to provide the support that teachers require. Ms. Ryan frequently brought her problems to the office, yet, like parents, the office often could not be counted on to help.

Ms. Ryan's relationship with other teachers is not a source of comfort either. Her isolation has become acute these last two years because her classroom is now "tucked away in a corner" without immediate access to other first-grade rooms. Because of their location and similar schedules, the other two first-grade teachers can more easily collaborate on projects, relieve each other in emergencies, get together for coffee and a chat. Ms. Ryan finds herself cut off from this casual social network, unable to find time to go out with her friends for a sandwich at lunch or for Chinese food some evening. She feels pushed, overwhelmed, harassed, and dispirited—feelings that are understandably exacerbated by loneliness and the loss of old friends.

"Today was a worthwhile day. I felt I was contributing something and the kids probably felt good about leaving school rather than leaving thinking 'Aw, that old witch . . . can't wait 'til 2:30 to get outta here.' You know I can just imagine these things going through the kids' heads." Said ruefully and with a tinge of shame, this statement provides the final clue to Ms. Ryan's predicament. Even the children in her class do not show her the love, respect, and appreciation that she needs to feel good about herself as a teacher. The school administration does not offer them, either, nor do her fellow teachers. In other years she has been successful; why not this year? In the next section we shall consider some possible answers to this question.

Synthesis   *Jean V. Carew*

One question that we asked of each teacher in our interviews was to put herself in an observer's place and tell what she felt was going on in her classroom. In response to this question Ms. Ryan offered a description that we can hardly improve on.

> Suppose an observer comes in when I'm taking reading groups and I have group three, the Helicopters, with me, which is like pulling teeth to try to read two pages. Here's what's happening with the Helicopters. Russell is falling off his chair; Jeff is walking back and forth; Greg is fidgeting with his pencil. Ricky is reading ahead into the next page; Lydia is ripping up her marker; Peggy is sitting there lost and waiting for something to go on; and Kenneth is cutting up somehow. There are eight kids in the group, so I have eight subdivisions.
>
> I have a triple role between trying to coordinate all the idiosyncrasies of these eight kids and monitoring the two other groups I have out

there. You know, Greg is sitting right beside me and he's reading in a nice loud voice but I can't even *hear* him. So I have to yell: "Jumbo Jets, didn't I just say if you wanted to use that up there you'd have to keep your voices down?" And so it goes. To an observer, to myself, I sometimes feel that it's very chaotic.

And again, we have another underlying factor: Is Kenneth in the classroom or not? I have two different classrooms, one when Ken is here and one when he is not. If Ken is here, then it definitely is chaotic.

Ms. Ryan is intentionally exaggerating her account for dramatic effect, but it is a remarkably accurate description, one that a visitor to her class-room might very well have recorded, not once but many times over the course of the year. Consider first the quantitative analysis of our observa-tions of Ms. Ryan's interactions with her first graders. This analysis shows that 68 percent of Ms. Ryan's interactions with children took place in aca-demic contexts, and, similarly, 46 percent of her interactions with individ-ual children had an academic task as their topic, the lowest proportions for the four teachers in the study. Conversely, 32 percent of these individual in-teractions were concerned with procedure and 11 percent with inappropriate child behavior, the highest and second highest percentages reported. Final-ly, in the light of Ms. Ryan's characterization of her class, it is not surpris-ing to find that only 25 percent of these teacher-focused observations were coded in terms of the Structured Interaction coding system. Her interac-tions with children seldom followed the clearly-structured, routinized pat-tern to which this coding procedure was adapted. These findings closely re-semble those for Ms. Edwards, Ms. Ryan's co-teacher at the Outer School, and differ markedly from those of the two teachers at the Inner School. Where Ms. Ryan and Ms. Edwards part company is in the data describing the quality of teacher-child relationships.

On all aspects of teacher behavior that seem to denote the teacher's inter-est in and responsiveness to children's individual needs, Ms. Ryan ranked third or fourth, her behavior being most similar to Ms. Prima's at the Inner School and contrasting strongly with Ms. Edwards', her co-teacher at the Outer School. Thus, in Ms. Ryan's class, the percentage of "open" ques-tions was 8 percent (compared to 17 percent for Ms. Edwards); the percent-age of "free" questions was 4.3 percent (versus 5.7 percent); the percentage of positive evaluations of children's responses was 5 percent (versus 19 per-cent); and the percentage of negative reinforcement of children's behavior was 23 percent (versus 18 percent).

The contrast between the two teachers at the Outer School is also appar-ent in the data describing the behavior of children in interaction with their teachers. Of the four classes, Ms. Ryan's ranked lowest on appropriate and expressive behaviors (13 percent and 18 percent, versus 27 percent and 26 percent for Ms. Edwards) and highest on dependent and inappropriate behaviors (40 percent and 29 percent, versus 27 percent and 20 percent for Ms. Edwards).

The following observations in Ms. Ryan's classroom convey the quality of her relationship with children more vividly than these statistics. The first comes from a Show and Tell session.

TEACHER: Did anyone do something they would like to share?
DONNA: I went ice skating.
TEACHER: Indoors?
DONNA: Yeah, indoors.
TEACHER: Cheryl?
CHERYL: I went to a friend's house.
TEACHER: That must have been a nice surprise. Barbara! Kenneth! Be quiet! Madeline?
MADELINE: My cousin came over yesterday and someone else came, too.
TEACHER: Good. [Donna starts to talk.] Donna, raise your hand first. How many people went to the dolphin show? [Several raise their hands.] That's a lot!
VANESSA: I went two times.
TEACHER: Good for you. Russell? [Russell tells about how he was chased around the football field.] So you were playing football in Park Terrace? Sounds like fun . . . Let's stand up now so we can do the pledge. [Teacher observes class.] We're waiting for five people to be ready. [Kenneth is sitting on a table, not paying attention. He stands up.] Cheryl, would you please start? [Cheryl leads the class in the pledge.]

In this observation Ms. Ryan is composed, calm, and patient. From time to time children are noisy and inattentive, but on the whole her interactions with them are pleasant. By way of contrast, consider the next observation. The children are supposed to be discussing a safety lesson they had earlier that day in the assembly room.

TEACHER: [Looks through papers on her desk.] I don't think we're ready yet for anything. [She looks at the class sternly.] Russell, put your scissors away. [Russell complies.] Nina and Ingrid, turn around please! [To Karen] What's one thing we should remember from the assembly today?
KAREN: Safety.
TEACHER: [To Andrew] Tell us what are safety helpers, Andrew.
ANDREW: People who help you cross the street.

VANESSA: [Raises her hand.] I never get a turn!

TEACHER: Okay.

VANESSA: The boy in the movie we saw looked like Ricky.

TEACHER: Yes, he did look a little bit like Ricky. [Tells class to take out their workbooks and tear out page 43. By now the class has become very noisy. Children are chatting and walking about at random. Teacher turns out the lights for a few seconds, a signal to be quiet. Teacher reprimands Vanessa.] I told you to just tear out that one page! [Teacher notices Kenneth climbing on the piano.] Kenneth, get down off the piano at once! [Kenneth ignores her and continues climbing. To class] Put two fingers up if you're ready to start your work. [To Jeff] Didn't I tell you to tear it out? [Lydia asks for directions.] What did I tell you to do?

TEACHER: [To class] Recess is getting *shorter* and *shorter* today. I still have several people who haven't torn out their page.

KENNETH: I can't tear it out.

TEACHER: You would be able to if you were sitting here when I went around helping!

TEACHER: [Looking at Jeff and Andrew] I'm waiting for two more people to tear out their pages. [Jeff complies.] I'm waiting for one more person. [Andrew slowly obeys.] We have only six minutes left of recess!

LYDIA: What are we waiting for?

TEACHER: For everyone to put their paper on their desks! Now we'll wait two minutes more. I waited for you, now you'll have to wait for me!

KENNETH: I didn't do anything!

TEACHER: I didn't say you did, but I waited for you, so now you'll wait for me. [To Karen] Turn around and put your head on your desk!

LYDIA: Barbara's paper fell on the floor.

TEACHER: Don't you worry about Barbara, you should worry about Lydia. [Teacher checks papers at her desk.] I have a feeling that we're not going to make it over to the playground today. That's it, keep up the humming! [In fact, the children are now all seated and relatively quiet. Teacher switches off the lights for a minute, turns them on again, then looks sternly at the class. To class] Big joke, huh? Think it's funny, huh? [A few children mumble no.] Neither do I! I think it's very sad that people in first grade cannot behave.

In this excerpt we see a pattern that was repeated many times in our observations: children noisy, inattentive, provocative, and disobedient, and

Ms. Ryan becoming steadily more frustrated and short-tempered with individual offenders until finally she punishes the whole class for the behavior of some.

Since the mode of controlling children just described is not unusual with Ms. Ryan, it is not surprising to find that of the four teachers she was the one most likely to distribute her attention unequally among her pupils. Four children—two "babies," Lydia and Madeline, and two "difficult children," Vanessa and Kenneth—received at least 50 percent more of her attention than the average child in her class. The two "babies" exhibited considerably more dependent behavior than the average child, and Ms. Ryan rejected their requests for help, materials, and attention much more often than the average child's. Similarly, the two "difficult children" displayed much more inappropriate behavior than the average child, and Ms. Ryan very much more often scolded and disciplined them. Thus, attention was disbributed unevenly in the sense that a few children received very many more negative interactions with her than others, but the converse was not true. There were no children who received much more positive attention from her than the average child, as was the case with Simone in Ms. Allen's class and Linda in Ms. Prima's.

Turning now to the question of race and sex discrimination, we note that Ms. Ryan's was the only class in which we found some evidence of racial and sex discrimination in the assignment of children to reading groups. Although 29 percent of the children in her class were black and 33 percent were boys, no blacks and only one boy were included in her top reading group. Conversely, of the seven children in her bottom reading group, four were black and four were boys. In discussing her reading group arrangements, Ms. Ryan pointed out that at the beginning of the school year the children differed greatly in their reading readiness, work habits, and motivation, and her reading group assignments were made entirely on this basis. Throughout the year the groups worked with very different materials and at a very different pace, so movement between groups was necessarily restricted (only two children were reassigned, swapping places in the second and third groups). These initial differences in the reading ability and habits of individual black and white children and boys and girls apparently effectively determined their reading-group assignments for the entire year. However, it must be emphasized that the quantitative analysis of Ms. Ryan's individual interactions with children showed that, on the average, she treated blacks and whites and boys and girls very similarly. These data showed no evidence of discrimination on her part against children as members of racial or sex groups.

One cannot describe Ms. Ryan or her classroom without considering Kenneth, her "child of the year." This seven-year-old black boy took up an astonishing amount of Ms. Ryan's time, attention, and energy and is one of the chief reasons for her mounting dissatisfaction with teaching.

Kenneth is the child of a single mother. He has an older sister in second grade and a younger brother also in first grade because Kenneth has been kept back a year. We know little firsthand about Ken's family, since his mother chose not to discuss personal matters in our interview with her. We hear only the rumors that his father committed suicide, that his mother has "bad feelings" about the school and is uncooperative and irresponsible, and that their disorganized and unstable lifestyle is at the root of Kenneth's behavior problems. In our visit to his home, however, we found a spacious, neat, well-kept apartment and a mother very guarded in her responses to our questions and clearly reluctant to say anything critical of her son's teacher or his school. She is satisfied with Kenneth's academic and social progress and sees Ms. Ryan as doing the best she can with him, considering that she has many other children to attend to and cannot constantly be giving him the attention he unreasonably demands. Kenneth's mother is herself overwhelmed with problems. Both of her sons are in serious trouble at school, and she is not about to impart information to a stranger, who for all she knows may be in league with the system.

So what we know of Kenneth is what Ms. Ryan tells us and what we observe in our many visits to her classroom. Ms. Ryan describes him as a child with many different sides to his personality. He is lovable, affectionate, gregarious, and very popular with other children, especially girls. He is also insecure, dependent, lacking in confidence about his academic abilities, and constantly in need of approval and encouragement. And he is also aggressive, defiant, unruly, and uncontrollable, especially vis-à-vis Ms. Ryan. The quantitative analyses of our observations—both those focused on Ms. Ryan and those centered on Kenneth himself—bear out Ms. Ryan's statements accurately. Of the eighty-odd children observed in this study, Kenneth displayed the highest percentage of inappropriate behavior in interaction with his teacher and received the highest percentage of negative reinforcement from her (table 20). Conversely, of all the children in his class, he was least involved in academic activities with Ms. Ryan. The child-focused observations tell much the same story. Of the eight children for whom we can make comparisons, Kenneth spent the least time in concentrated work and the most time interacting with other people, mostly playing and chatting (table 21). Finally, in 9 percent of these observations Kenneth engaged in wild and disorderly activities, again the highest percentage recorded.

First let us consider Kenneth's endearing qualities. In Ms. Ryan's words, "He is the most lovable kid on a one-to-one basis. When I can work with him one-to-one, he's beautiful. He responds to any kind of affection . . . he's an easy kid to love, but the next moment you could strangle him!"

Table 20. Kenneth versus average child: teacher-focused observations.

Variable	Kenneth	Average child[1]
Interaction topic		
Academic	27.0%	44.9%
Nonacademic	7.5	5.7
Procedural	34.0	30.6
Privilege	5.7	4.7
Appropriate C behavior	0.0	0.04
Inappropriate C behavior	25.2	10.3
Health, distress	0.6	0.6
Selected child and teacher behaviors		
Appropriate C behavior	6.3	4.2
Positive T reinforcement	5.0	4.0
Expressive C behavior	5.7	6.2
T humor, conversation	4.4	3.0
Dependent C behavior	13.2	12.6
T grants request	10.7	8.4
T rejects request	6.3	2.7
Inappropriate C behavior	23.3	9.4
Negative T reinforcement	40.9	16.9
T open/free question	1.9	3.2
T process question	0.6	2.5
% total teacher-child interactions[2]	8.1	5.0

1. Average of all children in Ms. Ryan's class.
2. Percentage of all teacher-child interactions for which the child was present and was a potential recipient.

Kenneth, however, is less concerned with enticing his teacher than he is in ensuring his popularity with his classmates. "The other children love him, absolutely love. A few may have a fear of him so they don't dare not be nice, but I would say they honestly love him. He's the king!"

Girls in particular succumb to his winning ways. From time to time he goes around "collecting his kisses" and it is not at all unusual to see him casually put his arm around his "wife" Alice or one of his many girlfriends, give her a hug or a kiss or a soft pinch on the cheek, whisper "girls are for kissing," and flash his handsome smile. Kenneth's supreme insult to a girl is

Table 21. Kenneth versus average child: child-focused observations.

Variable	Kenneth	Average child[1]	Range
Child activities			
Work	25.4%	46.3%	25.1-69.0%
Play	15.9	8.6	1.0-19.6
Talk	27.0	18.6	8.2-27.0
Self-care	1.0	3.0	1.0-7.5
Idle	13.3	15.4	2.7-29.6
Wild/disorderly conduct	8.5	2.8	0.0-8.5
Interacts with others	65.2	45.9	32.4-65.2
Child behavior when interacting with others			
Exhibits appropriate behavior	6.4	2.9	0.4-6.4
Receives appropriate behavior	5.5	2.3	0.8-5.5
Exhibits inappropriate behavior	22.8	5.9	0.4-22.8
Receives inappropriate behavior	6.6	2.4	0.7-6.6

1. Average of children observed individually in the four classes.

"You're too ugly to kiss." So, on his birthday the girls flock for his embraces, and it is amusing to see him for once embarrassed by an avalanche of attention. Kenneth is certainly not backward in the arena of sex appeal. In this class of thirteen girls and eight boys he has already secured a sizeable harem.

Ms. Ryan searches for a phrase to describe Kenneth's social personality and comes up with the term "class clown." What she means to convey is that "Ken is the sort of child who really grates on the teacher's nerves but whom the kids think is the greatest. Ken can do something which in another child would be bratty or silly, but coming from Ken, they just laugh and giggle. Andrew might have done the same thing the day before and the kids would laugh him to scorn, but if Ken does it the next day, everybody thinks it's hysterical. It's like some people can tell a joke and others can't."

Kenneth is certainly something of a comic. But his clowning has a happy/sad quality that is at once both moving and alarming. In the next observation we see something of the two sides of Kenneth: his showmanship joined with a lack of confidence in himself, a sense of incompetence, a pathetic need for reassurance that he is valued. Like a clown at a circus, he makes a joke of his ineptitude but the subtext is somber. Ms. Ryan has asked the children to draw pictures of themselves.

KENNETH: I ain't making my face any stupid color.

TEACHER: Use the color of your jersey.

KENNETH: I don't like my gray jersey. I don't like it. I ain't making it. How do you make tan? I know, make it with my pencil! [To Ricky] What's that? That's a head? Ha ha ha ha! How you making a head? All I know how to make is a circle. Want to see me make a straight line? I can't even make a straight line. No, I can't. [Pretends to cry like a baby] Wa Wa Wa! [and wipes his eyes. He draws a picture.] See, this one didn't come out right. I tried as hard as I could. [He pretends to cry, then laughs so hard he falls off his chair . . . To himself] I don't know how to make me! I'm a stupid nut. I'm a dumb-dumb! I don't know how to make nothing! . . . Don't have no ears, my ears got cut off. Everything I make is a girl. Can't draw, can't color nothing. I'm a creep. I'm a dumb-dumb. I'm a nothing. [To himself] I'm making myself. I'm making me good! [He starts to draw the picture again.] Look at mine. Ain't it stupid? [Goes to Ms. Ryan.] Is it okay?

TEACHER: Yes.

KENNETH: I'm making myself good. I'm a rootin' tootin' showdown! Lookit, Jeff, I'm a rootin' tootin' showdown [as he makes picture of a cowboy with guns drawn]. Don't have a hat. The Indian shot my hat off. Now lookit me, I'm mad! [Kenneth draws a sad face to complete his picture.]

Kenneth's feelings of inferiority and his need to have others affirm his worth can be glimpsed in other observations. More often, though, we see only the tough, obstinate, aggressive side of him—a Kenneth refusing to join a reading group, refusing to get started on his papers, rejecting both the stick and the carrot with a rude "Who cares? I don't have to!" At earlier times Ms. Ryan would alternately coax and threaten Kenneth when he defied her in this way, but not anymore. "It did no good." So, over the course of the year, Kenneth's behavior has steadily deteriorated, becoming more disruptive, wild, and uncontrollable. Ms. Ryan keeps a notebook, and one spring day she grimly read this abstract: "Tuesday, Kenneth Brown. Today Ken poured soap onto the table and had suds and water all over the room. Wrapped a wire around the pencil sharpener. Took papers off the bulletin board and books from the bookshelves. Kicked around a piece of styrofoam. Did no work. Was climbing and walking on the furniture and banging on the piano. Was yelling and talking back to me. Would not hang up his coat. Went out on the patio whenever he felt like it. Was taking the artificial flowers from my vase and breaking them up all over the room and the hallway. Was sitting on my desk, knocking over books, folders, and papers.

Was taking things belonging to other children away from them. Was wrestling, fighting, antagonizing other children. Took the wooden divider which had nails on it and was swinging that at people. Most of this happened between 8:30 and 11:00 because the minute he came in after lunch I carted him off to the office. This was Tuesday. *Ms. Ryan versus Kenneth Brown."*

Ms. Ryan's summary might very well have been written by one of us, for we observed Kenneth that very day and saw firsthand the turbulence he created. Such scenes no longer struck us as unusual; by now we had become accustomed to seeing Ken act out his "bad feelings." As he put it himself, "I'm a good kid sometimes. When I try. Sometimes I bother people. If I don't feel good, I be bad."

Kenneth is not yet a hardened case. He does try to accommodate, although less and less to Ms. Ryan. At least with his classmates, we still see him engaged for long stretches at a time in pleasant and productive activities. Surprisingly, he enjoys books, although he may not like to stumble through his primer for his teacher. Consider the following observation:

KEN: [Goes to the reading table, picks up a book, and flips through it, looking at the pictures.] I like this book! I like this one! [He goes through the book very fast and comes up to a picture.] Oooh! I love this one! [Jeff comes over. Ken, excitedly:] Jeff, look at this! [Ken interprets the picture for Jeff.] See, he's turning off the water. Look at his boots and all that, Jeff, and the wash cloth!

JEFF: Want to start it again backwards?

KEN: Okay. [The two flip through the book backwards, commenting enthusiastically about the pictures and making up dialogue for the characters.]

Kenneth is not averse to "playing school" so long as it is with one of his buddies and of his own choosing. Again we come upon him looking at a book with Jeff.

KENNETH: [Names the letters and pictures in an alphabet book.] I is for Indian, J is for Jam . . . M is for Mouse. N is for Nest. O is for Owl. P is for Pig . . . V is for Vase. W is for Wheel.

TEACHER: Kenneth, put your papers in your folder!

KENNETH: [Mocking Ms. Ryan] Put my papers in my folder. Put my papers in my folder.

TEACHER: Now do it!

KENNETH: Okay!!

To repeat her own words, Ms. Ryan is "hung up on academic progress" and feels constantly pressured by the school administration and parents to guarantee that each child is adequately mastering the basic skill curriculum. Knowing Kenneth is far behind, she sees his activity—intellectually productive and absorbing though it may be—as an evasion of work. One of Ms. Ryan's shortcomings as a teacher, as she herself admits, is that she does not spontaneously notice "good" behavior except as she defines it. Compared to Ms. Allen, for example, her definition of what is appropriate is relatively narrow and heavily biased toward obedience, good manners, and concentration on the task she has selected. She puts up with Kenneth's play-academics, though she does not see them as particularly worthwhile. "It's nice to have good behavior acknowledged. The kids appreciate it, they feel good about it. But I have to say that I'm guilty of not acknowledging these things often enough. I try to gear myself at certain times to do it . . . but I have to make a *conscious* effort to find the good things they are doing."

Ms. Ryan talks about experimenting earlier in the year with behavior modification procedures, specifically with Kenneth but also with all the children in her classroom. This experiment helped her to appreciate the good in children, but eventually she abandoned it for several reasons. First, it clashed with her principles to single out Kenneth for systematic reinforcement of good behavior, since "the other kids deserved it, too." So, instead of focusing only on Kenneth, she devised a check system for the class as a whole and awarded stars and stickers each day to every deserving child, which were accumulated for a more substantial treat at the end of the week. At the same time Ms. Ryan made special deals with Kenneth permitting him to earn his treats with fewer points and to receive extra bonuses via his reading tutor. Predictably, Kenneth was soon working less and less hard for these rewards and the other children also began to find the loopholes. They soon forgot the main point, and the procedure became just another empty ritual.

The experiment may also have failed in that it did not basically change Ms. Ryan's definition of good behavior in six-year-olds. For her the main element is still good conduct—being quiet and orderly, obeying the rules. Significantly, she describes a "beautiful day" when the behavior modification strategies seemed to have paid off, in these terms: "One day last week we just had the most beautiful day that we probably had all year. I just wanted to take them all home and hug them. Just a beautiful day. We were going upstairs to the movies and it turned out they were being shown in another classroom . . . so I had all the kids outside the auditorium while I was writing a note to the teacher to find out if we could come . . . and three different people went by and commented what a good class they were. And they were good! They shocked me! They had gotten a beautiful line. I told them what a great line they had made . . . It just happened spontaneously . . . it was just an automatic response on my part. It's so nice to get that feeling that you're not making any conscious effort to think of the good things, but it just comes naturally."

For once we see Ms. Ryan feeling really good about her class. Unfortunately, there were not many beautiful days in her classroom to tell us about. More often what we heard were "horror stories" about how Kenneth had gotten the upper hand and forced Ms. Ryan to call for help from the office, publicizing to the school administration once again the problems in her classroom. In our last interview she tells this story:

Today I had to meet with Peggy's mother at lunch so I'd left my tray with some potato chips, a brownie, and half a sandwich on my desk. Kenneth came along and started to eat my potato chips. So I spoke to him and he brought them back to his desk. I said, "Okay, you've eaten one, but you had no right to. Now put the rest of them back. You have no right to take anything that belongs to me." But he was just being downright defiant, so I said to him, "How would you like it if I came along and took things that belonged to you?" At which point I took a paper from his desk and then I took his sneaker. I figured some things won't mean much to him . . . he wouldn't mind walking around with one shoe on . . . but the thing is when he went home, he'd need his sneaker. He'd need his shirt, he'd need his jacket. "You wouldn't like it, would you?" He said, "I don't care." Well, that might not have been the right thing for me to say and maybe it wasn't, but he ended up just being kind of smart. He handed me his book, he handed me his folder, he handed me everything from inside of his desk, and I said, "You don't have to be like that. You know what I'm talking about."

At which point he took the desk, took everything and knocked it out of the desk, his chair and his desk and everything from inside his desk was all over the floor and, you know, it was a real violent action. And then he just stood there, didn't move, just stood there in the middle of the floor and at one point I think he was crying because I saw him rubbing his eyes and then he realized he can't cry, he's not supposed to cry. At which point I wasn't going to just scream and yell. I had had it. It wasn't doing me any good, so I just called for Mr. O'Connor.

By the time Mr. O'Connor came down, a good two minutes, three minutes, maybe even longer had passed. Here was Kenneth still standing there, hadn't moved, in the middle of all of his junk and Mr. O'Connor came in. So Mr. O'Connor told him to clean it up, he wouldn't budge. Mr. O'Connor went over to him, spoke to him, shook him. "Clean it up!" He still wouldn't budge. At which point Mr. O'Connor just picked up the sneaker and him and carried them out the door.

Like I said, maybe that wasn't the best thing to do with him, but obviously it wasn't penetrating when I told him to put the potato chips back. *A lot of it was just principle,* but at the same time . . . why should he go around eating my lunch? And why should he go around thinking that he has the right to take anything from anybody that he feels like? Which he does with the other kids. There are some days that I really feel he has improved. But at other times, it seems to reach a peak where it all unloads and comes out in a violent thing.

What then is to become of Kenneth? Ms. Ryan: "I just hope that he gets in with a teacher who has the patience of a saint . . . and hopefully he'll grow up. That's the only thing I can really anticipate. All I can hope for is that he'll survive."

And what is to become of Ms. Ryan? "I really feel I need a change . . . something to pick me up. I talk to people and they say, 'Pat, you're a smart kid, you're pretty sharp, you can get a lot of jobs.' And then others say, 'Oh Pat, how could you ever . . . it's people like *you* that we need to keep in schools.' They give me some incentive to stay. But I feel, you know, I don't need this. I can go someplace else where people will give me the respect I feel I deserve."

Like many of us, Ms. Ryan does not have sufficient insight into why she does not receive the respect and appreciation that she needs. She blames the school administration, parents, particular children like Kenneth, as well as herself. To her credit, she does realize that there is something fundamentally wrong. She searches for solutions in teacher workshops, she tries to use behavior modification procedures, she chronicles her feelings and actions in a diary, and she also turns to "experts," the observers in her classroom, to give her the answers. Ms. Ryan is the only teacher who continued to ask us to provide feedback about "what is really going on" while the study was still in progress, despite our explanations that we were not there to counsel but to learn. We, in turn, feel guilty at raising false expectations, ashamed at eavesdropping on trouble when we have neither the resources nor the intent to help her in an immediate, practical way.

Observing her frustration, her disquietude, her reluctance to reveal failure, conscience pricks: "There but for the grace of God go I." Faced with a Kenneth Brown, would we do any better? But then again, another voice says, is Kenneth really such a difficult child? Any more so than Jesse in Ms. Allen's class or Daniel in Ms. Edwards'? We have not carried out a scientific experiment; we have only watched the classroom scene unfold and talked with some of the actors. We have no conclusive answers to our questions.

Epilogue

From the beginning, we considered the teachers involved in this research to be collaborators in the sense of their having a unique perspective on the classroom scene which was to be an integral part of our study. We also felt that our final interpretations of our observation and interview material might be at variance with theirs and, if so, both points of view should be expressed. Accordingly each teacher was provided with a copy of the introductory text and of her own case study and was invited to meet with us personally at her convenience to discuss her reactions. Only two of the four teachers, Ms. Allen and Ms. Ryan, responded. As one might expect, their reactions were very different, for the portraits we had drawn of them contrasted sharply. Overall, Ms. Allen thought our account very positive and fair, but Ms. Ryan found much to protest. Both teachers requested that we delete a paragraph on their personal history from the text and suggested minor editorial changes, which were immediately made. However, Ms. Ryan's criticisms went considerably beyond questions of privacy. In fairness to her and as a counterbalance to our interpretation, we therefore present her point of view in detail below.

Our conversation with Ms. Ryan took place away from the school, at Ms. Ryan's request, on a gray, rainy afternoon. During the first twenty minutes or so we chatted about the weather and other neutral topics. We realized that we were all avoiding the difficult issue at hand—Ms. Ryan's reactions to her case study—but it was clear that Ms. Ryan was deeply uspet and that we needed time to become reacquainted with each other, for it was now over a year since our last meeting. Eventually it was Ms. Ryan who broke the ice. With courage, candor, and tenacity but without rancor or disrespect she delineated her reactions to the research and to the writing.

Ms. Ryan had expected the project to be a collaborative one in which we would provide information from time to time that might increase her understanding of the children or her skills as a teacher. She recalled asking several times when she would obtain this feedback but, receiving what seemed to be evasive answers, eventually realized that this would not occur until long after the school year had ended, when it would be of no value to her in teaching this particular class and perhaps of no practical value at all. She was not looking for "a magical cure" to the problems in her classroom, just constructive feedback from an outsider who she believed was in a position to give it. She felt her interest in gaining greater insight into the processes of teaching was deep and sincere, as attested to by her attending a workshop which included videotaping and analysis of her interactions with children in the year after our study ended. Ms. Ryan found this workshop much more helpful than our research in pinpointing her strengths and weaknesses as a teacher.

Ms. Ryan recounted how she flipped through the first few chapters of the report while at school, came to the case study of herself, read the first two paragraphs, and stopped short. She could not believe this was a description of her. Clearly she would need to read it in the privacy of her own home.

When she finally brought herself to do so, Ms. Ryan described her reaction to the writing as very intense and emotional. She was "devastated." She felt betrayed. Reading it was "like opening up an old wound and pouring salt on it." The report was all the more hurtful and unbelievable because it came at a time when she was really feeling confident and satisfied with her teaching. "I was having such a good year. Really enjoying my kids. They were really learning. At the end of the day they'd say to me, 'Have a nice day, Ms. Ryan.' It's so good to get a response like this from them. It means you're getting through. Then this report comes and makes me feel awful and doubt everything I've been doing. I don't feel like a *failure*. Sure, I have some problems, but I don't feel like a failure."

Her reactions to the case study were a bit calmer and more balanced when she read it a second time, but its impact was still mostly negative in that it made her unnaturally self-conscious, threw her timing off, and affected her spontaneity in the classroom. "The second time I read it, I was a bit less emotional. I could step back a little bit and see some of the things that were helpful to me. It opened my eyes to some things, made me sensitive to some things I do, but almost too much so . . . to the point that I was being *unnatural* in class . . . I was second-guessing everything I did. This lasted for about a week then I just tried to forget the whole thing."

The most serious of Ms. Ryan's criticisms was her feeling that we had deliberately distorted the evidence in order to write a good story. Looking at us intently she asked: "I want you to give me an honest answer and I hope you will tell me the truth. Did you *need* to picture me like this? Did you need to have four *different* types of teachers, including one who looks really bad?" Clearly her suspicion was that we had biased the data, whether consciously or not, so as to emphasize a good-bad contrast in the case studies. She saw evidence of this in the content as well as in the writing style. "Well, I think it reads like a *novel*. It doesn't sound like me at all . . . I had two of my friends, both teachers, both very honest people who know me well and would tell it to me straight . . . I asked them to read this chapter and give me their frank reactions. They both said it doesn't sound anything like me. And I'm sure they didn't say that just because they're my friends."

As to the style of writing, Ms. Ryan had this to say: "Whenever you presented me, you would begin by saying negative things, and then almost as an afterthought, you would then say something positive. First you would say something negative, then you would say 'even though' to make it sound as if I rarely did anything positive." Our choice of fictitious names also seemed to suggest to Ms. Ryan an unconscious process of stereotyping, although she found it difficult to specify exactly why she thought this.

Ms. Ryan was also concerned about our tendency to take her remarks too literally, disconnecting them from their expressive context and the easygoing, candid relationship established in the interviews. She felt that her personal style of communicating was candid, expressive, and sometimes ironic. Words taken out of context might mean something quite different if the nonverbal content, the tone and attitude with which they were said, had been noted. As an example she pointed out that the statement that she had had "guarded" contacts with Kenneth's mother was not true if it implied that she had a poor relationship with her. Ms. Ryan acknowledged using the term in describing a conference with Kenneth's mother, but what she meant by it was that she had deliberately used a low-keyed approach that would make Ken's mother feel less suspicious and afraid of the school and more able to relate to her as a person rather than as her child's official teacher.

Fundamentally what Ms. Ryan seemed to be saying was that we had not fully taken into account her unique style of expressing herself and the possibility that she had talked to us more like friends (with whom it is not always necessary to be explicit and verbally unambiguous) than like researchers who would later analyze and interpret only her disembodied words divorced from their expressive, interpersonal, and situational context. Ms. Ryan also noted that we always interviewed her at the end of the school day when she was more often than not tired, drained, and discouraged. Although she herself had chosen this as a convenient time, Ms. Ryan was sure she would have made quite a different impression had we seen her when she was more relaxed and refreshed. "Sometimes I would go home and say to myself, Why did you say those things? Why didn't you keep your big mouth shut? Did they understand what you meant? Well, if not, too bad . . . the damage is done."

This interview with Ms. Ryan forced us to consider again the ethical dilemmas that our research created. We had thought that giving each teacher an opportunity to react to our portrayal of her was the fair and decent thing to do. Yet two of the teachers had ignored our invitation, and for Ms. Ryan it turned out to be mostly a painful and destructive experience. In her case, we cannot escape responsibility for having raised false expectations, although we had taken precautions not to do so, and for having withheld what little assistance we might have given. We also cannot help feeling deeply wounded by her suspicion that we might have distorted and manipulated the data for our own ends.

Having reread the case study and the notes and observations on which it was based, we still think that our account was fair and true to the information we had. But Ms. Ryan's criticisms have made us more acutely aware than ever of the limitations of this evidence and the ultimately subjective nature of our interpretations. We can hardly perceive, much less correct, the distortions that our own values, predilections, and writing style may have engendered as we tried to distill and convey the personality of another human being. Despite the many-layered evidence we have gathered, despite the many perspectives we have tried to uncover and combine, despite all our efforts to see the whole person, we know we have only glimpsed each teacher through a glass darkly.

10

Conclusions

Jean V. Carew

IN CHAPTER 1 we discussed three main ways in which teachers have been thought of by researchers: as the central figure in the classroom, dominating and controlling the activities of children; as an automaton manufacturing a standardized child product; and as a powerful judge of ability and character, on whose pronouncements hangs the fate of his defenseless students. In this exploratory research we have tried to move beyond these narrow and often misleading concepts to provide a more complex, multidimensional and authentic depiction of teachers and teaching. In this concluding chapter we shall summarize what we have learned and consider our findings in the light of concepts that have dominated previous research.

The Teacher as Central Figure   Not all teachers are or wish to be the central figure in their classrooms. Even in these "traditional" public-school classrooms, teachers like Ms. Allen and Ms. Edwards sought to free the children from dependence on their authority and direction and to help them to function autonomously and cooperatively. We saw this objective realized in our observations in which children in these two classes were less likely to request direction and help from Ms. Allen and Ms. Edwards, although when they did so, they were more likely to receive positive responses. Both teachers also seemed to think of interactions among children as valuable learning opportunities. Thus, in organizing reading groups and seating arrangements, both teachers took interpersonal dynamics seriously into account, exposing the shy to the gregarious, the playful to the diligent, so that one could help and inspire the other. They conceived of basic skill groups as contexts for academic, personal, and social growth and used them as occasions to observe and encourage individual development. Ms. Allen carried her commitment to personality and social development a step further by keeping her reading groups as open and hospitable as possible, allowing children, including those receiving remedial tutoring, to "move themselves up" to more advanced groups as they gathered confidence and skill. Further, she continually changed the seating arrangements in her class so that each child could get to know a large number of seat neighbors over the course of the year. Ms. Allen and Ms. Edwards also seemed to place a higher value on casual conversation, play, and other more relaxed, child-centered modes of engaging children, perceiving these as contexts for encouraging interpersonal understanding and self-expression. Nor did they dominate their classrooms in the sense of constantly calling for discipline and order. In Ms. Allen's case there seldom was any need for overt control, for her students were nearly always remarkably orderly, well-behaved, and industrious. We speculated that this happy state of affairs was the result of her not nagging, of seeing but not noticing every transgression, and of the quiet, firm, but nonthreatening way in which she delivered reprimands when these were called for.

Despite these many similarities, Ms. Allen's and Ms. Edwards' first-grade curricula differed greatly in academic emphasis. Ms. Allen's stress on academic subjects was consonant with her focus on personal and social development, for she genuinely believed that the mastery of basic skills such as reading was fundamental to a first grader's self-esteem. Learning to read helped a six-year-old feel competent, confident, and proud of himself, more so perhaps than the mastery of any other skill. Her commitment to this belief was evident in her interactions with children in reading groups (her liberal use of praise, her sparing use of criticism, her delight in relating the reading material to children's everyday experiences, her excitement when the "magic day" dawned and "it all suddenly clicked"), and in her collaborative efforts with the reading specialist to design and implement a tutoring curriculum that would truly help children who needed it without making them feel stigmatized. Ms. Allen took enormous pleasure in teaching children to read. She was convinced that all normal children were capable of learning to do so and that it was the teacher's responsibility to ensure that they did. For many years she had been outstandingly successful in producing classes of children reading at and usually well above grade level, and the year we conducted this study was no exception. This record of success was a source of quiet satisfaction to Ms. Allen but not more so than her equally well-attested ability to "channel" her students' psychological and social development.

Though similar to Ms. Allen in her general child-centered style of interacting with children, Ms. Edwards evidently did not believe that the process of learning basic skills in structured groups was conducive to her main objective: personal and social development. Consequently, Ms. Edwards deliberately diluted the academic component of her curriculum, reasoning that the learning of social skills (how to get along with other children, how to resolve problems without resorting to physical aggression, how to behave cooperatively with regard to the needs of others) and the development of concomitant personal attributes (independence, self-direction, impulse control, persistence in the face of failure or frustration, confidence, self-esteem) were prerequisites to the mastery of cognitive skills in first grade. The systematic, routine teaching of basic skills also seemed not to be congenial to Ms. Edwards' temperament. She preferred one-to-one interactions with children and sometimes seemed bored by the repetitive rituals of reading turns and the spoon feeding that working with less advanced groups entailed. Her style was slow-paced and methodical, well-suited to the task at hand. But inwardly she seemed to question the point of the exercise, when what her first graders should really be engaged in was the drama of self-actualization and mutual understanding.

The other two teachers, Mses. Prima and Ryan, fitted the image of the teacher as the central figure more closely than Mses. Allen and Edwards, although they were by no means equally successful in playing the part. Ms. Prima, for example, spent as much time as Ms. Allen teaching reading and was equally successful at it. She was also an extremely efficient manager of her classroom, ensuring that activities followed one another briskly and that little time was unnecessarily wasted on procedural matters. For this teacher, however, the main objective was academic progress, not personality or social development. After a brief period of observation and experimentation, she structured her reading groups strictly on the basis of skill, and, once formed, they remained virtually unchanged throughout the year, although in some cases the initial distinctions justifying differential assignments were minimal. In organizing or interacting with her reading groups, Ms. Prima paid relatively little attention to the mix of personalities, to friendships and enmities, or to the children's perceptions of hierarchical distinctions among the groups. In her view, all students in her class got along well with one another anyway, they were not aware of status differences between groups (despite the fact that only children in the top cadre were designated as class helpers or surrogate teachers of other children), and her more advanced groups were as likely to envy her less advanced ones as vice versa, since her fast-paced, challenging, humorous approach to teaching guaranteed that a good time would be had by all. To consider social and psychological factors as criteria for composing reading groups seemed to Ms. Prima an unnecessarily complex approach to a straightforward academic task. Ms. Prima's relative lack of interest in personality was also apparent in her practice of giving group evaluations for behavior and performance. Every day each reading group was praised or criticized as a group, and individual children were occasionally chastised for making their group lose points. Ms. Prima seemed to see children primarily as members of a team (a reading group or the whole class) who were in a game to win. Winning—producing a class full of readers and of academically competent children—was the primary objective, and questions of personality and social growth were distractions from the main event.

Ms. Prima's overriding concern with academic success seemed to us very much related to her recollections of her mother as a "superwoman," to her many experiences of failure in school and college, and to her present urge to vindicate herself by surpassing her colleagues in reputation as the best teacher around. Her brisk, single-minded approach and lack of interest in the subtleties and contradictions of individual and social development expressed her personal need to structure and control her environment, to move forward quickly and linearly toward clearly defined academic goals, unimpeded by the baggage of unnecessary probing and introspection. Her self-esteem as a teacher derived from her ability to guarantee that all children in her class would be academically successful. It did not depend very much on opinions of how the coach related to the players or the players to one another. When, however, psychological and social problems created obstacles to academic success—and they often did—they needed to be tackled head on, for a good teacher is one who makes no excuses for academic failure.

The fourth teacher, Ms. Ryan at the Outer School, spent relatively less time on reading and academic subjects than Ms. Prima but this was not because of a competing priority. Indeed, she thought of herself as "hung up on academic progress" but obstructed from realizing it by the behavior of children in her classroom—the disorderly conduct of a few and the dependent, babyish ways of many. Consequently, much of Ms. Ryan's time was spent on procedural matters and on behavior control. Like Ms. Prima, Ms. Ryan seemed to place less importance on personality and social development but attended to various dimensions of psychological functioning insofar as they created behavior problems in her classroom.

The Teacher as Automaton Past research conveys the impression that teachers typically perceive and treat all children in their classes uniformly and that their primary objective is to turn out a standardized child product whose knowledge, skills, and character are readily measured by tests. The findings of this research hardly accord with this assumption as a general statement about teachers. First, as we have seen, the four teachers varied strikingly in their valuing of academic, personal, and social development as educational objectives. It is not surprising, then, that Mses. Allen and Edwards also exhibited a much greater interest in individuality and in the process of individuation, that is finding the appropriate methods of relating to individual children. The contrast between this pair of teachers and the other two was apparent in their overall positive views of their six-year-old students, in the subtle and differentiated nature of their perceptions of children, in their reasoning about appropriate strategies of intervention, and in our observations of their actual interactions with their first graders.

For example, when asked in our interviews to describe individual children in their own terms, both Ms. Allen and Ms. Edwards gave vignettes that emphasized positive characteristics, complexity, and variation. Each child seemed to be regarded as truly unique. The origins of individuality were myriad and a child might have many different sides to his personality which he displayed chameleon-like in different contexts. Both of these teachers took an intense interest in monitoring and mapping individual development, so as time went on their descriptions of children became even more complex and variegated as they detailed the changes and contradictions they had observed. Ms. Allen in particular seemed to have enormous tolerance for immaturity. For her a first grader's distractibility, dependency, attention seeking, aggressiveness, and the like were merely age-related, developmental phenomena that, with patience and sensitivity on her part, would gradually disappear. A six-year-old, however difficult, was not a threat to an adult nor should his behavior be regarded as a personal affront.

In contrast to Ms. Allen's, Ms. Ryan's perceptions of children seemed to start with the negative. Asked to describe her first graders at the beginning of the year, she depicted three quarters of them as "spoiled babies" or disruptive and uncontrollable "difficult children." Ms. Ryan admitted she had to make a "conscious effort" to think of the good things in her students, so much so that for a while she experimented with a behavior modification procedure to enable her to perceive and respond to their good behavior. The experiment failed because it did not fundamentally change Ms. Ryan's definition of goodness in a six-year-old. For her, the main elements continued to be displaying good manners, being quiet and orderly, and obeying the rules.

The four teachers' perceptions of parents also varied along with their perceptions of children. With their busy schedules none of the teachers reported visiting students' homes or talking with parents other than on the telephone or at scheduled parent-teacher conferences, occasional meetings, and social events in school. Parents seldom visited or observed the classroom, some evaded conferences with the teachers, and most ignored PTA meetings. Again, Ms. Allen was the teacher who seemed most interested in getting to know parents. She was very active in the PTA, allied herself with parents against the school administration on several political issues, and, at least in the case of Simone's mother, maintained extraordinarily close contact, talking with her on the telephone almost every week. Ms. Allen was also less wont than Ms. Prima or Ms. Ryan to make sweeping generalizations about categories of parents. She was pleased to know parents of many different social backgrounds and lifestyles and collaborated with some whom she suspected were abusive or neglectful so long as she was sure that they would not retaliate against the child for exposing the deficiencies of the home. Parents who did so were the one group that incensed her. Ms. Prima, on the other hand, seemed to favor only one group of parents, those from the lower-middle class who kept their distance from school, appreciated the teacher's authority and skill, and sent their children to school clean, well behaved, and eager to learn. To other categories of parents she seemed less sympathetic, including the supercilious, pushy university students and the disorganized, irresponsible militants.

The four teachers were also far from being automatons in the sense that they treated all children in their classes uniformly. Mses. Allen and Edwards in particular stressed in their interviews the importance of finding the appropriate way of intervening with different children. Thus, the strategy that Ms. Allen used with Jesse was quite different from the one she adopted with Mona or Simone. Matching the treatment to the child did not imply that Mses. Allen and Edwards were likely to distribute their attention grossly unequally among children. Our observations in fact demonstrated the reverse. The other two teachers, Mses. Prima and Ryan, who seemed less sensitive to children as individuals, were *more* likely to give some children conspicuously more attention than others, especially negative forms of attention. This finding suggested that the individualizing teacher was one who adopted a general child-centered method of interacting with children (that is, a mode rich in praise, sparing of criticism, responsive to requests for help, and encouraging of children's initiative and self-expression) but who at the same time was conscious of the inequity inherent in varying either the quantity or quality of her attention too much.

The Teacher as Judge and Arbiter   In research on the self-fulfilling prophecy the teacher is seen as a powerful judge of her students' characters and abilities and a potential maker or breaker of their lives. It is assumed that teachers quickly form basic expectations or judgments about children based on information relayed by the grapevine, or given by experts, or derived from their own cursory observations, and that these expectations influence the teacher's behavior in such a way as to fulfill the prophecies they imply. This research depicts the teacher as an uncritical, even malicious judge, ready to concur in the condemnation of others, quick to indict and to sentence her defenseless students. This harsh and simplistic portrayal obviously fits none of the four teachers in this study. Rather, as on every other point that we have discussed, their behavior neither corresponded to the research concept nor followed a uniform pattern from teacher to teacher. All four teachers, for example, said they disregarded readiness scores in their initial organization of reading groups, relying instead on personal observation of children in the first few weeks of school. In other words, they ignored the assessment of experts in favor of their own evaluations. But the teachers varied among themselves in the kinds of behaviors they considered relevant and in the flexibility of their decisions. Ms. Allen, for example, believed that the child's confidence in himself was fundamental to learning to read, and with increased confidence born of familiarity and experience, children would "move themselves up" to more advanced groups. Thus, her initial assignments to reading groups were not necessarily permanent nor were her original judgments self-fulfilling. In fact, one might say that she was loath to prophesy; her basic expectation was of change. In contrast, Ms. Prima attended only to academic skills and work habits in forming her initial reading groups, and once formed, they remained virtually unchanged for the year. Nevertheless, it would be misleading to describe her behavior as likely to fulfill prophecies of failure. For Ms. Prima, the judgment that a child was slow academically was a challenge to work harder at teaching, motivating, and disciplining him—in other words, to invalidate the prophecy.

The four teachers in this study also differed in interesting ways in their views of themselves as responsible for and capable of influencing the "whole child." Consider Ms. Allen once again. She strongly believed that the classroom teacher should shoulder total responsibility for her students. Referring more than a very few children from a class to remedial tutoring or relying on tests and psychological experts to diagnose behavior problems or calling the office for help with discipline were all "cop-outs" from teaching. The "complete" teacher took responsibility for all children in her class, turning to parents first as collaborators if they were cooperative and to outsiders only as a last resort. Ms. Allen was as good as her word. Although she was unable to prevent some of her students from receiving the remedial tutoring mandated by city law, she worked hard to make the specialist's curriculum and methods compatible with those used in her classroom and to prevent children from being stigmatized. She arranged medical check-ups when she suspected a physical problem, and she devised her own methods of classroom therapy with problem children like Jesse, Mona, and Simone. She never involved the school administration in disciplining recalcitrants, considering this to be demeaning to children and a betrayal of their trust in her.

Ms. Prima may also be thought of as a "complete" teacher in the sense that she took full responsibility for children in her class and was highly skeptical about involving experts in solving her students' problems. The main difference between her and Ms. Allen was that Ms. Prima made much less of a distinction between academic and behavioral inadequacies. She saw them as having much the same roots and as calling for much the same kind of intervention, namely discipline, control, and structure. Temperamentally primed to move quickly and decisively, she was impatient with the subtleties and contradictions of psychological diagnosis. In Nicky's case, for example, she resisted both his mother's and his counselor's attempts to get her to consider other ways of perceiving and responding to the boy although, as our own observations showed, the degree of control and criticism she heaped upon him was probably not warranted.

Ms. Ryan exemplified a third pattern. Unlike the two teachers at the Inner School, she often turned to outside experts for help—remedial tutors, counselors, the school office, behavior modification experts, even the observers in this study. Kenneth, for example, went for academic or behavioral therapy to three different people outside of her classroom several times a week. Of the four teachers in our study, she was perhaps the least confident in herself as capable of diagnosing and responding effectively to the problems of her students. She confessed herself baffled by her first graders' behavior and perplexed by the ineffectiveness of her own attempts to change them. By focusing unduly on deficiencies rather than strengths, she seemed to create problems in children by defining them to be so, trapping herself in a no-win situation that only increased her frustration, impotence, and anxiety and gradually eroded her pride in herself as a teacher.

The teachers' differing reactions to test assessments and to psychological evaluations by experts were also instructive. Discussing the results of an IQ test administered to her class, Ms. Allen disputed two thirds of the scores. In almost every case she claimed that the child in question was considerably brighter than his score indicated, his poor performance being attributable to the group setting, to inexperience with test procedures, to poor motor control, to perfectionist standards, and so on. For Ms. Allen, none of the children in her class were intellectually deficient. If the tests were properly constructed and administered, all her children would obtain at least average scores and their relative standing would more closely parallel her own judgments of their intellectual ability observed in many different contexts and over a long period of time. For much the same reasons Ms. Allen also challenged the reading readiness scores which automatically determined whether or not a child needed remedial tutoring and the psychological evaluations mandated for alleged "problem" children. Both devices, she felt, were insidious ways of labeling children as inferior and often served to bring about the kind of negative self-fulfilling prophecy that she sought to eliminate from her own relationships with children.

None of the other three teachers was as discerning or as adamant in her

opposition to these school practices as Ms. Allen, for none was so thoroughly an advocate for children. Ms. Prima did take up Nicky's cause and
worked hard to allay his mother's fears that he might be minimally brain-
damaged. But neither she nor the other two teachers seriously disputed
other cases of referral to counselors or remedial tutors. In her role as child
advocate Ms. Allen had from time to time fought with the Inner School administration and the Conroy school bureaucracy. She sought to "raise their
consciousness" and to persuade them to consider the deleterious nature of
these school practices. Getting no results, she took steps to protect her own
brood by inventing, in her quiet, canny way, every ruse and stratagem she
could think of. Thus, Ms. Allen confessed to having "spilled coffee" all
over her students' test scores when she found them invalid, she disputed
reading readiness assessments in order to prevent children who did not need
it from receiving remedial tutoring, she strongly advised parents against
consenting to the school's psychological evaluations, she refused to record
unfavorable remarks about children in their folders, and she was careful in
her conferences with her students' future teachers to emphasize the good in
each child and how best to "work around" the less good.

The other three teachers had little taste for Ms. Allen's brand of sabo-
tage. Perhaps with twenty years of experience at the Inner School behind
her, Ms. Allen could better afford to take such risks. For the other teachers,
the classroom and their day-to-day interactions with students was the place
where they proved themselves as teachers. In this more modest arena of interpersonal relationships they did not perceive themselves as "making" or
"breaking" children's lives, only as enhancing or diminishing them a little.
In each classroom, though, there were special children to whom these
teachers felt deeply committed and whose fate was a matter of intense personal concern. With these special children the teachers saw themselves in a
uniquely influential role that might indeed profoundly affect their lives. But
watching the classroom drama unfold from the sidelines, we saw something
else as well: the powerful impact that these children in their turn exerted on
their teachers. This two-way, intense, even passionate affair was nowhere
more vividly seen in this study than in the relationships between Ms. Allen
and Simone and Ms. Ryan and Kenneth.

We do not know exactly what it was about Simone, a talented, vivacious,
determined black girl, that captivated Ms. Allen, the former nun. Perhaps
Ms. Allen saw in Simone the freedom of individual expression denied her in
her years at parochial school and the convent. Perhaps it was that Simone
exemplified the predicament of a black child capable of succeeding in the
system by sheer brains and charisma but equally likely to be cut down by it
for being poor, black, and aggressive. Perhaps this child captured Ms. Allen's interest as ammunition for her political battles with the school admin-

istration. Perhaps Simone was special to Ms. Allen because she challenged all her skills as an educator, a person who brings out the best possibilities in another. Each of these explanations is plausible and probably true. For Ms. Allen is a complex teacher whose perceptions, reasoning, and motives are not so nimbly deduced.

Thus, with no particular effort on her part, Simone could have made Ms. Allen think and feel deeply about her. But Simone was not a child to sit back and wait for attention to come her way. By sheer force of personality, intelligence, and drive—when not by her histrionic pouting and sulking—she compelled Ms. Allen to take exceptional notice of her as an individual. In another classroom Simone might have been written off as a disruptive, egocentric attention seeker. In Ms. Allen, however, she met a teacher who well understood why she needed to play so grand a role. The challenge for Ms. Allen was to help Simone discard its more extravagant and gratuitous features and seize the essence of the part. We expect that Simone will be a child whom Ms. Allen will remember all her life, just as Ms. Allen may be a teacher whom Simone will look back on with appreciation and respect. In a very real sense Ms. Allen has helped to create the Simone we see at the end of first grade. She has tried to educate her, to help her actualize her extraordinary possibilities and to understand what it is within and outside herself that might endanger their realization. But Ms. Allen knows that even at age seven, a child as intelligent, gifted, and self-willed as Simone plots her own destiny. All Ms. Allen can do is to hope that the little wisdom she has tried to give her will stand her in good stead.

In his relationship to Ms. Ryan, Kenneth exemplified a different kind of special child. This "difficult, demanding, exhausting" black boy was Ms. Ryan's "child of the year," the one she would not let get the best of her. Ms. Ryan's words are apt, for it seemed to us that she often saw herself in combat with Kenneth. It was not that Ms. Ryan felt malice toward the boy. On the contrary, she really seemed to care deeply about him. Affectionate, gregarious, entertaining, Kenneth was a boy that other children, especially females, found easy to love. Kenneth was also an easy child to pity. Dependent, insecure, clowning to hide his lack of confidence in himself, he begged a teacher's compassion. Kenneth's problem was simply that he required too much of Ms. Ryan—too much perhaps of any teacher without special training, special experience, or special talents. Like Simone, he compelled his teacher to take exceptional notice of him as an individual, but the mode he chose—disruption, defiance, provocation, and even physical aggression—was one with which Ms. Ryan could not cope for very long.

Kenneth gained his objective but at great cost to himself and Ms. Ryan. Ms. Ryan's definition of the good child—orderly, disciplined, industrious—was so much affronted by this boy's attention-seeking unruliness that a large part of their time together was spent on a futile contest of wills. As she herself acknowledged, one of Ms. Ryan's shortcomings as a teacher was that she found it difficult spontaneously to see the "good" in children when this was juxtaposed with the "bad." Kenneth was the extreme case. He stretched Ms. Ryan's definition of the acceptable and her ability to cope to the utmost, and in the end she gave up trying.

So Kenneth achieved his Pyrrhic victory. At year's end he was promoted to second grade, hardly able to read and even less able to come to terms with himself. His success, however bizarre, was in making sure that he was a special child for Ms. Ryan, although in a tragically different sense than was true for Ms. Allen and Simone.

Objectivity We cannot claim that our description of these teachers and their classes is complete or objectively true. We do not know, for example, how teachers' and children's behavior was affected by the presence of an observer in the classroom. We also do not know how the responses of interviewees were influenced by our personalities and style, by our race, age, sex, appearance, or status as researchers. We also do not know how either type of data was affected by our explanation of the purposes of the study, its collaborative nature, or its practical benefits. Most important, we do not know what distortions in these data were engendered by our own training, values, beliefs, and temperaments as these influenced our selection and definition of observation codes, our perceptions of, reactions to, and interpretations of behavior and interview responses, and our selection of themes and details to present in our writing.

We see social science research as a selective process that combines empirical data, rational thinking, intuition, and evaluation. Researchers do not function like the lens of a camera; they filter and interpret information in the light of their own training, culture, and personal predilections. For example, Lightfoot's interest and training in the psychodynamic origins of personality and the manifestation of personality in behavior is apparent in her writing. One of her obvious personal preferences is for the "reflective" teacher who is aware of and takes into account subtle and complex aspects of context and individual personality before acting. Similarly, Carew's interest in and prior research on the effects of day-to-day social interactions on child development is evident in the case studies she constructed. One obvious personal preference in her case is for the teacher who genuinely delights in young children and is interested in and tolerant of their immaturity. Furthermore, as black researchers we have a more than merely scientific concern about the teachers' perceptions and treatment of minority students. This concern is evident in our accounts of special children in the four classes.

Our admission of our own personal failings and our images of ourselves as sensitive, tolerant, and helpful human beings also created conflicts with our role as detached researchers. Conscious that interpretation and evaluation is at the core of social-science research, it nevertheless distressed us to play the role of witness and judge without offering any practical help. The uneasiness created by our inability to resolve this ethical dilemma influences our writing, producing tensions, ambivalences, and compensating distortions that are not easy to pinpoint. Looking back, we worry most about the legitimacy of the nonactor's judgments of the actor, of the nonpractitioner's evaluation of the practitioner. We recall Ms. Allen's explanation for joining the study: "We felt it was about time that we not let only those who could do all the verbalization . . . have their say . . . I've seen what some of them have done to kids and then they've got the nerve to get up and give their opinions . . . and I start thinking about the people who really care about children . . . I'm not a show-off, not an exhibitionist . . . but we felt we had really sat back long enough and said nothing, and it's not right because there's a lot of good going on."

Appendix A:
Teacher-Child
Interactions Coding Manual

Jean V. Carew, Gloria S. Chao, and Sara Lawrence Lightfoot

The main purpose of this observation system is to describe dyadic interactions between teacher and children. By always identifying the particular child with whom the teacher interacts (when he or she is interacting with individuals separately or as members of small groups), the system allows the user to isolate each child's individual experiences with the teacher and to create a profile of each child's experiences either for a single observation or for a series of observations. Children of the same sex, race, social class, achievement level, or other characteristics may be grouped and profiles for these groups created by averaging individual scores. Or, if the interest is in comparing one teacher with another regardless of variation in student characteristics, profiles for all children in the class may be averaged and a class or teacher profile generated.

The system thus allows the user to compare the interactive experiences of individual children in one classroom, of groups of children in one classroom, or of individuals, groups, or entire classes of children across different classrooms. The main research application of this system is in investigating to what extent different individuals or groups of children may encounter substantially different experiences within the same classroom and how this differentiation in experiences may vary across classrooms as a function of independent variables describing the teacher, curriculum, school, or other characteristics.

The observation system includes two coding instruments, the Structured Interaction (SI) instrument and the Unstructured Interaction (UI) instrument. The SI instrument is used for on-the-spot coding of interactions occurring in question-answer sessions, reading turns, work recitations, paperwork, and the like. (In traditional classrooms these activities usually absorb most of the day.) Interactions occurring in those activities that do not involve questions or demands to perform or that cannot be coded on the spot plus interactions occurring in other activities are coded in terms of the UI system.

The target of observations is the teacher. Using a stopwatch and the SI coding sheets attached to a clipboard, the observer watches the behavior of the teacher during the first 30 seconds of each minute of observation, then codes (in terms of the SI) or describes (for later coding in terms of the UI) the observed behavior during the next 30 seconds. After a little practice, an observer usually finds it more efficient to observe and code/describe the behavior simultaneously during the first 30 seconds rather than waiting to do all of the latter task in the next 30 seconds. Interactions that cannot be coded on the spot in terms of the SI system are coded in terms of the UI system as soon as possible after the observation is completed.

The SI and UI coding sheets are both formatted to indicate consecutive time units (horizontal blocks) and identification or behavior dimensions (columns). Each time unit includes as many interaction units (rows) as occurred in the 30-second observation interval. Interaction units are numbered consecutively within the time unit, one row being devoted to each interaction unit. One code (a digit or a blank) is recorded under each column for each interaction unit, a new unit being coded each time a change in the identities or behaviors of the participants in the interaction requires a change in the coding. Thus both the SI and UI systems allow the observer to record as many interactions as occur in the 30-second interval and to code these along multiple dimensions describing the identities and behavior of the teacher and child interactors.

CODING SHEETS AND CONVENTIONS

Information at the Top of the Page

Identifying items listed at the top of the UI and SI coding sheets are coded identically as follows. These items need be coded only on the *first* page of each set of coding sheets so long as the activity context (variable 8) or the participants involved in the activity (variables 10, 11, 12) do not change. A change in activity or participants is signaled by continuing the coding on a new coding sheet and making appropriate changes in the codes at the top of the new page.

Variable	*Code*
Page number	Consecutive number in the top right corner of the page.
1. Class ID	1, 2, 3, etc.
2. Date	
3. Observation number	Number of the visit consecutively per teacher.
4. Start	Time at the beginning of the observation (e.g., 9:05).
5. Stop	Time at the end of the observation or period (as in cases where there is a break in the observation).
6. Duration	Time in minutes elapsed between Start and Stop.
7. Observer ID	1, 2, 3, etc.
8. Activity context	Use code numbers listed below and write in a description of the activity or event. Each new activity or change in group involved in the activity must be coded on a new page.

Variable	*Code*

Academic: nos. 1-6

1 = Subject matter lesson; emphasis is on content vs. skill; child's task is to receive knowledge or demonstrate understanding, vs. to show a skill (e.g., T lectures on the change in seasons)

2 = Reading and phonics

3 = Math, counting

4 = Penmanship

5 = Other academic work or work recitation (e.g., reciting memorized verbal material, retelling a story, telling riddles)

6 = Seatwork, homework, or paperwork review; T reviews C's written materials or work; if this occurs in the context of 2, 3, or 4 then code 2, 3, or 4

Nonacademic: nos. 7-10

7 = Self-reference recitation (e.g., Show and Tell)

8 = Nonacademic activity which T suggests or participates in as a main actor (e.g., story reading, role playing, Simon Says, art projects, etc.)

9 = Nonacademic activity which C chooses in the play area during "choice" time or at his desk between academic activities (e.g., drawing, games)

10 = Conversation

Other: nos. 11-13

11 = Rest and recreation (recess, breaks during the day)

12 = Transition periods between organized activity

13 = Morning routine; standard operating procedure at the beginning of the day (e.g., getting settled into seats, pledging to the flag, singing songs, noting the day's assignments, noting the date, weather, etc.)

9. Activity number	Number of the activity context consecutively per observation, i.e., 1 = first activity context observed, 2 = second activity context observed, etc.
10. Number of children	Number of children involved in an activity. If this is potentially the whole class, then code the total number of children minus absentees. If this is a subgroup, then code the number of children in the subgroup.
11. Who?	Circle the ID numbers of specific children involved in an activity context. If the whole class is involved, circle all ID numbers except for absentees.
12. Rank of reading or math groups	If reading or math groups are ranked, code 1 = top group, 2 = group next in rank, etc.

Structured Interaction Coding System

The Structured Interaction coding system is to be used in questioning sessions, reading turns, work recitation, and evaluations of seatwork and paperwork for on-the-spot coding. The SI instrument is not applicable and should not be used when a child initiates an interaction with the teacher.

Column Headings

Variable	*Code*
13. Time (unit no.) and interaction unit	Consecutive number of the time unit and consecutive number of the interaction within a given time unit. A new interaction unit is coded each time a change in the identities or behaviors of participants in an interaction requires a change in coding of the previous interaction unit.
14. Initiator (1st col.)	Who starts the interaction (e.g., asks a question, makes a demand or approach, etc.). Code the race/sex identification number of the initiator. In the SI system this code is always 0 = teacher.
15. Initiator (2nd col.)	Individual ID number of the initiator. In the SI system this code is always 01 = teacher. If a child initiates an interaction with the teacher, the event is recorded in the Notes section of the coding sheet and later coded on a UI sheet.
16. Recipient (1st col.)	The individual child involved in the interaction. Code the race/sex identification number for the recipient as follows.

1 = white girl
2 = white boy
3 = black girl
4 = black boy
5 = non-English-speaking girl
6 = non-English-speaking boy

Asian children are coded as white children unless they are learning English as a second language (codes 5-6). If desired, additional codes may be created for Asian children, Spanish-speaking children, etc. When more than 3 children are the recipients, code 0 = subgroup.

17. Recipient (2nd col.)	Individual ID number of the recipient. If one child, code the individual ID number (02 through 99). If 1-3 children are the recipients, code each child's ID number on a separate line as though individual interactions had occurred. If more than 3 children are the recipients, code 0.
18. Group context of the interaction (Gp.)	The number of children who are witnessing the interaction. This is usually equivalent to the number of children involved in a given activity (e.g., 6 children in a reading

Variable	*Code*

group). Code the number of children in the group in which the interaction occurs. If this is the whole class, code the number of children present. When the teacher is involved with a subgroup and momentarily interacts with a child who is not a member of that subgroup, code 50 on the SI sheet if (a) the teacher initiated the interaction *and* (b) the topic of the interaction is academic (see variable 19). In all other cases the event is recorded in the Notes section and later coded on the UI sheet.

19. Interaction topic — The content of the interaction (i.e., what the interaction is about). The interaction topic may be the same or different from the *activity context* coded at the top of the page. For example an interaction concerned with procedure (Read more slowly or Turn to page 5) or with a nonacademic topic (You look nice today) may occur in an academic reading activity context. Conversely, an academic topic may be the focus of an interaction occurring in a nonacademic context. Only academic interaction topics and self-reference recitation are coded in the SI. Procedural, nonacademic, or other interaction topics occurring in an academic activity context are coded on the UI sheet. Thus, in the SI system the specific interaction topic is nearly always coded identically with the activity context (e.g., in a reading activity context [variable 8, code 2] individual children are asked to read [interaction topic, code 2]). Occasionally the academic topic of the interaction is different from that implied by the activity context and the codes differ (e.g., in a reading activity context [variable 8, code 2] the teacher asks a child to count [interaction topic, code 3]).

Use code numbers 1-7, as defined for variable 8.

1 = Subject matter lesson
2 = Reading and phonics
3 = Math, counting
4 = Penmanship
5 = Other academic work/recitation
6 = Seatwork, homework, paperwork review
7 = Self-reference recitation

20. Question/ demand mode — Enter 1 in the appropriate column defined below. Leave the other two columns blank (only one entry is possible for each interaction unit).

Direct question (Dir.). T selects C to answer a question without waiting for children to raise hands, or if she does wait, she selects C who has not raised his hand. Often the

Variable	*Code*

form of questioning is: Mary, what is X? What is X, Mary? or, What is X? Mary? Code a direct question unless the observer is sure that T waited for hand-raising, then selected from among the hand-raisers.

Open question (Open). T selects C who has indicated he wishes to be asked by raising his hand or some other means.

Call out (Call). C calls out the answer before T has a chance to select someone.

21. Question/ demand type — Enter 1 in the appropriate column. Leave the other three columns blank (only one entry possible per interaction unit).

Process question/demand (Pcss.). Requires C to think through or figure out an answer. Question often begins with Why? How? How do you know?

Product question/demand (Prod.). Seeks to elicit a single, short, correct answer. Usually begins with Who? What? When? Where? How many?

Choice (Choice). C is presented with choices from which to select an answer (e.g., Is it this or that?) Usually only one of the choices is correct.

Free question (Free). Pertains to academic or self-reference questions. No right or wrong answer seems to be expected, although the child's answer must be relevant to the topic at hand (e.g., C may be asked to share an experience, or to describe a picture in his book). Self-reference free questions refer to personal experiences, opinions, preferences, or feelings.

N.B. Code always in terms of teacher's intent. Is she trying to get the child to talk as opposed to testing his knowledge?

22. Assessment — Enter 1 in the appropriate column. Leave the other 4 columns blank (one entry per interaction unit).

No response (NR). C makes no response to question.

Response (R). C gives a response to question, but teacher does not assess this response. (E.g., Johnny answers, $2 + 2$ is 4, but T says nothing, makes no gesture or facial expression, and goes on to another question. Susan reads a sentence correctly, T gives no feedback.)

Correct/complete (+). T indicates (verbally or gesturally) that the answer or product is correct or complete. (E.g., Okay, that's right. Yes. You've finished that. T repeats C's correct answer.)

Variable   *Code*

Partially correct (±). T indicates that some part of the answer is correct/complete, and some part is incorrect/incomplete. (E.g., You got this right, but that's wrong. You did this, but you have to finish that.)

Incorrect/incomplete (−). T indicates that C's answer or product is incorrect or incomplete. (E.g., No, you didn't do it right. No, you haven't done this paper yet. Be careful with your writing [meaning it was not correctly done].)

N.B. Throughout this section, code only what the teacher actually says or does in response to a child's answer, not whether the answer was correct or incorrect to the observer. This means that *all* answers which are not responded to by the teacher (both correct and incorrect answers) are coded under Response, no assessment (R).

CODING ASSESSMENT: SPECIFIC SITUATIONS

Extended turns (such as reading turns). Code each teacher response as often as it occurs. Each error correction is coded on a new line. Overall assessment or evaluation at the end of a turn is coded separately on the last line coded for that extended turn, and the Global (All) column is checked. Two separate feedback responses are coded on separate lines. (E.g., C reads, The cat sat. T: That's right [code in 1st row]). On the man. T: Not man, mat [code in 2nd row].)

For extended turns, the row no. column is coded indicating sequentially the row number of each teacher response in the series of interactions with a single child. In the example above, a "1" would be coded in the row no. column for the first teacher response, and a "2" would be coded in the row no. column for the second teacher response.

Paperwork review. Code only the teacher's actual verbal or gestural response in the assessment section. For example:

(a) The first two letters are right, but the last is wrong (±)
(b) This page is finished, but you forgot the other side (±)
(c) Something is missing on this paper (−)
(d) Child shows completed paper, teacher nods (+)

In paperwork review, the teacher may use rhetorical questions, implying criticism:

(e) Did you circle the numbers? (meaning, you did not complete the task) (−)

Distinguish this from work-procedure questions which occur when the teacher is not actually reviewing work.

(f) Aren't you supposed to circle the ones that are greater than? (meaning child did not do the task correctly) (−)

Variable	*Code*
23. Evaluation	Enter 1 in the appropriate column. Leave the other three columns blank. Only one entry is possible per interaction unit. No entry is also possible.

High Praise (‡). T gives special privilege or reward to C, calls the attention of the group to C's performance, or shows approval physically (e.g., hugging).

Mild praise (+). T makes statement such as Good, Very good (said in a matter-of-fact way), Fine, Thank you.

Praise and criticism (±). Good, but you have to do this one over. Fine, but you forgot to write your name.

Criticism (−). Includes both mild and severe criticism and sarcasm.

N.B. No response and ambiguous or quizzical teacher responses are not coded (E.g., Hmmm. You think that X will do Y?)

| 24. Terminal feedback (end) | Enter 1 in the appropriate column. Only one entry or no entry is possible per interaction unit. |

Process (Pcss.). T provides the process answer.
Product (Prod.). T provides the product answer.
Other (Other). T calls on another C to supply the answer.
Call out (Call). Another C calls out the answer before T has a chance to respond.

| 25. Sustaining feedback (go on) | Enter 1 in the appropriate column. Only one entry or no entry is possible per interaction unit. |

Repeat (Rept.). T repeats the question/demand, although not necessarily in the same form. (E.g., T may ask, What color is this? then repeat, What color? Do you know? Well?)

Clue (Clue). T gives a clue or rephrases the question to help C. T seeks the same answer as for the original question. (E.g., What color is this? Is it red or blue? It's the same color as your dress.)

New question (New Q). T asks a new question which seeks to elicit a different answer, or makes a new request for C to read. The new question may be easier or harder than the original, or may be on a different theme. (E.g., Well, what color is this one? Is the color brighter or duller? Is it square or round?)

N.B. Criticism questions should not be coded here (e.g., Haven't you been paying attention? is coded as criticism). If a child responds to criticism *or* to sustaining feedback, code it on a new line and number the first line "1" and the second line "2," etc. in the row no. column. Sustaining feedback is coded as often as it occurs as long as the teacher pauses long enough for the child to respond and he does so.

Variable   *Code*

Redundant repetition of questions (without pause) is coded only once. (E.g., Well? Do you know?)

Sustaining feedback for paperwork

Repeat. T asks that the task be done again. T repeats the demand for the task, or asks C to correct/complete work. Often T hands the paper back to C after he or she has stated that the work is incorrect/incomplete.

Clue. T asks that the task be done over, but gives information/help as to what is wrong or as to how to correct or complete it.

New question. T requests C to do a new task or go on to a new part. E.g.:

(a) T to Mary: Did you circle the numbers? (implying that the task is incomplete). T hands paper back to Mary. Code assessment (–) and Clue.

(b) T to Mary: Are you supposed to circle those that are greater than? (implying that task was done incorrectly). T hands paper back to Mary. Code assessment (–) and Clue.

(c) T to Mary: This isn't right. T hands paper back to Mary. Code assessment (–) and Repeat.

(d) T to Mary: Okay. Now go on to the next page. Assessment (+), New question.

(e) T to Mary: You didn't do this right. Go back to the first page and review the steps. Code assessment (–), New question.

A frequent case is that the teacher makes ✓ and X marks on the paper, then hands the paper back, saying, Okay, but correct these (incorrect items). Code assessment (–), Repeat. Although the assessment is probably (±), it would be difficult to see what was actually marked on the paper.

26. Global evaluation (all)

Teacher is responding to a global performance rather than to a discrete child performance (e.g., in a global evaluation at the end of reading). Use this code sparingly. Limit use to occasions when T gives error feedback, but also gives a positive evaluation at the end regarding overall performance. In paperwork review, T may say, All of this is correct, but you made an error here. Code assessment (±) but do not code Global. If T says, All of this is correct, now do the next page, Code assessment (+) and New question but not Global.

27. Row number

Number consecutively within a 30-second unit, the rows belonging to an interaction chain between the teacher and one child.

STRUCTURED INTERACTION PROTOCOL (SAMPLE) [1]

PAGE 8

1. CLASS ID 4   2. DATE Jan. 5   3. OBSERVATION # 6   4. START 9:30   5. STOP 9:45   6. DURATION 15   7. OBSERVER ID 2

8. ACTIVITY CONTEXT 2 reading   9. ACTIVITY # 3   10. + OF Cs 7   11. WHO? 7   12. RANK 2 "The Fat Cats"

02 03 04 (05) 06 07 08 09 (10) 11 (12) 13 14

15 16 (17) (18) 19 (20) 21 22 (23) 24 25 26 27

DESCRIPTION OF CODING INTERVAL

32. T gives procedural directive and converses with C. See UI protocol, line 32.

33.
1. Asks what "chair" begins with, calls on Cindy.
2. Cindy: "ch". T: Yes, very good. John, what word begins with "ch" in this sentence? John: no response.
3. T: Dick can you tell us? Dick: choose. T no assessment.

34.
1. T: Can someone tell us what this picture shows? Sue? Sue talks, T listens.

35.
1. T: Debbie, where does a waiter work? D: I forget.
2. T: Look on this page. D looks. T: Is it in a restaurant or in a bakery? D: Restaurant. T: Yes.

Time	Gp	Topic	Init	Recip	Question/Demand Mode (D-R / O-R / T / FFD)	Question/Demand Type (PROC / OPIN / ANSW / FACT)	Assessment (N / R / + / +I / -)	Evaluation (+ / ++ / + / +I / -)	End (CONV / PROC / OTHER / JAIL)	Go On (RALL / ENER / ELEQ / ENEW)	A O W L L #
32.											
33.1.	7	2	0 01	3 18	1	1	+	I			
2.	7	2	0 01	2 05	1	I	I				
3.	7	2	0 01	4 23	I	I	I				
34.1	7	2	0 01	1 17	I	I	I				
35.	7	2	0 01	3 18	I	I	I	I			1
	7	2	0 01	3 18	I	I	I				2

[1] The order of columns for variables 14–19 has been changed slightly to facilitate on-the-spot coding of structured situations.

Unstructured Interaction Coding System

The Unstructured Interaction coding system is used to code all teacher-initiated interactions that do not involve questions or demands to perform or that cannot be coded on-the-spot in terms of the SI system, and *all child-initiated* interactions. The UI variables are coded from notes made in the SI Notes section during the SI observations.

Column Headings

The first 7 variables below (numbers 13-19) are similar to those in the SI system but with certain exceptions and additions.

Variable	*Code*
13. Time (unit no.) and interaction unit	Same as in SI.
14. Initiator (1st col.)	Same as in SI, except that in the UI system either the teacher or the child may be the initiator of an interaction. Use information from the time elapsed before the 30-second observation unit if known. Code the teacher as initiator when she starts an interaction by reacting to a child's behavior (e.g., Jimmy is talking loudly and T says, Jimmy, please be quiet.). Code the initiator's race/sex identification number below.
	0 = teacher
	1 = white girl
	2 = white boy
	3 = black girl
	4 = black boy
	5 = non-English-speaking girl
	6 = non-English-speaking boy
	Asian children are coded as white children or as non-English-speaking children, or additional codes may be added for Asian children, Spanish-speaking children, etc.
15. Initiator (2nd col.)	Individual ID number of the initiator. Teacher = 01. If one child, code the individual ID number (02 through 99).
16. Recipient (1st col.)	Same as in SI.
17. Recipient (2nd col.)	Same as in SI.
18. Group context of the interaction (Gp.)	Same as in SI.

Variable	*Code*
19. Interaction topic	Same as in SI, except that procedural, nonacademic, or other interaction topics are coded as well as academic topics (for interactions which do not involve questions or demands to perform or which the child initiates). The coding of the interaction topic depends primarily on the behavior and intentions of the initiator of the interaction. (E.g., T says to Billy: Do the math problem on page 3. Billy: I don't want to! [Interaction topic Academic, code 3]. C to T: Can you help me with these words? T: Go back to your seat. Can't you see I'm busy! [Interaction topic Academic, code 2].)
19. Interaction topic: academic	Interactions related to academic content and especially to the subject matter of activities. Select corresponding code numbers 1-6, as defined for variable 8 (activity context).

1 = Subject matter lesson
2 = Reading and phonics
3 = Math, counting
4 = Penmanship
5 = Other academic work/recitation
6 = Seatwork, homework, paperwork review

(E.g., T: Come to the board and tell us which has less. C points to answer [code 3]. T: Let's make a nice tall H [code 4]. T explains Chinese New Year to class. C: I love fortune cookies! [code 1].T: Find 10 hearts. C: Is it a game? T: On your paper [6]. T: Does man begin with m or n? [2]. T administers IQ test to class [5]. C: I know this is orange. T: How can you tell? [code 1]. C: This letter is a hook with a dot. I made it perfect [code 4]. C: Here's a set of 4, and here's a set of one more [3]. C: I can make a sentence with "is." T: Please be more quiet [2].

| 19. Interaction topic: nonacademic | Interactions related to nonacademic content as in storytelling, games, and conversation. Select corresponding code numbers 7-10, as defined for variable 8. |

7 = Self-reference recitation
8 = Nonacademic activity suggested by teacher
9 = Nonacademic activity chosen by child
10 = Conversation

(E.g., T: Did you do something special during vacation? C: I went to the Ice Capades [code 10]. C: I colored all my valentines already! T: They're very pretty [code 8]. C: I've got my Show and Tell ready. T: Tell us all about it [code 7].) C: I made a big block tower. T: Try not to knock it over [code 9]. C: Can I be the dragon? I never get a turn. T: Okay, and Billy can be the knight [code 8].)

Variable	*Code*

19. Interaction topic: other

Interactions related to specific events of the day such as rest periods or morning routine. These codes are rarely used because most interactions in the context of rest and recreation, transitions, and routines are procedural (topic 22, below) (e.g., T takes attendance or collects lunch money, T directs clean-up time). In appropriate cases, select corresponding code numbers 11-13, as defined for variable 8.

11 = Rest and recreation
12 = Transition periods
13 = Morning routine

(E.g., C: We have recess every day but not parties. T: Yes, parties are special [code 11].)

19. Interaction topic: procedure

21 = Work related procedures

The interaction is concerned with if to do, when to do, how much to do, completion of, neatness, speed, care, and form of work rather than the substantive content of work. Distinguish between concern with mastery of a problem (academic topic) vs. the *manner* of doing it or giving/receiving directives (procedure). (E.g., C: How do I do this/What do I do? T: Match the numbers with the objects. Look at the picture, then circle the letter with the same sound [academic topics 3, 2]. In contrast, C says: What do I do? T: Do this paper over. Write your name. You have to color here and here. Finish both sides, etc. [procedural topic 21].)

(E.g., *Form*. T: Don't go over the line. Speak up. Raise your hand first. C: I did it backwards. I made it too big.

When to do, order in which to do. T: Do this paper now, and the other one later. Don't start until I tell you. C: Which page do I do first?

Directive to do. T: Open your workbooks. Tear out this page. Bring up your folder so I can check it.

If to do. C: Should I do page 1 or 2? Should I do this paper now?

Completion. T: Have you finished your paper? Did you miss any problems? C: I'm all done. Here's my phonics paper. I colored every bit of it.

Neatness, speed, care, waste. T: Your paper's a mess. Don't hurry so much. Be sure you read each question carefully before you answer it. Don't use so much paste.

22 = Class management procedures

The interaction is concerned with supplying materials, giving permission to do something other than work, giving

Variable	*Code*
	instructions on where and how to sit, line up, etc., and when to do a task or activity other than work. (E.g., T: You may return to your seats now. When I call your name, bring up your lunch money. No, you may not play cards now. Clean your desks and get ready for lunch. C: Can I move my desk? Do we have gym today? I need a scissors. 23 = Self-care procedures
	The interaction is concerned with the child's routine basic care such as dressing/undressing, going to the bathroom, getting a drink of water, blowing his nose. (E.g., T: Do you need help tying your shoes? Do you need a tissue? Don't forget to wear your mittens. C: My tights keep falling down. I need to fix my ponytail. Can you help me untie this knot? I can't get my boot off.)
19. Interaction topic: privilege	24 = Privilege
	The interaction is concerned with a special or privileged role which the teacher gives a child or which a child requests, or a favor the teacher asks a child to do. (E.g., T: Mary, will you please take this to the office. Bill, you be the leader today. Please pass out the papers. Let's all sing Happy Birthday to David. C: Can I hold the door? Can I lead the Pledge? I want to be first in line. Can I erase the board?
19. Interaction topic: child behaviors/ characteristics	Child behaviors or child characteristics can become the topic of an interaction when the teacher actively takes notice of them or makes reference to them (e.g., in praising a child for his appropriate behavior or scolding him for his inappropriate behavior). The following child behaviors/characteristics are to be coded as the topic when it is clear that the interaction is concerned with the child's behavior/characteristics. *Appropriate child behaviors* 31 = Teaching, helping behaviors. C acts as a teacher surrogate with peers, and teaches or helps another child on academic or nonacademic tasks, games, basic care, etc. (E.g., C: You're supposed to do it this way. T: You're such a good helper. Thank you for helping me.) 32 = Overt acceptance of teacher and school values, standards and rules. C shows T he/she is "with" her by making comments which reflect T's values and standards. (E.g., C: It's nice to read. We must all take turns/share/help. All you have to do is try. T: That's a good attitude to have. I'm glad to hear that.)

Variable	*Code*

33 = Enthusiastic comments; contribution and sharing of ideas. C expresses enthusiasm about an activity, contributes ideas or makes suggestions. (E.g., C: Let's do it this way. T: That's a wonderful idea, Johnny.)

34 = Exhibition of pride in product or performance. (E.g., C: Boy, I really did a good job. T: You deserve to be proud of it.)

35 = Seeking of opportunities to perform or showing an eagerness to perform. (E.g., C: I know the answer! I want to do it. T: You're such an eager beaver!)

36 = Seeking evaluation of product or performance. Also includes times when C brings work to T and indicates he has completed it. (E.g., C: Is this right? Is this good work? T: Do you have to ask me every time?)

37 = Spontaneous helping behaviors; volunteering to do a nonacademic task or favor for the teacher (other than seeking a privilege). (E.g., C picks up chalk from floor and gives it to T. C erases blackboard without being asked. T: Thank you).

38 = Overt compliance to a teacher request or directive. (E.g., C: Okay, I'll do it. I'll clean my desk. T: You're so obedient. Thank you.)

Inappropriate child behaviors

41 = Resisting authority, challenging, criticizing, or defying the teacher; also includes cheating on work. (E.g., C: I won't do that paper! You're a *mean* teacher! T: That's enough of your backtalk. Are you ready to join the group nicely? You've got wandering eyes again.)

42 = Display of aggression. Includes physical or verbal fighting, grabbing, pushing, hitting, kicking, breaking, tearing, etc. (E.g., T: Hands are not for punching and hitting. If you push in line, you can't come along. Stop this wrestling right now! It's dangerous to throw things at people.)

43 = Personal disruption of other children. Includes teasing and "bugging" others, mimicking, annoying, criticizing, preventing others from working, interrupting, name calling, belittling. (E.g., C: John is a cry baby! That's an ugly picture. T: Don't bother your neighbor, he's working. It's not necessary to be rude. You're really a pest today.)

Variable

Code

44 = Disruption of class or group activities or order. Includes loud talking, noise, humming, running around, horseplay, singing, dancing, etc. (E.g., T: Are you quite through clapping? Keep your feet still, we have enough noise. Please don't shout, we can hear you. If you can't sit quietly, you'll have to leave the room.)

45 = Nondisruptive off-task behaviors. Includes inattention, passive resistance (no response), noncompliance, ignoring directions, idling, walking around, coming late to school, etc.; also includes noncooperative behaviors such as refusing to help or follow instructions. (E.g., T: You're not listening. Pay attention. It's not play time, it's work time. Don't wander around, do your seatwork. I asked you please to get in line. I told you to put that toy away, or T takes toy away.)

Distress

46 = Showing of distress, discomfort, or fear. (E.g., T: What's bothering you? Are you afraid? Tell me what's wrong. Why are you crying?)

Personal qualities

51 = Intellectual ability. Refers to a child's intelligence, ability in school and on academic tasks, ideas, attentiveness, task orientation (hard worker vs. lazy). (E.g., T: James, you're a really bright boy. My, you work so hard.)

52 = Social/leadership ability. Refers to a child's ability to get along with peers and carry out leadership functions such as leading the Pledge of Allegiance, leading the class to lunch. (E.g., T: Sally is really a good leader, and you should all try to be more like her.)

53 = Appearance. Refers to a child's way of dressing, neatness, cleanliness in appearance. (E.g., C: Do you like my new clothes? T: Very nice. You look so handsome today! Tuck your shirt in. Your face really needs to be washed.)

54 = Health. Refers to the way a child feels physically. (E.g., C: Did you know I was sick? My ear hurts. T: Do you have any medicine? You don't look well. Are you tired? You have a bad cold, don't you.)

Expressive qualities

61 = Affection, happiness. Refers to a child's good mood, happiness, or expressions of affection on the part of the child. (E.g., T: I'm glad to see you're so cheerful!)

Variable	*Code*

62 = "Bad mood." Refers to a child's expressions of moodiness or negative attitude. (E.g., T: Mike, why are you so grouchy today?)

28. Child behavior The specific behavior exhibited by the child *in interaction with the teacher*. If the behavior does not occur in the context of interaction with the teacher, it is not coded. As noted above, the child's behavior occurring outside of an interaction with the teacher can become the *topic* of an interaction which she initiates (e.g., to make an issue of that behavior). However, to be coded in this column the child's behavior must have occurred during the interaction with the teacher. In some cases the child's behavior initiates the interaction. In other cases the child's behavior is simply responsive to the teacher's initiation (e.g., T: Read this sentence. C: Yeah, I love to read), or occurs incidentally in the context of the interaction.

Child Behaviors Coded in the UI system

Appropriate work-related behaviors

11 = Teaching, helping. C acts as a teacher surrogate with peers, and teaches or helps another child on academic tasks. (E.g., T designates C as a "class helper." C to peer: You're supposed to do it this way.)

12 = Overt acceptance of teacher and school values, standards and rules. C shows T he's "with" her, by making comments which reflect T's values and standards. (E.g., It's nice to read. All you have to do is try. We must all take turns/share/help. Those who won't keep quiet won't get a turn.)

13 = Enthusiastic comments; contribution and sharing of ideas. C expresses enthusiasm about an activity, contributes ideas, or makes suggestions. (E.g., Yea! I like that game! Let's do it this way.)

14 = Exhibition of pride in product or performance. (E.g., Look at my drawing! Boy, I really did a nice job this time.) To be distinguished from an evaluation-seeking statement, which asks T to make a judgment about his product or performance. (E.g., Do you like this picture? Is it good work?) If there is doubt, code 16, evaluation of product or performance.

15 = Seeking of opportunities to perform, or showing an eagerness to perform. (E.g., I know the answer! I want to do it. Can I have another turn? Can I be with that group?)

Variable   *Code*

16 = Seeking evaluation of product or performance. Also
      includes times when C brings work to T and indicates
      that he has completed it. (E.g., Is this right? Is this
      good work? Ms. Jones, I'm done with this [i.e.,
      please look at it].)

17 = Spontaneous helping behaviors, volunteering to do a
      task (nonacademic) or favor for T. (E.g., C picks up
      chalk off the floor and gives it to T. C cleans off the
      blackboard for T without being asked.)

18 = Overt compliance in response to a T request or direc-
      tive. (E.g., Okay, I'll do it. Okay, I'll clean my desk.
      Okay.) To be coded only when an overt response by C
      occurs within 30-second time unit of observation.

19 = C makes a comment, gives an opinion, or converses
      with T. Comments may focus on substantive aca-
      demic material, procedures, or C's personal experi-
      ences, perceptions, and feelings. (E.g., C to T, On
      Sunday we made a snowman!)

Child requests

21 = C asks for clarification or information. Requests for
      both procedural and cognitive information are in-
      cluded. (E.g., Where should I put this? What time do
      we leave? Do this page? What's this word? Why does
      $2 + 2 = 4$?)

22 = C asks for help. (E.g., I can't find my crayons. Please
      tie my shoelace. I can't do this work [please help me
      with it]. I made a mistake.)

23 = C asks for materials. (E.g., May I have a pencil? I
      need a piece of paper.)

24 = C asks for permission or asks to do something. (E.g.,
      May we play the color game? May I go to the bath-
      room? May I sharpen my pencil? Will *you* [teacher]
      read this book?)

Mild inappropriate behaviors

31 = C complains about academic work, not being per-
      mitted to do something, feeling bad, etc. (E.g., This
      work is too hard. I wish I could play now. I'm tired.)

32 = C tells tales, tattles on another child. (E.g., Johnny
      pushed me! Ms. Smith, Ann is cheating!)

33 = C makes excuses for unfinished work, inappropriate
      behavior, not following directions, etc.; i.e., attempts
      to justify his actions or behavior. (E.g., I haven't had
      time to finish my paper. I couldn't help that, because I
      was tired.)

34 = C bosses other children, tells them what to do, or threatens them. (E.g., If you don't stop it, I'm going to tell the teacher! You shouldn't do that! You're not supposed to touch that.)

35 = C denies wrongdoing. (E.g., I didn't do it. I wasn't the one.)

Clearly inappropriate behaviors

41 = Resisting authority, challenging, criticizing, or defying the teacher; also includes cheating on work. (E.g., I won't do that paper! If you would stop reminding me, I could finish it! No, I won't help her! I don't like that picture you drew. Someone said you were a mean teacher.)

42 = Display of aggression. Includes physical or verbal fighting, grabbing, pushing, hitting, kicking, breaking, tearing, etc.

43 = Personal disruption of other children. Includes teasing and "bugging" others, mimicking, annoying, criticizing, preventing others from working, interrupting, name calling, belittling. (E.g., John is a crybaby! That's an ugly picture.)

44 = Disruption of class or group activities and order. Includes loud talking, noise, humming, running around, horseplay, singing, dancing, etc.

45 = Nondisruptive off-task behaviors. Includes inattention, passive resistance (nonresponse), noncompliance, ignoring directions, idling, walking around, coming late to school, etc. Also includes noncooperative behaviors such as refusing to help or follow instructions.

Expressive behaviors

51 = C expresses affection. (E.g., I love you. I like you. C hugs T or takes hold of T's hand.)

52 = C expresses humor, jokes. (E.g., C laughs in the context of a riddle or joke. C tells a joke and laughs.)

53 = C asks for sympathy or attention. (E.g., My stomach hurts. I have a headache. I hurt my finger.)

54 = C displays shyness or embarrassment. (E.g., C withdraws when approached, or speaks in a very soft voice when asked a question, etc.)

55 = C shows distress, discomfort or fear. (E.g., C cries or whimpers. I'm afraid of it, etc.)

56 = C apologizes to T for misbehaving, wrongdoing, etc.

Variable   *Code*

29. Teacher behavior   The specific behavior of the teacher occurring in interaction
                        with the child or children.

Teacher Behaviors Coded in the UI system

Teaching/giving information

11 = States rules, values, standards. (E.g., you always raise
      your hand when you want to speak. Hitting people is
      not a nice thing to do. When we come to school, we
      must sit quietly. We do not play games during reading
      period.)

12 = Instructs, explains how to do academic work. (E.g.,
      We write "d" like this [T writes on board]. Now, on
      this page, you are to circle the pictures that begin with
      "c." Read this page silently to yourself. Please color
      the pictures on that page.)

13 = Gives substantive, nonroutine information on aca-
      demic or nonacademic subject matter. Includes read-
      ing a story, explaining how one can tell that the 2
      math sets are the same, etc. (E.g., This word is called
      a compound word because it's made up of 2 smaller
      words. That word is read "sunlight.")

14 = Gives routine information on class routine, proce-
      dures, etc. (E.g., Today we're going to the library at
      10:00. First do your phonics paper, then do your
      math paper.)

Checks up/questions

21 = T asks a procedural or other nonacademic question
      (not in the context of topics 1-6). (E.g., Where's your
      work? Did you do your homework? Have you fin-
      ished your work? What's this? Is this your paper? Did
      you put it on my desk?)

22 = T asks a question concerning C's grasp or under-
      standing of academic subject matter, or work-related
      procedures. (E.g., Do you understand this? Do you
      know how to do it? Do you know what to do on this
      paper?)

23 = T asks C to report on another child. (E.g., What was
      David doing? Tell me, was Mary a good girl at lunch
      time?)

Controls/directs

31 = Encourages, reassures C about something. (E.g., Go
      ahead, you can do it. Go on. Don't worry about it.
      That's okay, it will be all right.)

Variable	*Code*

32 = Directs C to do something, gives a directive to promote behavior rather than to inhibit it. (E.g., Please
put everything away now. Come here please. Do your
work.) A directive such as, Sit down and be quiet!
would be coded as 34, directs C not to do, as it inhibits a behavior (noisiness).

33 = Gives C a choice of what to do. (E.g., You may do
this now, or do it after lunch. You may work now, or
play now.)

34 = Directs C not to do, or to cease doing. This is coded if
the observer is certain that the directive was made to
inhibit, rather than promote behavior. (E.g., I'm
waiting for you . . . [to be quiet]. Don't do that now.
Be quiet. Sit down and do your work [if C is idling].
Andy! [when T only uses C's name, but wants to inhibit C's present behavior, as in noise, inattention,
etc.].)

35 = Reprimands or scolds C. This may be phrased as a
question. (E.g., John! Weren't you supposed to clean
your desk? You *know* that you weren't supposed to
do that, don't you? Didn't I ask you to be quiet? I
don't know what to do with you! You're just acting
like a little baby today! I wish you would *listen* to
what I say, and follow directions!)

36 = Harsh scolding, including verbal or physical punishment. (E.g., Okay, you can't go outside with the rest
of the children, because you were so naughty this
morning.) T physically restrains C from going out, or
pulls him outside the classroom for misbehaving.
(E.g., Susan! Go to the principal's office.)

Justification of action

41 = Gives an "objective" or other "good" reason for
actions. (E.g., We can't play outside today because
it's too cold.)

42 = Appeals to rules. (E.g., Now that it's rest time, we
should all be quiet. We can't do that because it's not
fair.)

43 = Appeals to authority ("Because *I* say so"). (E.g., The
principal says we can't eat in the classroom. Be quiet,
because I say so.)

Consequences

51 = Offers positive inducement, incentive. (E.g., If you
are quiet, we can go to the playground. If you're good
today, we'll have a surprise. If you work really hard
now, we can have recess later.)

Variable   *Code*

52 = Threatens punishment, withdrawal of privilege, etc.
(E.g., If you're not good today, we won't have any
recess. Anyone who talks will have to go to the principal's office.)

Permission

61 = Gives permission. (E.g., Yes, you may play with that.
Yes, Mary. You may get in line. You may join us.)

62 = Defers permission or makes permission contingent.
(E.g., You may do that when you finish your work.
You may go after lunch.)

63 = Refuses permission. (E.g., No, you may not. No, you
can't have another turn.)

Help

71 = Gives help, including providing materials, tying shoelaces, rolling up sleeves, helping C on academic or
nonacademic tasks, etc. Often, C first approaches T,
then is given help.

72 = Questions C in response to a request for help. (E.g.,
John comes up with his paper to ask for help. T says,
What do the directions tell you to do? Mary asks how
to read the word "sunshine." T asks, How do you
sound it out?)

73 = Defers help, refers C to another for help. (E.g., I'll
help you later, Mary. Please wait until I'm done with
this group. Ask John, he knows how to do it. You'll
just have to wait.)

74 = Refuses help. (E.g., No, you should know that. I'm
not telling you, figure it out yourself. You know what
to do, so I won't tell you. I explained it once, and I'm
not saying it again.)

Feedback (academic or nonacademic tasks)

81 = Correct/complete/wholly satisfactory. (E.g., That's
right! Okay. You did this page correctly.)

82 = Partly correct/partially satisfactory. (E.g., No name!
[on this paper]. This is right, but this one is wrong.
This is okay, but fix your letters.)

83 = Incorrect/incomplete/wholly unsatisfactory. (E.g.,
You haven't finished it. No, this isn't right. I want
you to correct this page [meaning it's unacceptable].)

Evaluation

91 = High praise. (E.g., Oh, what an excellent paper!
You're such a good leader! That's really a great idea!)

Variable　　　　　　　　　　　　　　　*Code*

92 = Praise. (E.g., That's good. That's nice. Fine. Good. That's interesting. Thank you [in response to a child's doing a favor, etc., for teacher].

93 = Praise and criticism. (E.g., This is good work, only this one needs to be corrected. This is a nice picture, but it's a little messy.)

94 = Criticism only. (E.g., No, that's bad. What a mess you are! No, you're silly today, not sharp. That's not good work.)

95 = Accepts apology. (E.g., That's okay. Okay, you're forgiven.)

96 = Refuses to evaluate. (E.g., I don't have time to look at it now. I'm busy.)

Sustains task

101 = Repeats question, repeats a demand to do a task (in a complete or correct way). Assume that the task is not complete or correct when coding this. (E.g., T says, Mary, I said please do your work. Go back and finish it/do it correctly.)

102 = Directs C to do a new task. (E.g., Okay, now go on to the next page. Go back and do some different pictures. Why don't you do another one?)

Participates

111 = T joins in an activity with the children, such as in role play where she tries to guess what roles the children are playing. Singing or playing games are also included, when T is involved as a member of the activity.

Listens

121 = T listens to comments or opinions of C, without making any comments in return. (E.g., Mary tells T about what she did on Sunday, and T nods and smiles. John tattles on Bill; T listens to John, then scolds Bill.)

Teasing, joking

131 = T shares in the expression of humor with the children. Included are laughing, telling jokes and riddles, teasing C. (E.g., Oh, poor Mike gets caught every time! I give up, why does a fireman wear red suspenders?)

Variable   *Code*

Conversation

141 = T engages in conversation with C. Topics could be
related to academic or nonacademic tasks, or some
aspect of C's perceptions, feelings, preferences, or
personal experiences. (E.g., C: That was a nice story
we read. T: Yes, I liked that too. C: My mother had
a baby yesterday. T: Oh really? Is it a boy or a girl?
T: Dick, how are you today?)

142 = T defers response, or refuses to respond, when it is
clear that she has heard C. Includes, I don't know,
Not now.

143 = T responds with sarcasm. (E.g., Oh, really? As if I
didn't know!)

Concern

151 = T shows concern for the welfare or well-being of C.
(E.g., What's the matter? Are you all right? Why are
you feeling bad? I hope you're feeling better today.
Better take care of yourself.)

Affection

161 = T shows affection for C. (E.g., I love you, too!
You're my little girl! Includes physical affection
such as hugging, etc.)

N.B. for child and teacher behaviors. In any given row of
interaction between the teacher and a single child, up to
three child behaviors and three teacher behaviors may be
coded, as long as the *topic* of the interaction has not
changed. All of these *must* have occurred within the 30-
second time frame of observation, and must be part of the
same interaction chain between the teacher and the child. If
the *topic* changes, the interaction should be coded on a new
row, and the *Link* column should be coded.

30. Link   Code this column when more than one row is required to
completely code an interaction chain. Number consecutively
within the 30-second time unit the rows belonging to a
chain.

UNSTRUCTURED INTERACTION PROTOCOL (SAMPLE)

1. CLASS ID **4**   2. DATE **Jan. 5**   3. OBSERVATION # **6**   4. START **7:30**   5. STOP **9:45**   6. DURATION **15**   PAGE **19**
7. OBSERVER ID **2**

8. ACTIVITY CONTEXT **2 Reading**   9. ACTIVITY # **3**   10. + OF Cs **7**   11. WHO? 02 03 04 (05) 06 07 08 09 (10) 11 (12) 13 14 / 15 16 (17) (18) 19 (20) 21 22 (23) 24 25 26 27   12. RANK **1** "The Fat Cats"

Time	Init		Recip		Gp.	Topic	Child Behavior	Teacher Behavior	Link	DESCRIPTION OF CODING INTERVAL
32. 1.	0	01	0	0	7	22		32		T: Fat Cats, put everything away and come up here. Close your workbooks. C: My mother says I have a molar.
2.	1	17	0	01	7	54	19	14		T: Oh, is it coming up?
34.	0	01	4	09	50	22		33		T: Bobby, hang up your jacket or put it on, one or the other.
35. 1.	0	01	3	11	7	21		32		T: Barbara you may come up with this group. T gets a chair for her. Tim: Not many words start with "ch"
2.	2	20	0	01	7	2	19	31		
3.	0	01	4	23	7	45	18	34		T: Well, you have to think. Phil, sit right. Phil complies.

Appendix B:
Child-Focused
Observation Coding System

Jean V. Carew and Josefa Rosenberger

The main purpose of this observation system is to describe the behavior of select-ed children during unstructured activities such as individual seatwork or free play rather than in structured contexts such as reading or math groups. The target of ob-servations is the child rather than the teacher. Using a stopwatch, the observer watches the behavior of the selected child for 15 seconds, then describes (for later coding in terms of the child-focused variables below) the observed behavior during the next 15 seconds. Many of the child-focused variables are defined in much the same way as the corresponding child behavior codes in the teacher-focused UI sys-tem and permit the user to compare the child's behavior when he is and is not direct-ly interacting with the teacher.

The child-focused coding sheet is formatted to indicate consecutive 15-second time units (horizontal blocks) and identification or behavior dimensions (columns). Each horizontal line of coding corresponds to one 15-second observation unit.

IDENTIFYING INFORMATION AND BEHAVIOR DIMENSIONS

Variable	*Code*
Name and page number	Name of focus child and consecutive number of the coding sheet.
Date/time	Date of observation and time at the beginning of the obser-vation or portion (in cases where there is a break in the ob-servation).
Unit number	Consecutive number of the coding unit or line, each line comprising one 15-second observation segment.
Interactive (Inter.)	Whether the focus child interacted verbally or nonverbally with another person or persons or was not interactive. If the child was not interactive, code 0. If the child was interactive, code the identity of person or persons involved using indi-

Variable	*Code*
	vidual ID numbers, initials (e.g., T = teacher; Mr. X = principal/visitor/aide, etc.; FS, MA, JL = peers), titles, abbreviations, or other descriptive phrases (e.g., "reading group"; "a boy" or "two girls" if identities are unknown). The exact manner of identification of interactors in this column is left to the coder.
Verbal	Whether the focus child spoke to another person or persons or was silent. If the child was silent, leave the column blank. If the child talked, whispered, shouted, etc., to someone other than himself, enter a check mark (✓). Do not enter checks for singing, humming, sound effects, reading aloud, counting, comments to self, noises, etc. Such utterances may be recorded in notations such as "self," "laughs," "uggh!" "Shhh!" "pow! pow!" etc., to indicate that the focus child was not silent although not conversing. If another child, adult, teacher, etc., spoke to the focus child who was not verbal, the identity of the speaker (ID number, initials, title, abbreviation) is recorded in the column followed by a check mark, e.g., T✓, RJ✓.
Exhibits appropriate or inappropriate behavior	Whether the child exhibited an appropriate or inappropriate behavior, usually in interaction with others. A code is entered only if such a behavior was observed during the 15-second unit. If only "neutral" behaviors occurred (i.e., those not defined below as appropriate or inappropriate), the column is left blank.

Appropriate child behaviors
Code a plus (+) in this column if any of the following was observed.

From UI coding system
Variable 28, codes 11-18, 51, 52, and 56 (see appendix A for expanded definitions):
teaching, helping others, offering help
acceptance of values, rules
enthusiastic comments, sharing ideas
exhibition of pride in product or performance
eagerness to perform
seeking evaluation of performance
spontaneous helping, volunteering
overt compliance to directive or request
expresses affection, friendship
expresses humor, enjoys jokes
apologizes for wrongdoing

Variable   *Code*

Other appropriate behaviors
C expresses sympathy, comforts another. (E.g., Does it hurt
very much? Don't cry, we can fix it.)
C shares, lends own things, gives things away. (E.g., You
can borrow my crayons. This cookie is for you.)
C encourages, praises others. (E.g., Wow, did you make
this? You got all the right answers! You can do it.)
C invites others to join in, includes others. (E.g., You can
play too. Wait for Mary.)

Inappropriate child behaviors

Code a minus (−) in this column if any of the following was
observed.

From UI coding system
Variable 28, codes 31-35 and 41-44 (see appendix A for expanded definitions):
C complains
tells tales, tattles, threatens to tattle
makes excuses
bosses other children, threatens them
denies wrongdoing
resists authority
displays aggression, roughhouses, fights
disrupts other children, class or group (by loud talking,
noise, running around)

Other inappropriate behaviors
breaks rules. (E.g., C leaves the room)
teases, torments, insults children, calls them names
excludes other child from play. (E.g., Go away. Don't
bother us. None of your business.)
refuses help. (E.g., I'm not telling you.)
criticizes other child. (E.g., You made a big mess.)
threatens child. (E.g., I'll beat you up.)
pouts, sulks, stews, is in a bad mood. (E.g., C broods, mut-
ters to self, has a tantrum)

Receives appropriate   Whether the child was the recipient of appropriate or inap-
or inappropriate   propriate behavior directed to him by other children or of
behavior   positive or negative teacher reinforcement. Code (+) or (−)
for the appropriate or inappropriate behaviors defined
above or for positive or negative teacher reinforcement
defined below. If none of these were addressed to the focus
child, the column is left blank.

Variable	*Code*

Positive teacher reinforcement
From UI coding system, variable 29, codes 31, 51, 61, 92, 131, 151, and 161 (see appendix A for expanded definitions):
T encourages, reassures child
T offers positive inducement, incentive
T gives permission
T praises child, shows approval
T shares humor, jokes with child
T shows concern for child
T shows affection

Negative teacher reinforcement
From UI coding system, variable 29, codes 34-36, 52, 63, 74, 94, 142, 143 (see appendix A for expanded definitions):
T inhibits child, directs not to do
T reprimands, scolds
T scolds harshly, punishes
T threatens punishment
T refuses permission
T refuses help
T criticizes child
T refuses response, defers response
T responds with sarcasm

N.B.: The child may exhibit and be the recipient of positive and/or negative behavior/reinforcement in a single 15-second observation, e.g., child and peer call each other names ($-/-$) or share toys ($+/+$); child lends peer a book, peer throws it on the floor ($+/-$).

Child activities

The predominant activity or event in which the child was engaged. Only one entry (a check mark in the appropriate column) is possible per 15-second unit. If more than one activity occurred equally during a single observation unit, a hierarchical selection is made based on the order of the activities given below.

N.B.: Coding decisions are based on what the child is actually doing, not on what he *should* be doing. Thus, if a child is supposed to be working on a math paper but instead discusses "Star Trek" with his neighbor, then Talk is the correct coding.

Work. Any academic task or quiet, constructive activity such as paperwork, coloring, drawing, reading a book, doing a puzzle, listening to a story, cleaning up. Included are class rituals such as the Pledge of Allegiance, lunch

Variable   *Code*

count, singing songs. The child may be interactive (e.g., C and peer discuss phonics paper) or noninteractive. If child is preparing to work (e.g., arranging papers, choosing a crayon, borrowing an eraser, etc.), code Work. If child is looking at and listening to others working or discussing work (e.g., Teacher helps another, C looks on; children compare drawings, C listens), code Work.

Play. Any concentrated "fun" activity such as play with toys and objects (e.g., clay modeling), games, make-believe, role playing, Simon Says, etc. Does not include unfocused, restless, or daydreaming behavior, which is coded as Idling. The child may be interactive and/or talking, or noninteractive in the context of Play. Preparation for play is also coded as Play.

Talk. All social chitchat, comments other than about work, general conversation. The child may be talking or simply listening silently to another addressing him. Talk is coded when talking is the main activity, whereas talk related to the larger context of work or play is coded as Work or Play.

Self-care. Taking care of personal needs such as going to the bathroom, tying shoelaces, getting a drink of water, hanging up clothes, dressing/undressing, grooming, getting one's lunchbox, etc.

Idling. No clear activity. Child is doing nothing in particular. Includes daydreaming, staring, fidgeting, wandering about, looking around, etc. Child is off-task, passing the time or fooling around when he should be busy (occupied). Not to be confused with Play.

Wild/disorderly. Clearly disruptive, aggressive, or out-of-place activity. Includes running around the room, chasing children, wrestling, fighting, hitting, kicking, climbing on things, jumping, noisiness, rowdiness (e.g., C pounds on furniture), other unruliness (e.g., C hides in coat closet).

No code. Any activity which is not codable in terms of the previous 6 variables, e.g., transitional activities other than preparation for work or play such as getting on line, waiting one's turn, or standing by waiting for the teacher's attention. Occasionally the child may be receiving a scolding or defending himself against aggression. The No Code is used in any unusual or ambiguous situation.

Variable	*Code*
	Hierarchical coding decisions. When two or more activities seem to occur equally often or to be of equal duration in a 15-second observation unit such that no one activity is clearly predominant, coding is determined by a hierarchy proceeding downward from Work through Wild/disorderly. For example, a child may alternately work and daydream (idle) for 15 seconds; the correct code is Work. The child may stop to blow his nose (self-care) during a card game; the correct code is Play.
Notes	A space is provided at the right of each coding line for comments or notations the coder may wish to make.

B-6

CHILD-FOCUSED OBSERVATION PROTOCOL (SAMPLE)

NAME: _Jim Jones_   PAGE: __1__

Date/Time	Unit	Inter.	Verbal	Exhibits +/-	Receives +/-	Work	Play	Talk	Self-Care	Idle	Wild	No Code	Notes
4/28/76	1	O				✓							C colors paper
9:00 a.m.	2	O				✓							Colors
Morning	3	O	sings			✓							Works, taps feet
paperwork	4	AB	✓			✓							"Look at my paper!"
	5	AB	✓					✓					Chat re birthday
	6	T	Tv	–								O	T scolds C for noise
	7	O				✓							colors, yawns
	8	O								✓			Stares out window
	9	O								✓			Chews pencil
	10	CD	✓	+									Gives help to CD
	11	O				✓							Works, makes faces
	12	O	self			✓							Reads aloud to self
	13	O						✓					Ties shoelace
	14	O				✓							Chooses crayon
	15	O	oh rats!			✓							Breaks crayon
	16	T	✓			✓							"I'm finished now!"
	17	EF	✓				✓						Cs play w/blocks
	18	EF	✓	–			✓						Knocks over EF's tower
	19	EF	✓	–	–						✓		Cs wrestle, fight
etc.	20	T	Tv									O	T calls C to read

Appendix C:
Supplementary
Statistical Information

Table C.1. Frequencies of individual items included in SI and UI coding systems.

Variable	Allen		Prima		Edwards		Ryan	
	n	%	n	%	n	%	n	%
STRUCTURED INTERACTION CODING SYSTEM[1]								
19. Interaction topic								
1 = Subject lesson	82	5.8	91	6.1	25	3.4	20	3.6
2 = Reading/phonics	1217	86.6	1236	83.1	336	46.3	400	71.4
3 = Math	80	5.7	70	4.7	227	31.3	94	16.8
4 = Penmanship	9	0.6	59	4.0	1	0.1	0	0
5 = Other	0	0	8	0.5	6	0.8	15	2.7
6 = Seatwork	1	0.1	18	1.2	71	9.8	0	0
7 = Show and Tell	6	0.4	0	0	49	6.8	14	2.5
20. Question/demand mode								
Direct	1041	74.1	1284	86.3	538	74.2	484	86.4
Open	347	24.7	150	10.1	125	17.2	45	8.0
Call out	17	1.2	54	3.6	61	8.4	31	5.5
21. Question/demand type								
Process	69	4.9	278	18.7	85	11.7	35	6.3
Product	1276	90.8	1200	80.6	598	82.5	501	89.5
Choice	0	0	1	0.1	1	0.1	0	0
Free	60	4.3	8	0.5.	41	5.7	24	4.3
22. Assessment								
No response	97	6.9	135	9.1	51	7.0	42	7.4
Response	645	45.9	430	28.9	138	19.0	198	35.4
Correct/complete	476	33.9	629	42.3	384	53.0	239	42.7
Partially correct	9	0.6	8	0.5	28	3.9	6	1.1
Incorrect/incomplete	174	12.4	285	19.2	124	17.1	75	13.4

Table C.1 (*cont.*)

Variable	Allen		Prima		Edwards		Ryan	
	n	%	n	%	n	%	n	%
23. Evaluation								
High praise	75	5.3	47	3.2	29	4.0	0	0
Mild praise	163	11.6	58	3.9	110	15.2	28	5.0
Praise and criticism	1	0.1	1	0.1	2	0.3	0	0
Criticism	4	0.3	7	0.5	1	0.1	0	0
24. Terminal feedback								
Process	4	0.3	14	0.9	10	1.4	4	0.7
Product	32	2.3	24	1.6	23	3.2	10	1.8
Other	45	3.2	94	6.3	21	2.9	13	2.3
Call out	5	0.4	8	0.5	2	0.3	7	1.2
25. Sustaining feedback								
Repeat	60	4.3	78	5.2	47	6.5	32	5.7
Clue	82	5.8	65	4.4	25	3.4	45	8.0
New question	210	14.9	141	9.5	129	17.8	55	9.8
26. Global evaluation	17	1.2	9	0.6	10	1.4	4	0.7
Total SI interactions	1405		1488		725		560	

UNSTRUCTURED INTERACTION CODING SYSTEM[1]

19. Interaction topic

	Allen		Prima		Edwards		Ryan	
Academic								
1 = Subject lesson	0	0	0	0	5	0.3	4	0.2
2 = Reading/phonics	196	16.9	359	23.2	113	7.9	217	12.8
3 = Math	38	3.3	34	2.2	156	10.9	76	4.5
4 = Penmanship	23	2.0	27	1.7	26	1.8	0	0
5 = Other	2	0.2	1	0.1	25	1.7	25	1.5
6 = Seatwork	52	4.5	26	1.7	63	4.4	66	3.9
Nonacademic								
7 = Show and Tell	0	0	0	0	28	1.9	36	2.1
8 = T-suggested activity	41	3.5	52	3.4	25	1.7	70	4.1
9 = C-chosen activity	11	0.9	26	1.7	15	1.0	23	1.4
10 = Conversation	45	3.9	64	4.1	44	3.1	36	2.1
Other								
11 = Recreation	0	0	0	0	3	0.2	14	0.8
12 = Transition	1	0.1	1	0.1	1	0.1	1	0.1
13 = Morning routine	0	0	0	0	0	0	5	0.3

(*cont.*)

Table C.1 (*cont.*)

Variable	Allen		Prima		Edwards		Ryan	
	n	%	n	%	n	%	n	%
Procedure								
21 = Work-related	161	13.9	210	13.5	218	15.2	237	14.0
22 = Class management	360	31.1	279	18.0	462	32.2	510	30.1
23 = Self-care	20	1.7	30	1.9	32	2.2	22	1.3
Privilege								
24 = Privilege	37	3.2	41	2.6	56	3.9	85	5.0
Appropriate child behavior								
31 = Teaching/helping	2	0.2	10	0.6	1	0.1	1	0.1
32 = Acceptance of values	1	0.1	2	0.1	1	0.1	1	0.1
33 = Enthusiasm	0	0	0	0	0	0	0	0
34 = Exhibition of pride	0	0	0	0	1	0.1	0	0
35 = Seeking to perform	2	0.2	1	0.1	2	0.1	1	0.1
36 = Seeking evaluation	0	0	0	0	1	0.1	0	0
37 = Spontaneous helping	0	0	0	0	0	0	0	0
38 = Overt compliance	1	0.1	0	0	0	0	0	0
Inappropriate child behavior								
41 = Defiance	0	0	7	0.5	0	0	2	0.1
42 = Aggression	1	0.1	3	0.2	2	0.1	10	0.6
43 = Disruption of another	26	2.2	62	4.0	19	1.3	14	0.8
44 = Disruption of class	81	7.0	190	12.3	95	6.6	146	8.6
45 = Off-task	30	2.6	98	6.3	30	2.1	73	4.3
Child distress								
46 = Distress/fear	1	0.1	5	0.3	2	0.1	4	0.2
Child personal quality								
51 = Intellectual	0	0	1	0.1	0	0	0	0
52 = Social/leadership	3	0.3	1	0.1	0	0	1	0.1
53 = Appearance	0	0	1	0.1	1	0.1	1	0.1
54 = Health	23	2.0	14	0.9	9	0.6	12	0.7
Child expressive quality								
61 = Happiness	1	0.1	4	0.3	0	0	0	0
62 = Bad mood	0	0	1	0.1	0	0	0	0
28. Child behavior								
Appropriate								
11 = Teaching/helping	0	0	10	0.6	3	0.2	0	0
12 = Acceptance of values	1	0.1	3	0.2	5	0.3	0	0
13 = Enthusiasm	4	0.3	17	1.1	5	0.3	4	0.2

Table C.1 (*cont.*)

Variable	Allen		Prima		Edwards		Ryan	
	n	%	n	%	n	%	n	%
14 = Exhibition of pride	2	0.2	15	1.0	12	0.8	6	0.4
15 = Seeking to perform	11	0.9	23	1.5	9	0.6	16	0.9
16 = Seeking evaluation	33	2.8	40	2.6	83	5.8	40	2.4
17 = Spontaneous helping	5	0.4	4	0.3	5	0.3	5	0.3
18 = Overt compliance	7	0.6	9	0.6	22	1.5	23	1.4
19 = Comments/converses	87	7.5	129	8.3	140	10.0	130	7.7
Requests								
21 = Information	39	3.4	96	6.2	63	4.4	156	9.2
22 = Help	19	1.6	120	7.7	32	2.2	78	4.6
23 = Materials	7	0.6	9	0.6	13	0.9	10	0.6
24 = Permission	31	2.7	39	2.5	34	2.4	45	2.7
Mild inappropriate								
31 = Complains	5	0.4	18	1.2	13	0.9	21	1.2
32 = Tattles	11	0.9	51	3.3	17	1.2	12	0.7
33 = Makes excuses	1	0.1	4	0.3	6	0.4	13	0.8
34 = Bosses others	0	0	2	0.1	1	0.1	0	0
35 = Denies wrongdoing	1	0.1	3	0.2	2	0.1	1	0.1
Clearly inappropriate								
41 = Defiance	0	0	8	0.5	4	0.3	27	1.6
42 = Aggression	1	0.1	1	0.1	1	0.1	4	0.2
43 = Disruption of another	10	0.9	21	1.4	7	0.5	8	0.5
44 = Disruption of class	25	2.2	65	4.2	40	2.8	67	4.0
45 = Off-task	20	1.7	52	3.4	16	1.1	59	3.5
Expressive								
51 = Affection	2	0.2	2	0.1	0	0	0	0
52 = Humor	2	0.2	19	1.2	2	0.1	0	0
53 = Sympathy	0	0	3	0.2	0	0	1	0.1
54 = Shyness	0	0	1	0.1	2	0.1	0	0
55 = Distress	0	0	3	0.2	2	0.1	2	0.1
56 = Apology	0	0	0	0	0	0	1	0.1
29. Teacher behavior								
Teaching								
11 = States rules	7	0.6	6	0.4	5	0.3	2	0.1
12 = Instructs/explains	67	5.8	82	5.3	90	6.3	116	6.9
13 = Gives information	40	3.5	55	3.5	58	4.0	91	5.4
14 = Routine information	20	1.7	58	3.7	43	3.0	103	6.1

(*cont.*)

Table C.1 (*cont.*)

Variable	Allen		Prima		Edwards		Ryan	
	n	%	n	%	n	%	n	%
Checks up/questions								
21 = Procedural	57	4.9	81	5.2	139	9.7	145	8.6
22 = Understanding	0	0	7	0.5	9	0.6	9	0.5
23 = Asks C to report	1	0.1	0	0	0	0	0	0
Controls/directs								
31 = Encourages/reassures	22	1.9	21	1.4	22	1.5	23	1.4
32 = Directs to do	454	39.2	284	18.3	496	34.5	509	30.1
33 = Gives choice	2	0.2	0	0	0	0	2	0.1
34 = Directs not to do	136	11.7	328	21.2	158	11.0	220	13.0
35 = Reprimands/scolds	27	2.3	121	7.8	55	3.8	116	6.9
36 = Scolds harshly	0	0	1	0.1	0	0	6	0.4
Justification of action								
41 = Objective reason	1	0.1	0	0	1	0.1	2	0.1
42 = Appeals to rules	6	0.5	5	0.3	3	0.2	3	0.2
43 = Appeals to authority	0	0	1	0.1	0	0	2	0.1
Consequences								
51 = Positive inducement	0	0	1	0.1	4	0.3	8	0.5
52 = Threatens punishment	1	0.1	28	1.8	6	0.4	22	1.3
Permission								
61 = Gives permission	46	4.0	28	1.8	45	3.1	52	3.1
62 = Defers permission	8	0.7	6	0.4	5	0.3	7	0.4
63 = Refuses permission	17	1.5	21	1.4	16	1.1	29	1.7
Help								
71 = Gives help/materials	122	10.5	132	8.5	102	7.1	141	8.3
72 = Questions C	3	0.3	12	0.8	4	0.3	11	0.6
73 = Defers help	6	0.5	29	1.9	9	0.6	22	1.3
74 = Refuses help	2	0.2	11	0.7	7	0.5	12	0.7
Feedback								
81 = Correct/complete	7	0.6	25	1.6	21	1.5	12	0.7
82 = Partly correct	3	0.3	8	0.5	17	1.2	2	0.1
83 = Incorrect/incomplete	21	1.8	25	1.6	30	2.1	12	0.7
Evaluation								
91 = High praise	24	2.1	23	1.5	19	1.3	8	0.5
92 = Praise	35	3.0	41	2.6	49	3.4	39	2.3
93 = Praise and criticism	2	0.2	2	0.1	1	0.1	1	0.1

Table C.1 (*cont.*)

Variable	Allen		Prima		Edwards		Ryan	
	n	%	n	%	n	%	n	%
94 = Criticism	5	0.4	31	2.0	15	1.0	7	0.4
95 = Accepts apology	0	0	1	0.1	0	0	1	0.1
96 = Refuses to evaluate	0	0	0	0	0	0	0	0
Sustains task								
101 = Repeats question	3	0.3	1	0.1	5	0.3	1	0.1
102 = Directs to new task	4	0.3	0	0	5	0.3	1	0.1
Participates								
111 = Joins in activity	27	2.3	3	0.2	5	0.3	4	0.2
Listens								
121 = Listens silently	5	0.4	20	1.3	11	0.8	6	0.4
Teasing/joking								
131 = Shares humor	3	0.3	28	1.8	2	0.1	1	0.1
Conversation								
141 = Converses with C	59	5.1	78	5.0	75	5.2	61	3.6
142 = Defers response	5	0.4	16	1.0	18	1.3	8	0.5
143 = Sarcasm	0	0	6	0.4	1	0.1	0	0
Concern								
151 = Shows concern	6	0.5	11	0.7	8	0.6	8	0.5
Affection								
161 = Shows affection	1	0.1	7	0.5	0	0	1	0.1
Total UI Interactions[2]	1159		1550		1437		1693	

1. Percentages are calculated separately for the SI and UI systems using the total number of interactions coded in the SI *or* the UI respectively as the base. This procedure differs from that followed in chapter 5, table 6, where the base is the total number of teacher-child interactions coded in the SI and UI combined.

2. All coded UI interactions including those addressed to a group of more than 3 children or to the whole class.

Table C.2. Items composing variable clusters.[1]

Clusters	SI Variables	UI Variables
Interaction topics	Variable 19, sum	Variable 19, sum
Academic	codes 1-7	codes 1-6
Nonacademic		codes 7-13
Procedure		codes 21-23
Privilege		code 24
Appropriate C behavior		codes 31-38
Inappropriate C behavior		codes 41-45
Health, distress		codes 46, 54
Appropriate C behavior		Variable 28, sum codes 11-18
Positive T reinforcement	Variable 23, sum codes High praise and Mild praise	Variable 29, sum codes 51, 91, 92, 151, 161
Expressive C behavior		Variable 28, code 19
T humor, conversation		Variable 29, sum codes 111, 131, 141
Dependent C behavior		Variable 28, sum codes 21, 22, 23, 24
T grants request		Variable 29, sum codes 61, 71
T rejects request		Variable 29, sum codes 62, 63, 73, 74
Inappropriate C behavior		Variable 28, sum codes 31-35 and 41-45
Negative T reinforcement	Variable 23, sum codes Praise and criticism and Criticism	Variable 29, sum codes 34, 35, 36, 52, 93, 94, 142, 143
T asks open/free question	Sum variable 20, code Open, and variable 21, code Free	Variable 29, code 33
T asks process question	Sum variable 21, code Process, and variable 24, code Process	Variable 29, code 72
T asks product question	Variable 21, sum codes Product and Choice	
T does not assess response	Variable 22, code Response	
T assesses response	Variable 22, sum codes Correct, Partially correct, and Incorrect	Variable 29, sum codes 11-13 and 81-83
T gives directive	Sum variable 20, code Direct, and variable 25, all codes	Variable 29, sum codes 31, 32, 101, 102
T procedural behavior		Variable 29, sum codes 14, 21, 22

Table C.2 (*cont.*)

Clusters	SI Variables	UI Variables
Variables omitted from clusters		
Interaction topics		Variable 19, codes 51-53 and 61-62
All others	Variable 20, code Call out; variable 22, code No response; variable 24, codes Product, Other, and Call out; variable 26	Variable 28, codes 51-56; variable 29, codes 23, 41-43, 95, 96, 121

1. This table consists of items that were summed together to produce the composite variables referred to in chapter 5, table 6, and tables 9-11. The items included in the composite variable may occur in the SI and/or the UI system, the rationale for summing them being their conceptual similarity. However, if more than one code signaling the same composite variable occurred in a single interaction, only one entry was accepted for that composite variable. This procedure ensured that the same composite variable was not counted more than once for a single interaction and that the data base (the number of SI plus UI interactions) was the same for all variables.

Table C.3. Frequencies of variable clusters.[1]

Variable	Allen		Prima		Edwards		Ryan	
	n	%	n	%	n	%	n	%
Interaction topics								
Academic	1655	69.6	1883	65.3	1000	51.0	850	43.4
Nonacademic	90	3.8	135	4.7	150	7.3	164	8.0
Procedure	438	18.4	442	15.3	617	31.3	635	32.2
Privilege	36	1.5	41	1.4	55	2.8	84	4.3
Appropriate C behavior	6	0.3	13	0.5	6	0.3	3	0.2
Inappropriate C behavior	132	5.5	350	12.1	133	6.7	220	11.2
Health, distress	22	0.9	19	0.7	11	0.6	16	0.8
Appropriate C behavior	63	2.6	121	4.2	144	7.3	93	4.7
Positive T reinforcement	305	12.8	206	7.1	217	11.0	85	4.3
Expressive C behavior	85	3.6	125	4.3	141	7.1	126	6.4
T humor, conversation	80	3.4	113	3.9	78	4.0	62	3.1
Dependent C behavior	96	4.0	262	9.1	144	7.3	280	14.2
T grants request	143	6.0	142	4.9	144	7.3	174	8.8
T rejects request	33	1.4	67	2.3	39	2.0	65	3.3
Inappropriate C behavior	74	3.1	220	7.6	107	5.4	205	10.4
Negative T reinforcement	185	7.8	544	18.8	264	13.4	376	19.0
T asks open/free question	392	16.4	158	5.5	162	8.2	58	2.9
T asks process question	75	3.1	292	10.1	94	4.8	50	2.5
T asks product question	1276	53.5	1203	41.6	599	30.3	501	25.4
T does not assess response	645	27.1	430	14.9	138	7.0	198	10.0
T assesses response	756	31.7	1060	36.7	689	34.9	445	22.5
T gives directive	1505	63.1	1577	54.5	989	50.1	914	46.3
T procedural behavior	71	3.0	140	4.8	170	8.6	234	11.9
Total SI + UI interactions	2384		2891		1974		1974	
Omitted UI interactions[2]	180		147		188		279	

1. This table consists of the frequencies of composite variables defined in table C.2 along with the percentage of combined SI and UI interaction units in which the variables were coded in each classroom. As noted in table C.2, only one entry per composite variable was counted when more than one code signaling the same cluster occurred in a single interaction. In addition, all UI interactions directed by the teacher toward a group of children or the whole class were omitted from the analyses of combined SI and UI interactions.

2. All UI interactions in which the recipient of the interaction was a group or the whole class rather than an individual child.

References

Adorno, T. W., E. Frenkel-Brunswik, D. J. Levinson, and R. N. Sanford. 1950. *The authoritarian personality.* New York: Harper and Bros.

Allport, G. 1953. *The nature of prejudice.* Boston: Beacon Press.

Anastasi, A. 1958. *Differential psychology,* 3rd ed. New York: Macmillan.

Becker, H. 1952. Social class variation in teacher-pupil relationships. *Journal of Educational Sociology* 25: 451-465.

———. 1963. *The outsiders.* New York: The Free Press.

Bellack, Arno, et al. 1966. *The language of the classroom.* New York: Teachers College Press, Columbia University.

Biddle, Bruce, and Ellena Williams, eds. 1964. *Contemporary research on teacher effectiveness.* New York: Holt, Rinehart and Winston.

Bonger, W. 1969. *Criminality and economic conditions.* Bloomington: Indiana University Press.

Brenton, M. 1970. *What's happened to teacher?* New York: Avon Books.

Brophy, J. E., and T. L. Good. 1970a. Brophy-Good system (teacher-child dyadic interaction). In *Mirrors for behavior: an anthology of observation instruments,* 1970 suppl., vol. A, ed. A. Simon and E. Boyer. Philadephia: Research for Better Schools.

———. 1970b. Teacher's communication of differential expectations for children's classroom performance. *Journal of Educational Psychology* 61(5): 365-374.

———. 1974. *Teacher-student relationships: causes and consequences.* New York: Holt, Rinehart and Winston.

Carew, J. V., I. Chan, and C. Halfar. 1976a. *Intelligence and experience in day care.* Final report to the National Institute of Mental Health, August.

———. 1976b. *Observing intelligence in young children: eight case studies.* Englewood Cliffs, N. J.: Prentice-Hall.

———. 1977. Observed intellectual competence and tested intelligence: their roots in the young child's transactions with his environment. In *Child development: a study of growth processes,* 2nd ed., ed. S. Cohen and T. J. Comiskey. Itasca, Ill.: F. E. Peacock Publishers.

Charters, W. W. 1963. The social background of teaching. In *Handbook of research on teaching,* ed. N. L. Gage. Chicago: Rand McNally.

Darwin, C. 1859. *Origin of species.* New York: The Mentor Edition of the New American Library of World Literature.

Dennison, George. 1969. *The lives of children.* New York: Random House.

Dewey, J. 1916. *Education and democracy.* New York: The Free Press, 1966.

Dreeben, R. 1968. *On what is learned in school.* Reading, Mass.: Addison-Wesley.

———. 1970. *The nature of teaching.* Glenville, Ill,: Scott, Foresman.

———. 1973. The school as workplace. In *Handbook of research on teaching,* 2nd ed., ed. R. Travers. Chicago: Rand McNally.

Dunkin, M., and B. Biddle. 1974. *The study of teaching.* New York: Holt, Rinehart and Winston.

Durkheim, E. 1893. *The division of labor in society.* Glencoe, Ill.: The Free Press, 1933.

———. 1897. *Suicide: a study in sociology.* Glencoe, Ill.: The Free Press, 1931.

Eddy, Elizabeth. 1967. *Walk the white line: a profile of urban education.* Garden City, N. Y.: Doubleday.

Elashoff, J., and R. Snow. 1971. *Pygmalion reconsidered.* Worthington, Ohio: Charles A. Jones.

Erikson, K. 1966. *Wayward puritans: a study in the sociology of deviance.* New York: Wiley and Sons.

Erlich, H. 1973. *The social psychology of prejudice.* New York: Wiley and Sons.

Farber, J. 1969. *Student as nigger.* New York: Pocket Books, Simon and Schuster.

Featherstone, J. 1971. *Schools where children learn.* New York: Avon Books.

Flanders, N. 1970. *Analyzing teacher behavior.* Reading, Mass.: Addison-Wesley.

Fuchs, E. 1969. *Teachers talk: views from inside city schools.* Garden City, N. Y.: Doubleday.

Getzels, J. W., and P. W. Jackson. 1963. The teacher's personality and characteristics. In *Handbook of research on teaching,* ed. N. L. Gage. Chicago: Rand McNally.

Goffman, E. 1963. *Stigma: notes on the management of spoiled identity.* Englewood Cliffs, N. J.: Prentice-Hall.

Good, T., and J. E. Brophy. 1970. Which pupils do teachers call on? *Elementary School Journal* 70: 190-198.

———. 1973. *Looking in classrooms.* New York: Harper and Row.

Goodlad, J. I., et al. 1970. *Behind the classroom door.* Worthington, Ohio: Charles A. Jones.

Grier, William, and Price Cobbs. 1968. *Black rage.* New York: Basic Books.

Henry, J. 1957. Attitude organization in elementary school classrooms. *American Journal of Orthopsychiatry* 27: 117-133.

———. 1965. *Culture against man.* New York: Vintage Books.

Hentoff, Nat. 1966. *Our children are dying.* New York: The Viking Press.

Illich, I. 1970. *Deschooling society.* New York: Harper and Row.

Jackson, P. 1968. *Life in classrooms.* New York: Holt, Rinehart, and Winston.

Jackson, P., and H. Lahaderne. 1970. Inequalities of teacher-pupil contacts. In

Learning in social settings, ed. M. Miles and W. W. Charters. Boston: Allyn and Bacon.

Kozol, J. 1967. *Death at an early age.* Boston: Houghton Mifflin.

Leacock, E. B. 1969. *Teaching and learning in city schools.* New York: Basic Books.

Lightfoot, S. L. 1973. Politics and reasoning: through the eyes of teachers and children. *Harvard Educational Review* 43(2): 197-244.

———. 1975. Sociology of education: perspectives on women. In *Another voice: feminist perspectives on social life and social science,* ed. M. Millman and R. Kanter. New York: Anchor Books.

———. 1976. Socialization and education of young black girls in school. *Teachers College Record* 78(2): 239-262.

———. 1978. *Worlds apart: relationships between families and schools.* New York: Basic Books.

Lightfoot, S. L., and J. V. Carew. 1976. Individuation and discrimination in the classroom. *American Journal of Orthopsychiatry* 46(3): 401-415.

Lortie, D. 1973. Observations on teaching as work. In *Handbook of research on teaching,* 2nd ed., ed. R. Travers. Chicago: Rand McNally.

———. 1975. *Schoolteacher: a sociological study.* Chicago: University of Chicago Press.

McPherson, G. 1972. *Smalltown teacher.* Cambridge: Harvard University Press.

Merton, R. 1957. *Social theory and social structure.* Glencoe, Ill.: The Free Press.

Merton, R., and R. A. Nisbet. 1966. *Contemporary social problems,* 2nd ed. New York: Harcourt, Brace and World.

Minuchin, P., et al. 1969. *The psychological impact of school experience.* New York: Basic Books.

Olson, W. C. 1966. Grouping and growth theory. In *Grouping in education,* ed. A. Yates. New York: John Wiley and Sons.

Parsons, Talcott. 1951. *The social system.* New York: The Free Press.

Piaget, J. 1932. *The moral judgment of the child.* New York: Harcourt, Brace and World.

Raths, J., J. Paucella, and J. Van Ness. 1971. *Studying teaching.* Englewood Cliffs, N.J.: Prentice-Hall.

Rist, R. C. 1970. Student social class and teacher expectations: the self-fulfilling prophecy in ghetto education. *Harvard Educational Review* 40(3): 411-451.

———. 1973. *The urban school: a factory for failure.* Cambridge: M.I.T. Press.

———. 1975. Becoming a success or failure in school: a theoretical and methodological synthesis. Unpub.

Rogers, C. 1951. *Client-centered therapy.* Boston: Houghton Mifflin.

———. 1961. *On becoming a person.* Boston: Houghton Mifflin.

Rosenshine, B., and N. Furst. 1973. The use of direct observation to study teaching. In *Handbook of research on teaching,* 2nd ed., ed. R. Travers. Chicago: Rand McNally.

Rosenthal, R., and L. Jacobson. 1968. *Pygmalion in the classroom.* New York: Holt, Rinehart and Winston.

Ryan, W. 1968. *Blaming the victim.* New York: Vintage Books.

Sarason, S. 1972. *The culture of the school and the problem of change.* Boston: Allyn and Bacon.

Silberman, C. 1970. *Crisis in the classroom.* New York: Random House.

Smith, L., and W. Geoffrey. 1968. *Complexities of an urban classroom: an analysis toward a general theory of teaching.* New York: Holt, Rinehart and Winston.

Snow, R. 1969. Unfinished Pygmalion. *Contemporary Psychology* 14: 197-199.

Thorndike, R. 1968. Review of R. Rosenthal and L. Jacobson's *Pygmalion in the classroom. Educational Research Journal* 5: 708-711.

Walberg, H. 1969. Physical and psychological distance in the classroom. *School Review* 77: 64-70.

Waller, W. 1932. *Sociology of teaching.* New York: John Wiley and Sons.

White, B., J. V. Carew Watts, et al. 1973. *Environment and experience: major influences on the development of the young child.* Englewood Cliffs, N. J.: Prentice-Hall.

White, W. F. 1969. *Psychosocial principles applied to classroom teaching.* New York: McGraw-Hill.

Withall, J. 1956. An objective measurement of a teacher's classroom interactions. *Journal of Educational Psychology* 47: 203-212.

Yee, A. H. 1968. Source and direction of causal influence in teacher-pupil relationships. *Journal of Educational Psychology* 59: 275-282.

Index